Off THE BEATEN PAGE

Off THE BEATEN PAGE

THE BEST TRIPS FOR LIT LOVERS, BOOK CLUBS, AND GIRLS ON GETAWAYS

❧ TERRI PETERSON SMITH ❧

CHICAGO
REVIEW
PRESS

Copyright © 2013 by Terri Peterson Smith
Published by Chicago Review Press, Incorporated
814 North Franklin Street
Chicago, Illinois 60610
ISBN 978-1-61374-426-0

Cover and interior design: Andrew J. Brozyna, AJB Design, Inc.
Cover photo: Kelly V. Brozyna

Library of Congress Cataloging-in-Publication Data
Smith, Terri Peterson.
  Off the beaten page : the best trips for lit lovers, book clubs, and girls on getaways
/ Terri Peterson Smith.
     pages ; cm
  Includes index.
  ISBN 978-1-61374-426-0 (trade paper)
  1. Travel—Guidebooks. 2. Book clubs (Discussion groups)—United States. 3.
Women—Books and reading—United States. 4. Literary landmarks—Guidebooks.
5. Festivals—United States—Guidebooks. I. Title.

  G155.A1S575 2013
  910.4—dc23

                            2012045867

Printed in the United States of America
5 4 3 2 1

To my mom, who taught me the love of reading,
and to Scott, Michael, and Patrick,
my favorite travel companions

Too young to go, I read about elsewheres, fantasizing about my freedom. Books were my road. And then, when I was old enough to go, the roads I traveled became the obsessive subject in my own books. Eventually I saw the most passionate travelers have always also been passionate readers and writers. —**PAUL THEROUX,** *The Tao of Travel*

Contents

APPENDIX

INDEX

INTRODUCTION

The Next Chapter

TAKING READING FROM THE LIVING ROOM INTO THE WORLD

Why do we travel? My favorite answer comes from an essay the great travel writer Pico Iyer wrote for *Salon* many years ago. He said, "We travel, initially, to lose ourselves; and we travel, next, to find ourselves. We travel to open our hearts and eyes and learn more about the world than our newspapers will accommodate. We travel to bring what little we can, in our ignorance and knowledge, to those parts of the globe whose riches are differently dispersed. And, we travel, in essence, to become young fools again—to slow time down and get taken in, and fall in love once more."

Why do we read? Substitute the word "read" for travel in Iyer's essay, and for me the answer is much the same. People read to leave their everyday lives and escape to unfamiliar places, to have new experiences, and to learn more about the world and its people. When we "escape with a good book," we lose ourselves and sometimes find ourselves along the way, like a traveler wandering the streets and alleyways of a foreign country. Through reading, we discover worlds we would otherwise never experience. Few of us have the time or financial wherewithal to climb Kilimanjaro, tour the Australian outback, or take a months-long "grand tour" of Europe, but we can go anywhere in a book.

To me, the best of all worlds is to combine reading with travel. Like pairing wine with a delicious meal, one enhances the other. I have loved that combination since grade school, when I read about the places we were going on our annual family vacations while Mom and Dad were loading up the car. For example, reading Esther Forbes's *Johnny Tremain* before a trip to Boston made the city's colonial history and historic places come alive for me. Many years later, when I took my own children to Boston, we read Robert McCloskey's *Make Way for Ducklings* before the trip. Once there, we all waddled across the street from the Old Corner Bookstore and on over to the Public Garden, diligently following the path of Mack, Jack, Kack, Quack, and the other ducklings. I'm sure the boys didn't enjoy it as much as I did; I got to be a kid again.

My book clubs, too, have traveled together to a variety of locales. (As a compulsive reader, I'm in two book clubs.) But rather than read in preparation for trips, we traveled in response to books. We started small, with "field trips" to author readings at local book shops, to movies adapted from a book we had read, and to literary places such as F. Scott Fitzgerald's neighborhood in St. Paul, Minnesota. Eventually, we ventured farther from home. We have gathered at members' cabins and eventually traveled to other cities. Each time we started with a story, took a trip related to the book, and, by doing so, forged a deeper connection with the literature, with the place, and with each other.

I began thinking about writing *Off the Beaten Page* after a book-club trip to Chicago inspired by Erik Larson's *The Devil in the White City*, a murder mystery that takes place during the 1893 world's fair in Chicago. We had a blast. Later, whenever I told other women about our adventure, they either remarked that they wished their book groups would do the same thing or began to very enthusiastically relate their own groups' travel experiences to me. I know there are about a zillion book groups out there, all meeting in their homes, libraries, or church basements month after month, so I decided to share a few ideas and encouragement to help them take their reading groups out into the world.

Traveling to the places we read about seems really important to me these days—not just because it's fun to travel or because it prevents book-group boredom, but also because traveling encourages *empathy*. We live in polarized times, when it seems just about everyone looks at the world through the prism of "us versus them," and the light that emerges is only two colors—red or blue, rich or poor, coastal and urban or midcontinent rural, black or white, the 1 percent or the 99. The list is endless. If your TV, laptop, or iPad is your sole source of information about the world, you might wonder how people who live in the same country can think, behave, and talk in ways so fantastically different from you. In some ways, it's easy to see why we can't understand each other, because the United States is a country with wildly distinctive regions, cultures, and people. For example, I'm always fascinated with the extreme contrast between Minneapolis, where I live, and New Orleans. They're both on the Mississippi River, but the view from our opposite ends of the river couldn't be more different. It's more than just "po-tay-to" versus "po-tah-to." A native Minnesotan visiting New Orleans for the first time, amid sounds and sensations of zydeco music, humid and hazy air, Spanish moss, "Who dat?" and crawfish étouffée, can probably sympathize with Marco Polo on his first voyage to the Orient. How in the world can we relate to each other?

Reading stories about diverse people and different places offers a degree of understanding. Stories teach a bit about the character of your destination, create a mental picture, and offer a small sense of belonging. If you've read a well-known book or two about the place you're visiting, you have a leg up, like a cultural passport to your destination. And when you travel to that place to connect and experience it personally, the combination of reading and travel helps you see the world in Technicolor rather than in black and white, in three dimensions instead of two. As Mark Twain said in *The Innocents Abroad*, "Travel is fatal to prejudice, bigotry, and narrow-mindedness, and many of our people need it sorely on these accounts. . . . Broad, wholesome, charitable views of men and things cannot be acquired by vegetating in one little corner of the earth all one's lifetime."

I traveled across the country to research this book and in the process became truly proud and passionate about our fascinating diversity. I want other people to read about it and experience it. Hence, in writing *Off the Beaten Page*, I hope to whet readers' travel taste buds by exploring the places where literature and travel intersect in destinations that are really fun to visit.

The first part of the book covers the basics of literary travel: what it is, how to do it, and ways for novices to dip their toes in the water of literary travel by taking a few field trips close to home. Thus equipped, your group, be it an organized book club or an informal group of friends, may expand and enrich the experience of reading beyond the wine-and-dessert discussions in the living room. And, hopefully, you'll find ways to understand the places you travel through the eyes of authors who have gone there before you, as well as open your eyes and hearts to the people who live there now.

In the next section, I describe fifteen of my favorite literary locales across the United States. There's no magic in the number fifteen. I could easily have doubled that number. In fact, while I was writing the book, everyone I talked to had a favorite place to recommend. How about Natchez? You're including Maine, right? Asheville? Nashville? Louisville? But writing, like traveling, requires choices and compromises. I've chosen places that are relatively easy to reach, no more than about an hour from a major airport. They're places where activities are concentrated, so once you get there you can stay in one inn or hotel, walk or take public transportation to most activities, and usually avoid a car.

These cities showcase some of the most distinctive parts of the country, hold special importance in our literary tradition and our cultural heritage, and offer interesting nightlife and cultural life. They range from the very urban New York City, the literary hub of the country, to the wide-open spaces of New Mexico. I admit that some places have more literary merit than others that I chose, but I included the latter locations because they are really fun for groups to visit. Each chapter opens with an essay that discusses a few works of literature—fiction or nonfiction—and how they evoke a sense of the destination. After that, you'll find a short vignette about an author who lives in that area. A reading list follows, filled with books that I not only love to tell my friends about but that also show a variety of American literary genres—classics from the 1700s to contemporary "noir" crime fiction. The reading lists include "good books"—works that your English teacher would approve of—but also books on the light side. Yes, *Moby Dick* looms large over the Boston reading list, but you'll also find *Twilight* in Seattle. Literary travel should be fun, whether you're thinking deep thoughts or just basking on the beach.

After the reading list, you'll find an itinerary for each destination, planned with book groups in mind. It's hard to get away sometimes, between kids, jobs, and other responsibilities, so these trips are mainly designed as long weekends. Also, travel isn't cheap, so each itinerary combines a few splurges with simple pleasures—fine dining with pizza, Broadway shows with just sitting and people watching. In the search for an authentic experience, I've opted for interesting boutique hotels with just a few larger chain hotels. I've rationalized the cost of staying in nice hotels in the middle of the action (instead of Mabel's Motel out by the freeway) with the notion that if you share rooms and go at off-peak times, it keeps the cost down. The itineraries emphasize activities that take you into the world of the books you've read but also include such beyond-the-book activities as Segway rides, kayaking, shopping, and plenty of local food and music. These itineraries are just a start. Feel free to tailor them to your interests and favorite books.

Hopefully *Off the Beaten Page* will inspire you to create your own book-related travel, shared memories, and tighter bonds with your traveling companions and your fellow citizens. So go forth and travel, but with a book in hand. I'd love to hear about your book group, your travels, and your suggestions for future volumes. My e-mail is tsmith952@comcast.net. And look to my blog, *Off the Beaten Page Travel* (www.offthebeatenpagetravel .com), for updates on new places to go and feedback on these and other trips from your fellow literary travelers.

Part 1

LITERARY TRAVEL BASICS

1

Literary Travel

LIT, LANDSCAPE, AND LAUGHS

Over the years, I have developed some of my closest friendships with the people in my book groups. We see each other every month, no matter what. We've watched our collective group of children grow up, celebrated the successes in our work and family lives, and propped each other up through our sorrows. That's why one of my favorite things is to share a literary getaway with these women. We've had more than a few—everything from trendy big-city outings to a rural Wisconsin road trip with ten women in an RV. The thrill of *seeing* and *living* the books you love in the company of some of your favorite friends is simply the best. Sure, you can curl up alone with a good book, vacation with your family, or meet up with your gal pals for dinner or happy hour downtown. But it's the combination of those three—lit, landscape, and laughs—that makes my book-club travels memorable.

I can't say that I invented the book-club getaway. Literature lovers have used books to inspire their travels since the early nineteenth century, when, novels in hand, British book lovers climbed into their carriages to tour the literary landscape of England and Scotland. There they gazed on the sites of their best-loved stories, absorbed the environment that inspired their favorite authors, and even walked the paths of fictional characters. They meandered through such places as Shakespeare's Stratford, the Scottish highlands of Robert Burns's poetry, and even the imaginary literary territories of Dickens's London or Hardy's Wessex. Thus began *literary tourism*, a form of travel inspired by and centered on great works of literature. It offered a way to experience the interrelation between the real place and the fictional story and was, according to Nicola Watson, author of *The Literary Tourist*, "a new way of living with reading."

Americans, too, caught the literary travel bug. Having few of their own literary landmarks to visit at the time, they crossed the Atlantic to personally experience their favorite novels' settings and perhaps even meet the authors. For example, Watson notes the 1816 journey of a young Washington Irving, author of classic American stories such as *The Legend of Sleepy Hollow* and *Rip Van Winkle*. He traveled to Abbotsford, near Melrose, Scotland, home of Sir Walter Scott, the author of *Ivanhoe* and other classics. Apparently not a shy fellow, Irving arrived at Abbotsford, knocked on the door, and presented a letter of introduction. Sir Walter himself gave Irving a tour.

Much has changed on the literary scene since then. We speak and travel with contemporary casualness. Our books come not only in print but also as audio books and e-books. And the celebrity of famous authors has been eclipsed somewhat by rockers, actors, and even reality-show "stars." Yet our desire to go to the places we read about is stronger than ever. Literary sites abound, tied not only to classic literature but also to popular fiction, and visitors flock to them. You can still visit Haworth Parsonage in Yorkshire, where Charlotte Brontë composed *Jane Eyre*, and walk the path to the valley that is the setting for her sister Emily's

Wuthering Heights. But now children and their parents take Harry Potter tours in London; teenage fans of Stephanie Meyer's *Twilight* series trek to tiny Forks, Washington, to see the rain-soaked real-life landscape where fictional vampires and werewolves clash; and readers of all stripes flock to Stockholm, spellbound by Stieg Larsson's Millennium Trilogy (*The Girl with the Dragon Tattoo*, *The Girl Who Played with Fire*, and *The Girl Who Kicked the Hornet's Nest*) and his unforgettable heroine, Lisbeth Salander. Now, with an estimated seven million book clubs in the United States, more groups than ever are on the road to lit locales.

But what fuels the literary wanderlust of today's readers, who can learn about places around the world on the Internet, almost like being there? There are several answers. One is that some things haven't changed. People still travel to literary locales for the same reason Washington Irving did: for a closer and more personal connection to a story that even the Internet can't provide. It's the same force that propels history buffs' travel to such places as George Washington's Mount Vernon or Thomas Jefferson's Monticello, or Gettysburg, or the beaches of Normandy. There they gain firsthand understanding of how early Americans' lives forged our modern society or how the terrain influenced the battle. Readers seek out the locales of their favorite novels for the same reasons art lovers visit Monet's home at Giverny or Vincent Van Gogh's sunflower field at Arles: they want to see for themselves places of such beauty and inspiration.

Readers also set out on lit trips because travel puts books in *context*. After I saw the immensity and behavior of whales in the ocean off the Massachusetts coast, my appreciation of both Captain Ahab and his adversary, the white whale, in *Moby Dick* multiplied tenfold. It's not that Mark Twain's description of "the magnificent Mississippi, rolling its mile-wide tide along, shining in the sun" falls short. But a riverboat ride near Memphis gave me a better grasp of the Mississippi's power and its importance to both antebellum cotton traders and modern-day Americans. Melanie

Halvorson shares a similar experience of when her Chicago book group traveled together to her family's cabin in La Crosse, Wisconsin. It's about five hours from Chicago and near where David Rhodes's book *Driftless*, about life in a tiny farming community, is set. "It really added to reading the book," she says. "To see the geography and the personalities there made it easier to picture the characters in the book." These urbanites also got the chance to taste the slower pace of Wisconsin's open, country setting. She even attended an appearance by the author (who lives nearby) at a La Crosse area bookstore before the group came.

I had read Truman Capote's *Breakfast at Tiffany's* years ago, and it seemed to me to pale in comparison to the movie. But before a recent trip to New York, I reread Capote's novella and several other books, all of them about people finding their place in New York and, more symbolically, in the larger world. That gave *Breakfast at Tiffany's* a whole new level of interest and poignancy. There's also a certain thrill that comes when the imaginary world and the real world merge. I felt the tiny shock of recognition standing outside Tiffany's and understood Holly Golightly's description of "the quietness and the proud look of it." And, with my face pressed against the glass, I grasped how looking at the gems in the window could indeed dispel the blues, or what Holly calls "the mean reds."

The beauty of reading about your destination before you set out is that literature can give you the inside scoop on where you're headed. Spending a long weekend in Charleston? There's no better guide than a writer like Pat Conroy, who grew up in the geography and the traditions of the South Carolina Low Country he writes about in *The Prince of Tides*, *The Water Is Wide*, and other books. Through fiction, writers such as Conroy convey the lives of real people in a particular region and provide insights that help us understand and appreciate the people and cultures we encounter when we travel there. If you plan to visit New Orleans and want to understand what happened during Hurricane Katrina and its continuing impact on the area, read Tom Piazza's fictional work *City of Refuge*. As author Richard Russo said of the book, "To read *City of Refuge* is to realize that is what fiction is for: to take us to places the cameras can't go." Plan your Seattle trip around *Snow Falling on Cedars* with an accompanying trip to Bainbridge Island, one of the places that inspired the author, and you'll discover the area's history, ethnic mix, industry, arts, and culture and have fun on the water, too. Fiction can layer events, explain people and their motivations, and distill their emotions in a manner that intensifies reality, which can make a reader a truly savvy traveler.

Camaraderie, too, is a key attraction of literary getaways. I love the time my book groups spend sharing perspectives on the book of the month over wine, dessert, and the occasional roaring fire. But traveling to a literary destination allows you to get away (at least for a while) from the pressures and distractions of work, motherhood, soccer practice, and so many other responsibilities. You gain just a little time to explore new places and ideas, try new things, and, if nothing else, have a lot of fun in each other's company. We're still sharing photos of each other riding Segways in Chicago and playing darts in a lakeside Wisconsin tavern.

Cindy Hudson, the author of *Book by Book: The Complete Guide to Creating Mother-Daughter Book Clubs*, knows the feeling. After her book group read Barbara Kingsolver's *Animal, Vegetable, Miracle*, which focuses on eating locally, her book group organized a wine-tasting day with a potluck lunch focused on ingredients from a local farmers' market. They talked to the winegrowers, sipped a bit of their wine, and ate incredible food. They discussed what they had learned about eating locally as well as ideas they had for changing their food habits going forward. Hudson says, "The pictures from that day show all of us with big smiles. The event was such a hit we knew that we'd be looking at other opportunities to take our group on the road at least once a year."

Bear in mind, you *can* go too far with all this. One of my favorite examples is in Wendy McClure's *The Wilder Life*, a hilarious story of truly over-the-top literary travel. A passionate fan of Laura Ingalls

Wilder's *Little House on the Prairie* stories, McClure attempted to experience what she calls "Laura World" by tackling Little House activities such as churning butter and making Vanity Cakes. Her results, simply put, were less than spectacular. When she visits the sites that Laura Ingalls Wilder wrote about, it becomes apparent that reality doesn't hold a hand-dipped tallow candle to the world Laura created in our imaginations. In many places, there isn't much left of the homes where the real-life Ingalls family lived, and the kitschy commercialism seemed to diminish the magic of the books. Writer and English professor Anne Trubek came to a similar conclusion on a tour of the homes of writers ranging from Hemingway to Poe to Langston Hughes, which she discusses in *A Skeptic's Guide to Writers' Houses*. Says Trubek, "We will never find our favorite characters or admired techniques within these houses; we can't join Huck on the raft or experience Faulkner's stream of consciousness. We can only walk through empty rooms full of pitchers and paintings and stoves."

But literary travel isn't about visiting authors' homes. Of course, you can't expect to see Jo, Amy, and the other "little women" if you visit Louisa May Alcott's home, though it's fun to imagine them dancing around in the author's brain as she sat at her desk. But a side trip to O. Henry's tiny house in Austin, Texas, is well worth the effort to hear a bit about his life and to see how people lived in that time period.

Still, the essence of the writer isn't in a house; it's in his or her words and ideas. And when you pack those along on your trip, they can elevate your travel from ho-hum to thrilling. To me, the intersection of literature and travel is a lot like a Venn diagram; it's that place where the mental and emotional imagery of a great book and its contemporary sights, sounds, and smells all overlap. The search for that "sweet spot" between imagination and reality is the hallmark of literary travel. Find it, and you're in heaven.

2

How to Avoid a Temperamental Journey

Mark Twain said, "I have found out that there ain't no surer way to find out whether you like people or hate them than to travel with them." I know exactly what he means. The power struggles, factions, shifting loyalties, emotional highs and lows, and cliff-hanging uncertainty can make a vacation resemble a trip through the pages of *Lord of the Flies*. What will happen next? Will someone save them? Will they kill each other?

Of course, your group has none of these issues. You're patient, considerate, and savvy travelers. You're cohesive and fun-loving—regular "BFFs." Still, you're all different people with different, shall we say, *quirks*. So let's review the concept of group dynamics, some of the reasons that conflicts arise, and how planning can help avoid friction before you hit the road.

After traveling with friends, family, couples, an Outward Bound group, and, of course, book groups, I know of what I speak. Simple personality conflicts are common partly because traveling forces people to be together far more than in normal life. Trust me, when you spend a lot of time together, the quirks take center stage. Little things you may not notice during, say, a book-club gathering or over lunch (for example, someone being too opinionated or pushy, always late, or not paying her fair share of the restaurant tab) become like nails on the blackboard. But there's hope for even the most unruly group.

So how do you minimize the risk that your sentimental journey might turn into a temperamental one? Two things—understanding group dynamics and careful predeparture planning—are paramount. And you don't need to travel with a clinical psychologist to be successful at both. Rather than avoiding or ignoring the issues, people in the group need to anticipate problems, voice their concerns, and come to a mutual understanding ahead of time. I'm talking about basic but important things, like how often will we eat? Raise your hand if you snore enough to rattle the windows. Who will be that person's roomie? Is there anyone in the group whose idea of packing light is to bring a giant purple suitcase, a duffel bag full of pillows and purses, and maybe a small dog? Pretrip planning sessions provide a venue for groups to ask such questions and establish the ground rules, a list of dos and don'ts for the trip. And put compromise at the top of that list. It's probably the most important part of traveling in a group. Other expectations may include respect, communication, contributing equally (in terms of effort and money), being inclusive, and helping others. While you want to be sure you yourself have fun, it's also important to be flexible and make an effort to ensure that the whole group has fun. If everyone takes this approach, everyone's needs should eventually get met.

Ironically, it's often the groups whose members have very similar personalities that have the most difficult time traveling together. One of the tensest trips I've taken was with a group of hard-driving type-A personalities. We were great friends at home, when we only had to decide where to go for the occasional dinner, but on the road each decision became a not-so-subtle battle of wills. Compromise? Never! We practically had to arm wrestle to decide what time to meet for breakfast. My experience was hardly unique. "The problems usually arise when a majority of the group is passive or a majority of the group is bossy," says Tim O'Connell, an associate professor in the Department of Recreation and Leisure Studies at Brock University in St. Catharines, Ontario, Canada, and coauthor of *Group Dynamics in Recreation and Leisure*.

By contrast, the groups with the least conflict are typically those with the most diverse personality types because they bring a variety of perspectives, ideas, styles, and ways of doing things to the table. In 2011, one of my book groups drove from Minneapolis to a member's Wisconsin lake cabin in a thirty-three-foot RV, dubbed the Bookmobile. I'll confess that it wasn't my idea. I had visions of us careening over curbs, knocking down streetlights, and sending pedestrians scurrying for cover. But one member of our group, who I'm sure was a long-haul trucker in a previous life, actually *wanted* to drive the rig. Another dedicated herself to the role of navigator. So we all jumped in with both feet. On the morning of our departure, we showed up looking like kids ready for camp, and in a stunning reversal, our kids took a picture of *us*. We had enough gear for a month-long trip and enough food to feed a marine platoon, but it all fit. We worked together to get our gigantic vehicle safely parked without knocking down pine trees, and the road trip was as much fun as the cabin. Multiple ideas and perspectives made the trip a success.

Conflicts also arise when members of the group have different goals for the same trip, for example, different expectations for the level of physical activity or for how lively the nightlife should be on a trip. Other lit-trip goals worth discussing might include delving more into a book by seeing the landscape where it takes place, learning more about the life and culture in a particular destination, meeting an author, or simply relaxing and spending time discussing a book in the environment that is the backdrop for the story. But what makes a group successful is that it merges individual goals and objectives into shared group goals. Establishing those up front creates conditions for everyone to have a good time, because they understand what the trip is all about from each others' perspectives. "Conflict," O'Connell summarizes, "can arise in any group if there is a lack of clarity about roles, goals, and expectations." Armed with this knowledge, lit trippers can proceed to the next phase—actually planning the trip.

PLOTTING THE PLAN

Making everyone sit down and get organized can feel a bit like herding cats. If your group needs a little extra motivation to do some detailed planning, read about some truly spectacular examples of *poor* planning, such as Candice Millard's book *River of Doubt* about Theodore Roosevelt's disastrous journey down a tributary of the Amazon, Susan Jane Gilman's travel memoir *Undress Me in the Temple of Heaven*, or other books listed in the "It Seemed Like a Good Idea at the Time" chapter of Nancy Pearl's *Book Lust to Go*.

Your group isn't likely to face starvation or malaria as Roosevelt did, but travel experts agree that no matter where you're going, planning is key. And the farther in advance, the better. Planning well ahead can help those on a tight budget save for the trip and for the group to find deals and discounts. Longer lead times also offer the opportunity to book tickets to high-demand shows and museum exhibits. And because many restaurants and tours can't accommodate a sizable group spontaneously, it's especially important to book them in advance.

Brainstorming for the trip can be an enjoyable experience as the group comes to a consensus on what activities, sights, and experiences they want to choose. The process generates energy, excitement, and enthusiasm for the trip, especially if the group is prepared with brochures, websites, or guidebooks for the destination. A pretrip planning session provides a great time for people to share their expectations. They can "put their cards on the table" so everyone else knows where they are coming from. This openness helps minimize surprises down the road.

For book lovers, it's fun to frame the discussion in terms of literature, so here's a list of questions to jump-start the process.

JAY GATSBY OR OLIVER TWIST?

Discuss your budget and finances to tailor a trip that's affordable for all. The budget will dictate how far you can go, whether you drive or fly, the type of accommodations you choose, and whether you share rooms. Don't forget that renting a house can be an economical option for a group.

EDITH WHARTON OR JACK KEROUAC?

Do you seek a taste of Gilded Age glamour, or are you blue jeans and jalopy types? A slim budget may still accommodate people who yearn for a little luxe, if only for an evening. Make sure you're on the same page when it comes to clothing so you don't have one friend in cutoffs and others in cocktail dresses. No matter what the dress code, take lots of pictures. Many people have photographs of themselves only with their families or, if they're the family photographers, they may have no pictures of themselves at all.

BEACH MUSIC OR *THE SNOWS OF KILIMANJARO*?

For northerners, finding warm weather provides an added incentive to travel in winter. Others prefer to "chill."

FAR FROM THE MADDING CROWD OR *BRIGHT LIGHTS, BIG CITY*?

For many, a spa or a western ranch holds more appeal than the fast-paced energy of a big city. Ditto for quiet evenings versus lively nightlife.

AROUND THE WORLD IN EIGHTY DAYS OR *WAITING FOR GODOT*?

What's the energy level of people in your group and the pace they hope to set? The answer will help determine how much to pack into your itinerary.

ULYSSES OR *THE CAT IN THE HAT*?

How bookish should the trip be? Discuss how serious the group is about cultural pursuits and book-related tours and activities and how you might balance the intellectual side of the trip with some good mindless fun.

SHERLOCK HOLMES OR DR. WATSON?

Every group has people who are natural, proactive doers, while others are happy to act as companionable sidekicks along for the ride. Some groups succeed by putting the trip into the hands of the most motivated planners. Still, people usually feel more excited about participating in a trip when the plan incorporates some of their ideas rather than being something that was forced upon them. The trick is to capitalize on the talents of the group and divide the planning tasks among people whose interests and talents match each job. So find out who might be the best and most motivated people to make restaurant reservations, book hotels, organize the finances, shoot photos, or research events and activities.

SCARLETT O'HARA OR MELANIE WILKES?

Do you have a bold personality with a zest to try new food, jump into adventurous activities, and meet new people? Or are you a little wary of the unknown? I heartily advocate erring on the Scarlett end of the scale by building new experiences into any trip. I think it's important to stretch yourself throughout life, and travel provides the perfect opportunity to get out of your comfort zone in ways large and small. What a shame it would be to come back from a vacation saying, "I wish I had . . ." rather than "I'm glad I did . . ." So, while planning your trip, encourage each other to seize the day, take a chance, and try something new, even if it's as simple as taking a short art class, listening to a different type of music, or getting your feet wet by kayaking for the first time. Then you can return to the "real world" with no regrets.

THE FINAL QUESTION: WHICH DO YOU PICK FIRST, THE BOOK OR THE PLACE?

Pick a place you've wanted to go and find books to match, or choose a book that has made your travel taste buds tingle enough to go where it takes place. "We've done it both ways," says Karen Johnson of St. Paul, Minnesota, whose group has taken trips both large and small. "We knew there was an exhibit about Jackie Onassis at the Field Museum in Chicago, so we all read different books about her and took a trip to Chicago to see the exhibit." Some book groups pick a destination and plan an entire year's worth of reading around it. Conversely, my book club enjoyed reading *The Devil in the White City*, which inspired a trip to Chicago to learn more about the 1893 world's fair, the history, and the architects behind the story, which was the inspiration for chapter 10.

AUTHORING THE ITINERARY

Everyone has shared their expectations, their goals, and the activities they'd like to pursue with the group. All that pretrip discussion actually takes shape when the group puts its plans into an itinerary, which is essentially a schedule. By folding in agreed-upon goals and objectives, the itinerary transforms individuals into a group. By creating an itinerary, you will eliminate the conflict that arises from uncertainty by providing structure, especially when the group as a whole has bought into the itinerary beforehand. Many free-spirited travelers prefer not to make a detailed itinerary, with the notion that it limits their experience "in the moment," but save that for when you travel by yourself or perhaps with one other person. For a group, an itinerary, even a very loose one, is critical. It simply keeps the group on track.

Yet just how tightly you design the itinerary depends on the nature of the group and individual members' personalities. A strict or loose itinerary depends, in part, on specific activities that require the group to be in a place at a particular time, such as dinner at a restaurant or theater reservations. Before our trip to Chicago, at first our book group planned only the basics—hotel and air transportation—but left out the details, thinking that the rest of the plans would fall into place when we got there. Fortunately, one person pushed the group to do more concrete planning. She took it upon herself to create an itinerary, make restaurant reservations, and book a show. If she hadn't, we would have done only about half of what we did, with about half the memories and probably some frustration at not being able to do what we wanted on a last-minute basis.

Choreographing all you want to get done into a seamless schedule may seem daunting. Start creating your itinerary by listing everything the group wants to see or do at your destination in order of priority. To get a feel for how much time to devote to various activities, consult guidebooks and websites (tourism bureaus' websites, such as www.nycgo.com, offer suggested itineraries) and post questions on Twitter or to online message boards, such as TripAdvisor. This research will make it easier for you to estimate what you can accomplish during, say, a three-day trip. A touch of technology makes the job easier. Websites such as Triporama or TripHub provide helpful itinerary planning and communication tools to keep the entire group up to speed. Microsoft and Apple also offer easy-to-use itinerary software. In addition, tourism sites such as Explore Chicago (www.explorechicago.org) provide online trip-planning tools.

Though it's tempting, resist the urge to jam activity into every minute of the trip, from the earliest morning flight to the final nightcap. Otherwise your trip will feel more like marine boot camp than a refreshing getaway. The trick is to think of free time, or down time, as an activity that you schedule. For example, it can be quiet time when the group decides to be in the same place to read or watch television or a movie. Trips often require lots of walking or other physical activity to which some group members might not be accustomed. Breaks help people stay both physically and emotionally fresh. Also, time alone can be a great way to fulfill individual needs and desires with little impact on others. Free time allows people to explore on their own, do things "their way," and take a break from the rest of the group.

If interests diverge or if some in the group want to keep going while others want a break, consider splitting the group and reuniting at an appointed time. A split group doesn't mean you don't like each other. Instead, it shows effective communication and an understanding of differences. It's a great way to accommodate both the frantic runners and the slow pacers, the party animals and the early-to-bed introverts.

ANTICIPATING PLOT TWISTS

Despite the emphasis here on creating a schedule, it's important to anticipate the unexpected on any trip. "A journey is like marriage," said John Steinbeck. "The certain way to be wrong is to think you control it." That's why a certain amount of flexibility in following the itinerary is as important as the itinerary itself.

In many ways, the anticipation of the trip and all that you've planned is part of the fun. But when individuals make a plan, they begin to play out the scenario in their heads, thinking about what to expect and how to react. So, without a little unanticipated excitement, it feels like they've already taken the trip in their minds: been there, done that. But surprises, even small ones, add zest to the experience. It's like receiving a surprise gift instead of opening a package you ordered yourself.

Sometimes flexibility just means taking the time to savor simple moments of serendipity, says Kathy Louise Patrick, owner of Beauty and the Book hair salon and bookstore in Jefferson, Texas. Patrick is also founder of the Pulpwood Queens and Timber Guys Book Clubs (which have sprouted forty-three chapters across the United States and several in Europe) and frequent leader of book-based trips. She and a group of Pulpwood Queens from Texas were on a tour in Venice, Italy, when they encountered the unexpected: "We were walking along a canal and a group of vendors started whistling the theme from *Dallas*. We cracked up and couldn't figure out how they knew we were from Texas. Then we realized our pink cowboy hats might have been the clue."

While visiting the home of the Nobel Prize–winning author Pearl Buck in Pennsylvania, Karen Johnson's St. Paul book group enjoyed a delightfully unplanned discussion with Buck's daughter, who had arrived for a board meeting and started a conversation with them. The group took extra time from their schedule to chat with her. "On another trip," says Johnson, "we went to Montgomery, Alabama, with a focus on Zelda Fitzgerald. But we found the F. Scott and Zelda Fitzgerald Museum a little dull, so we adjusted our itinerary to spend more time at Martin Luther King Jr.'s first church, which we found fascinating."

Following their itinerary too rigidly would have made both trips much less interesting. When great unplanned opportunities arise, hold a quick check-in with the group to approve a change; then go with the flow.

ADDING AN EPILOGUE

Adding one last component to your itinerary will conclude your literary tour de force on a high note: a final celebration of being together as a group. Whether it's the final breakfast, lunch, or dinner of the trip or a post-trip gathering, it's important and enjoyable to rehash the trip, share photos, and evaluate the pros and cons of the journey. What did you love and what would you do differently? In what subtle ways did the trip transform you or the group as a whole? What did you learn? Perhaps the trip will fuel future reading lists or new travel ideas. This final recap helps the group learn from its experiences and create an even better lit-trip sequel down the road.

3

Short Story

LIT TRIPS IN YOUR OWN BACKYARD

Don't get me wrong; I love to travel, especially with fellow lit lovers. But you don't have to travel to Bali in the footsteps of Elizabeth Gilbert in *Eat, Pray, Love* to take a "lit trip." Nor must the trip be long and expensive. I've found that book-based adventures close to home provide a great way to dip your toes in the water of literary travel and enrich your reading experience as well. Short trips also provide a tonic for book groups that could use a little variety to spice up their relationships.

Some groups simply opt for a weekend getaway together, perhaps to a spa or condo near the beach, where they bond over a book discussion in a new atmosphere. Fran Shea, whose suburban Minneapolis book club has been meeting since the 1970s, says their occasional simple trips together have strengthened their already tight bond. My own book group drove an RV from Minneapolis to a member's Wisconsin lake cabin, as I mentioned in chapter 2. At the cabin, we discussed Wallace Stegner's novel *Crossing to Safety*, which is set partly in the same area of the state, and also chose our books for the upcoming year.

Reading a book and going as a group to see a movie or play made from it provides a great local travel opportunity. Peggy Terry, cochair of the Folktales' Black Women's Literary Society in Austin, Texas, talks about the time her group traveled to San Antonio for dinner and to see the play *The Color Purple*. Terry notes the many literary organizations and associations of book clubs for African American women, such as the United California African-American Bookclubs or the Go On Girl! Book Club, that provide opportunities for book groups to come together, meet other groups, and support the literary contributions of authors of African descent. Countless other literary organizations and book festivals around the country offer opportunities for book lovers to meet and greet each other as well as their favorite authors (see the appendix on page 273). One of the more creative gatherings I've heard about is the Pulpwood Queens Book Club's annual themed "Girlfriend Weekend" in Jefferson, Texas, featuring dinners at which authors serve the food and culminating with the annual "Hair Ball."

Other book-bound activities may require only a couple of hours on a weekend afternoon or an evening out, perhaps something as simple as attending author appearances and signings at local bookstores. Booksellers, independent and chain alike, are eager to have groups in their stores, especially if they *buy books*. These people love books, they're widely read, and, given some notice, they're usually happy to discuss reading ideas and make recommendations. And don't forget that many colleges, universities, and local community education programs offer classes or seminars on particular books and authors that are great to attend as a group. For example, I joined an evening seminar at the University of Minnesota in which a university ethicist, Dr. Jeffrey Kahn, discussed the ethical aspects of *The Immortal Life of Henrietta Lacks*, a bestselling work about the woman whose cells revolutionized modern-day cancer and genomic research.

You don't have to wait for an outside organization to create such literary activities. You just need to pick a nearby destination or a topic and find a book to match. Think "field trip," like those trips you took in school, only without the long ride on a school bus or the "sack lunch." Live near New York City? There's hardly a place in the city where Jack Kerouac and his beat buddies didn't hang out or that didn't serve as the location for some classic novel. My Minneapolis book club read Laura Hillenbrand's *Seabiscuit* and then went to a local horse-racing track. We saw beautiful racehorses up close, watched their jockeys maneuver on the track, and even placed a few bets. We didn't win much, but we had a great time.

But small-town America is equally awash in opportunities for lit trips. Take, for example, Valerie Van Kooten, who is an instructor at Central College in Pella, Iowa, and who organizes literary trips in conjunction with a bookstore in Oskaloosa, Iowa, called the Book Vault. "After I put down a book," says Van Kooten, "I wonder what the place looks like, what the people there are like. It's an incomplete experience." Reading-related travel, she says, completes the picture. Through the Book Vault (so named because it's located in an old bank building), she assembles book-based trips that range from close-to-home locations to cross-country destinations. For example, her group read Fergus M. Bordewich's *Bound for Canaan: The Underground Railroad and the War for the Soul of America* and Mary Kay Ricks's *Escape on the Pearl: The Heroic Bid for Freedom on the Underground Railroad*. The next month, they traveled to historic Underground Railroad "stations" in Iowa. "No matter how great the book, there's nothing like actually standing in a tiny space meant to hide a runaway slave to drive home the runaways' experience," she says. In another example, they took a tour of "haunted Iowa" based on a book of the same name.

Sometimes, traveling around one's own community may offer a surprisingly eye-opening experience. The ultimate destination, as author Henry Miller said, "is never a place, but a new way of seeing things." Lit trips offer a way to see your own environment anew and discover people, buildings, works of art, and restaurants that you pass every day without noticing. That great writer and traveler Bill Bryson says, "To my mind, the greatest reward and luxury of travel is to be able to experience everyday things as if for the first time, to be in a position in which almost nothing is so familiar it is taken for granted." Bryson gained a huge following with his funny books about travels in Australia, *In a Sunburned Country*, and walking the Appalachian Trail, *A Walk in the Woods*. But he turned his focus to the great indoors and wrote about touring his own home in *At Home: A Short History of Private Life*. Who knew kitchens, fuse boxes, bedrooms, and attics could provide such fascinating material?

In his book *The Art of Travel*, Alain de Botton tells about a Frenchman named Xavier de Maistre who took the idea of travel close to home to an even greater extreme in a work called *A Journey Around My Room*. Says de Botton, "De Maistre's work sprang from a profound and suggestive insight; the notion that the pleasure we derive from a journey may be dependent more on the mind-set we travel *with* than on the destination we travel *to*. If only we could apply a traveling mind-set to our own locales, we might find these places becoming no less interesting than, say, the high mountain passes and butterfly-filled jungles of Humboldt's South America." I don't recommend inviting everyone over for a tour of your bedroom, but you get the point; the possibilities are endless.

Below you'll find a list of books grouped by subject area along with loosely related places to go and things to do, just to get you thinking. Bon voyage!

ANIMALS

READ:
Paul Auster, *Timbuktu*
Rita Mae Brown, *Hiss of Death*, *Murder Unleashed*, and others

Temple Grandin, *Animals Make Us Human*

John Grogan, *Marley and Me: Life and Love with the World's Worst Dog*

Julie Klam, *Love at First Bark: How Saving a Dog Can Sometimes Help You Save Yourself*

Jack London, *The Call of the Wild, White Fang*

Stephen McCauley, *The Man of the House*

Susan Orlean, *Rin Tin Tin: The Life and the Legend*

Garth Stein, *The Art of Racing in the Rain*

GO: Visit a local humane society or animal rescue group. Make a donation and you'll be doing a little pet-related philanthropy, too. Or attend a dog or cat show or agility competition (the kind where animals race at top speed through obstacle courses that include running through chutes, weaving in and out between poles, and leaping over jumps). Yes, there are agility competitions for cats, too.

ART

READ:

Steve Martin, *An Object of Beauty*

Steven Naifeh and Gregory White Smith, *Van Gogh: The Life* and *Jackson Pollock: An American Saga*

Irving Stone, *The Agony and the Ecstasy* (Michelangelo) and *Lust for Life* (Van Gogh)

Edmund de Waal, *The Hare with Amber Eyes: A Family's Century of Art and Loss*

Robert K. Wittman and John Shiffman, *Priceless: How I Went Undercover to Rescue the World's Stolen Treasures*

GO: Visit a gallery, attend a community education art or art history class, or go to a museum. Many museums across the country offer tours related to particular books.

BOOKS

READ:

Nicholas Basbanes, *A Gentle Madness: Bibliophiles, Bibliomanes, and the Eternal Passion for Books* and *Patience and Fortitude: A Roving Chronicle of Book People, Book Places, and Book Culture*

GO: Attend an antiquarian book fair or visit an author's home. If you live near a particularly fabulous library, go there for an event or tour.

BUILDINGS

READ:

Bill Bryson, *At Home: A Short History of Private Life*

Barbara Isenberg, *Conversations with Frank Gehry*

Michael Pollan, *A Place of My Own: The Architecture of Daydreams*

Ayn Rand, *The Fountainhead*

Books about Frank Lloyd Wright, such as Nancy Horan's *Loving Frank*, Brendan Gill's *Many Masks: A Life of Frank Lloyd Wright*, or T. C. Boyle's *The Women*. (Wright's personal life was as provocative as his design philosophy.)

GO: Tour an architecturally significant building or home. Chapters of the American Institute of Architects and some art museums also hold tours of important local buildings. Sightseeing companies often offer architectural tours, too.

CHALLENGE YOURSELF

READ:

Steve House, *Beyond the Mountain*

Amber Karlins, *My Year of Living Fearlessly*

Beryl Markham, *West with the Night*

Jane Robinson (editor), *Unsuitable for Ladies: An Anthology of Women Travellers*

GO: Try something new that takes you out of your comfort zone, even a little, such as scaling a climbing wall, sky diving, surfing, or cross-country skiing.

COOKING AND EATING

READ:

Julia Child, *My Life in France*

M. F. K. Fisher, *The Gastronomical Me, How to Cook a Wolf*, and others. John Updike called her "the poet of the appetites."

Gabrielle Hamilton, *Blood, Bones, & Butter: The Inadvertent Education of a Reluctant Chef*

Kate Moses, *Cakewalk: A Memoir*

Julie Powell, *Julie and Julia: My Year of Cooking Dangerously*

Ruth Reichl, *Tender at the Bone: Growing Up at the Table, Comfort Me with Apples*, and *Garlic and Sapphires: The Secret Life of a Critic in Disguise*

Calvin Trillin, *The Tummy Trilogy*. Trillin has been called the "Walt Whitman of American eats."

Patricia Volk, *Stuffed: Adventures of a Restaurant Family*

GO: Visit a restaurant, cooking class, wine shop, or bakery, or participate in any food-related activity.

CRIME

READ:

Raymond Chandler, *The Big Sleep, Farewell My Lovely, The Long Goodbye*

Agatha Christie, *And Then There Were None, Death on the Nile, Murder on the Orient Express*

Sir Arthur Conan Doyle, *The Hound of the Baskervilles, A Study in Scarlet*, and many others

Gillian Flynn, *Gone Girl*

Dashiell Hammett, *The Maltese Falcon, The Thin Man*

Patricia Highsmith, *Strangers on a Train, The Talented Mr. Ripley*, and others

P. D. James, *The Private Patient, Talking About Detective Fiction,*
Devices and Desires
GO: Tour the local police department or state police sheriff's
office. This sounds like a kids' field trip, but it can be cool for
grown-ups, too. Some departments offer tours of their crime labs.

FAIRS

READ:
Melanie Benjamin, *The Autobiography of Mrs. Tom Thumb*
Katherine Dunn, *Geek Love*
Sara Gruen, *Water for Elephants*
Erin Morgenstern, *The Night Circus*
Phil Stong, *State Fair*
GO: Attend a state fair, county fair, or circus.

FARMS

READ:
Timothy Egan, *The Worst Hard Time*
Michael Perry, *Coop: A Family, a Farm, and the Pursuit of One*
Good Egg
David Rhodes, *Driftless*
Jane Smiley, *A Thousand Acres*
John Steinbeck, *The Grapes of Wrath*
GO: Visit or volunteer on a farm (see Worldwide Opportunities
on Organic Farms, www.wwoofusa.org/About_WWOOFUSA) or
volunteer at a farm animal sanctuary (www.farmsanctuary.org
/get_involved/jobs/volunteer.html#farm).

HAUNTED HOUSES AND SCARY PLACES

READ:
Shirley Jackson, *The Haunting of Hill House*
Stephen King, *The Shining, Carrie,* and many others

Stephanie Meyer, the *Twilight* series (see chapter 16)
Edgar Allen Poe, *Edgar Allen Poe: Poetry and Tales*
W. Scott Poole, *Monsters in America: Our Historical Obsession with the Hideous and the Haunting*
Anne Rice, *Interview with the Vampire, Lasher, The Vampire Lestat*
Edith Wharton, *The Ghost Stories of Edith Wharton*
GO: Take a "ghost tour" offered by a tour company in your area or visit a Halloween haunted house.

HISTORY

READ:
Stephen E. Ambrose, *Undaunted Courage*
Taylor Branch, *Parting the Waters* and *Pillar of Fire*
Shelby Foote, *Shiloh*
David McCullough, *1776, Truman, John Adams, The Great Bridge*
Sarah Vowell, *Assassination Vacation, The Wordy Shipmates*
Or ask at your library or historical society about any great books that explore your local history.
GO: Visit your local historical society, battlefields, or landmarks.

MUSIC

READ:
Johnny Cash, *Cash: The Autobiography*
Peter Guralnick, *Lost Highway: Journeys and Arrivals of American Musicians* and other books by this author
Nick Hornby, *High Fidelity*
B. B. King and David Ritz, *Blues All Around Me: The Autobiography of B. B. King*
Kathleen Krull, *Lives of the Musicians: Good Times, Bad Times (and What the Neighbors Thought).* This is a kids' book, but people of all ages will have fun reading it.
Loretta Lynn, *Loretta Lynn: Coal Miner's Daughter*
Nancy B. Reich, *Clara Schumann: The Artist and the Woman*

Keith Richards, *Life*
Patti Smith, *Just Kids*
Sheila Weller, *Girls Like Us: Carole King, Joni Mitchell, Carly
 Simon—and the Journey of a Generation*
GO: Attend a concert that relates to the book.

SPORTS

READ:
Biking: James McManus, *Going to the Sun*
Fishing: Ernest Hemingway, *The Old Man and the Sea*; **Norman
 Maclean**, *A River Runs Through It*
Water adventures: Lisa Michaels, *Grand Ambition*; **Candice
 Millard**, *River of Doubt*
Horseracing: Laura Hillenbrand, *Seabiscuit*
Baseball: W. P. Kinsella, *Shoeless Joe*; **Bernard Malamud,**
 The Natural
Football: H. G. Bissinger, *Friday Night Lights: A Town, a Team,
 and a Dream*; **Taylor Branch,** *The Cartel: Inside the Rise and
 Imminent Fall of the NCAA*
Soccer: Franklin Foer, *How Soccer Explains the World*; **Chuck
 Korr and Marvin Close**, *More than Just a Game: Soccer vs.
 Apartheid*
GO: Attend a game or event related to the sport.

Part II
READING EAST TO WEST

4

Boston

ON LAND AND SEA

If there's an epicenter of the intersection of American history and literature, it's Boston. Running from *The Crucible* and *The Scarlet Letter* to *Mystic River*, the rich literature of the Boston area suggests opportunities for lit lovers and traveling book clubs unmatched anywhere else in the country. So many, in fact, that this chapter is a "twofer."

Consider, first, the pursuit of Revolutionary literature and history. If you find yourself attracted to guys adorned with tricorn hats, capes, knee breeches, and shoes with big brass buckles who stroll down the Freedom Trail while whistling "Yankee Doodle," option 1 is tailor-made for you. You'll experience Boston, the cradle of liberty and the birthplace of the American Revolution, but through the eyes of two heroines of that era—Abigail Adams and Phillis Wheatley. Option 2 focuses on the Boston area's maritime tradition, also central to a wealth of American history and literature from Herman Melville's whale tale, *Moby Dick*, widely regarded as *the* great American novel, to Sebastian Junger's contemporary tale of the sea, *The Perfect Storm*. You'll learn about and experience the lives of those who have for centuries gone "down to the sea in ships" and those who await their safe return.

So choose between the two itineraries, combine ideas from each, or do both. No matter how you choose, enjoy the combination of literary tradition and history and modern-day art, culture, cuisine, and outdoor recreation that makes Boston unique.

OPTION 1

YOU GO GIRL! ABIGAIL ADAMS AND PHILLIS WHEATLEY

> *If we mean to have Heroes, Statesmen and Philosophers, we should have learned women. The world perhaps would laugh at me, and accuse me of vanity, but you I know have a mind too enlarged and liberal to disregard the Sentiment. If much depends as is allowed upon the early Education of youth and the first principals which are instill'd take the deepest root, great benefit must arise from literary accomplishments in women.*
> —**Abigail Adams,** *The Letters of John and Abigail Adams*

Like most book lovers, whenever I read about some far-distant place or time, I try to imagine myself in that setting. But the American Revolution has always challenged my visualization skills. There were no cameras to photograph the battlefield as there were during the Civil War. We have none of the haunting photos of those young soldiers gazing solemnly at us through time. On top of that, the history books depict a Revolutionary "team" composed solely of males. Paul Revere made his midnight ride; Patrick Henry shouted, "Give me liberty or give me death"; and Washington crossed the Delaware. Meanwhile, the girls had Betsy Ross sewing a flag. In some ways that's understandable. During colonial times, women's roles were limited primarily to marriage and motherhood. If the main characters in our stories of the American Revolution were men, it's mainly because women weren't allowed a voice in political life. When they got married, they usually lost their property and legal rights. Most were poorly educated, even illiterate.

However, in recent years historians have started to recover from the gender amnesia that they have suffered through the years and begun to investigate the ways in which Revolution-era women kept the economy and the farms running while their men were away fighting. As it turns out, a few of them were fighting right alongside the men. The lives of two particularly remarkable women offer a way to look at the Revolutionary era from a different angle—founding mother Abigail Adams and her contemporary Phillis Wheatley, the first person of African descent to publish poems in English. Their accomplishments are astounding for their era and are even more inspiring when viewed from the twenty-first century. So, taking advantage of our time's more inclusive perspective, we can visit Boston and walk the cobblestones where the patriots, men *and* women, walked and where revolution took root.

Let's start with Abigail, as seen in Woody Holton's biography *Abigail Adams: A Life*. One of the great things for posterity—not so great for the couple—is that John and Abigail Adams were separated for much of their married life. John was either off working in other towns as a lawyer, in Philadelphia framing the Constitution, or in France working as a diplomat. Consequently, they wrote frequent and wonderful letters. Their correspondence survived largely because John Adams recognized that they were living in historic times and ordered all of his correspondence to be kept. So we have been left with a chronicle of both daily life and a view of crucial events in American Revolutionary history as seen through the eyes of a couple in the thick of it. The book shows the important ways in which Adams and other women of the era played important roles in the formation of the country, even though their efforts have been overshadowed by the stories of the

Founding Fathers. With her husband away so frequently, she had little choice but to fail or succeed on her own, beyond the limited expectations that society set for women. She ran the farm, built a business, purchased property, and owned it in her own right, all rare deeds for eighteenth-century women.

But Abigail's interests ran broader and deeper. Holton's view of Abigail emphasizes her interest in the politics of the day and her enduring interest in women's issues. In a famous letter to John, who was a delegate at the Constitutional Convention, she urged her husband to remember the rights of women while they were framing the basic principles of the nation. "I long to hear that you have declared an independency and by the way in the new Code of Laws which I suppose it will be necessary for you to make I desire you would Remember the Ladies, and be more generous and favourable to them than your ancestors." She urged him, "Do not put such unlimited power in the hands of the Husbands." These statements have made her a feminist icon.

The power of literature contributed greatly to Abigail's thinking. She constantly rued the lack of proper education for women; she obtained the bulk of her own education through reading and discussing books and ideas with her friends through correspondence. Describing Abigail's literary activities, which are reminiscent of today's book clubs, Holton writes, "She and her friends frequently read books and discussed them. They also exchanged numerous letters, not only trading gossip (although they did that, too) but making self-conscious efforts to teach and learn. Abigail cannot properly be described as self-taught, for she and her friends educated each other." He says there was one major difference from today's book groups: "Thoroughly impressed with the authors they read and at the same time modest about their own powers of observation, the young letter writers rarely found anything to criticize in the books they discussed."

Just down the street, but worlds apart from Abigail Adams, lived one of the icons of early American literature, Phillis Wheatley, the enslaved poet. There's no record that they ever met, but it's fun to imagine them crossing paths on the street or to picture Adams reading one of Wheatley's poems in a local newspaper. Harvard University professor Henry Louis Gates Jr. tells her story in *The Trials of Phillis Wheatley: America's First Black Poet and Her Encounters with the Founding Fathers,* a book that is an expanded version of the Thomas Jefferson Lecture in the Humanities that he gave before the Library of Congress.

Susanna Wheatley purchased the seven-year-old Phillis "for a trifle" on Boston's Beach Street Wharf and named her after the ship she arrived on, *The Phillis.* Highly unusual for slave owners, the Wheatleys taught Phillis to speak English and to read, and she studied Latin and the Bible. By watching others use a pen, she taught herself how to write and started writing poems, which Susanna Wheatley submitted on her behalf for publication in various local newspapers. She wrote a poem about the Boston Massacre, *On the Affray in King Street,* patriotic poems, elegies, and odes to people, including George Washington. Her poem about renowned English preacher, the Reverend George Whitefield, who was touring the country at the time of his death, was so popular that it was published multiple times in Boston; Newport, New York; Philadelphia; and, later, London. That, says Gates, "made her the Toni Morrison of her time."

Yet because she was an enslaved African, few people believed that she was really capable of writing such poetry. When Susanna Wheatley set out to have a collection of Phillis's poems published, not a single publisher accepted the authenticity of her works. In one of the truly odd events of American history, eighteen of the era's most important men, including Massachusetts governor Thomas Hutchinson and John Hancock, gathered for a trial, a sort of inquisition to determine if Phillis really authored the poems. Imagine how daunting it must have been for a slave, probably only in her late teens, to stand up to the questioning of these dignitaries. Although no one really knows exactly what transpired at the meeting, she passed muster. "She has been examined by some of the best Judges," they said, "and is thought qualified to write them." But American publishers still refused to print her poetry. Susanna Wheatley eventually found a publisher in England, and Phillis Wheatley's *Poems on Various Subjects, Religious and Moral* is now considered the genesis of the African American literary tradition.

Phillis became so famous that Gates likens her to another modern-day celebrity, Oprah Winfrey. The Wheatleys soon freed her, but her life was no happy *Oprah* episode. As a woman of color, she never garnered the appropriate respect for her work or prosperity from book sales. American publishers still refused to print her work, her husband left her, and she died at age thirty. Nonetheless, her aspirations were groundbreaking.

During the decades following the Revolutionary War, Boston became the cradle not just of liberty but also of American culture. It was a center for political thinkers, transcendentalists, reformers, and abolitionists. By the 1800s, the city had become the literary hub of the country and home to writers such as Louisa May Alcott (who was told by one publisher, "Stick to your teaching; you can't write"), Henry James, Henry David Thoreau, and Ralph Waldo Emerson. So if your last encounter with US history was when your parents dragged you to Boston for a family vacation or when you did the same thing to your kids, it's time to come back for a refresher. And while you're in Boston, take time to gather inspiration from your Revolutionary sisters.

A BOSTON ITINERARY WITH A REVOLUTIONARY FLAIR

Day One

2:30 PM

Boston Public Garden
You can download a free forty-minute audio tour of the garden to listen to while you walk.
www.audisseyguides.com/tour-overview-6

3:30 PM

Hit the Freedom Trail

Boston Town Crier takes you on a guided tour of the most important places on the Freedom Trail. Starts at the Boston Common visitor center.
139 Tremont Street, 617-794-7512
www.bostontowncrier.com

6:00 PM

Dinner at the Silvertone Bar & Grill

Comfort food in a retro atmosphere.
69 Bromfield Street, 617-338-7887
www.silvertonedowntown.com

8:00 PM

Boston Symphony or Boston Pops

Experience the power and excitement of the Boston Symphony Orchestra, one of the preeminent orchestras in the country, which plays both classical and pops, depending on the time of year.
301 Massachusetts Avenue, 888-266-1200
www.bso.org

Day Two

8:30 AM

Breakfast at the Thinking Cup

Great coffee and pastry.
165 Tremont Street, 617-482-5555
www.thinkingcup.com

10:00 AM

Literary landmarks

Walking tour that highlights the great figures of Boston's

literary heyday including Alcott, Thoreau, Hawthorne, and others. Tours are regularly scheduled for Saturdays at 10:00 AM, but if you have a group, call in advance to arrange a tour to suit your schedule.
Boston by Foot
617-367-2345
www.bostonbyfoot.org

12:00 PM

Lunch at Quincy Market
Pick up something at one of the counters inside and take it out, or eat at one of the many restaurants that surround the market.

2:00 PM

Kayak Boston Harbor (Saturday and Sunday only)
Charles River Canoe and Kayak offers guided tours leaving from the Charles River through the locks, under the fabulous Zakim Bunker Hill Bridge, and into the inner harbor.
617-965-5110
www.paddleboston.com/tours/harbor.php

If the weather is bad or if you're not in Boston on the weekend, you have two other great choices:

Isabella Stewart Gardner Museum
The museum houses the collection of another of Boston's visionary women, Isabella Stewart Gardner, and it is considered one of the most remarkable and intimate collections of art in the world today.
280 The Fenway, 617-566-1401
www.gardnermuseum.org

Museum of African American History
Composed of the African Meeting House and Abiel Smith

School on Beacon Hill. You can also follow the Black Heritage
Trail, a 1.6-mile walking tour encompassing the largest
collection of historic sites in the country relating to the life
of a free African American community prior to the Civil War.
Guided tours available year-round by appointment
(617-742-5415) and at 10 AM, noon, and 2 PM Memorial Day
through Labor Day.
46 Joy Street, 617-725-0022
www.afroammuseum.org

Afterward, do a little shopping in Newbury Street's great
boutiques.

7:00 PM

Dinner at Giacomo's

This Italian restaurant made its reputation on the North
End, but if you go there you'll find a long wait outside, no
dessert on the menu, and no reservations accepted. The
newer South End restaurant works better for groups because
it takes reservations and offers dessert and still has a great
atmosphere. Cash only.
431 Columbus Avenue, 617-536-5723
http://giacomosblog-boston.blogspot.com

9:00 PM

The Green Dragon Tavern

Established in 1654, the Green Dragon was a watering
hole for colonists and revolutionaries including Paul Revere.
Live music.
11 Marshall Street, 617-367-2114
www.somerspubs.com/green-dragon

Day Three

8:30 AM

Breakfast at your hotel

10:00 AM

Adams home in Quincy
Take the red line to the Quincy Center Station (about half
an hour). The National Park Service operates this historic
site (open April through November) and offers a guided
tour through the homes and property of US presidents John
Adams and John Quincy Adams and, of course, Abigail Adams.
617-770-1175
www.nps.gov/adam/index.htm

Where to Stay in Boston

Omni Parker House
Opened in 1855, the Parker House is right on the Freedom
Trail and is the oldest continuously operating hotel in the
United States.
60 School Street, 617-227-8600
www.omnihotels.com/FindAHotel/BostonParkerHouse

Courtyard Boston Downtown/Tremont
In the theater district.
275 Tremont Street, 617-426-1400
www.marriott.com

OPTION 2: THE CATCH OF THE DAY: BOSTON AND CAPE ANN

They that go down to the sea in ships,
That do business in great water;
These see the works of the Lord,
And his wonders in the deep.

—**Psalms 107:23–24**

A gentle mist drifts down from the gray sky. In the Midwest we might say it's a great day for ducks. But on the Atlantic Ocean, in the Stellwagen Bank National Marine Sanctuary, it's a great day to be a whale. We've made the hour-long trip out of Boston Harbor to the open ocean just outside Massachusetts Bay. About two hundred yards from our boat, two humpback whales are spouting, rolling, and slapping their fins and tails against the water like two forty-ton kids at the community pool. Then they dive and disappear. Herman Melville described a similar experience in *Moby Dick*: "The monster perpendicularly flitted his tail forty feet into the air, and then sank out of sight like a tower swallowed up."

The show is over, it seems. The fun of seeing the whales' antics has just about compensated for the seasickness I feel, my two predeparture Dramamine pills notwithstanding. I'm about to turn around and go inside to get out of the rain when, suddenly, a whale breaches. He launches his bulk straight up out of the water, twists, and splashes back down with a thunderous crash. Then his partner shoots up like a Polaris missile, water pouring off his body like a waterfall. My seasickness is temporarily forgotten.

In this marine sanctuary, we're floating amid the fishing grounds and shipping lanes from which coastal communities such as Boston, Gloucester, Plymouth, Salem, and Provincetown made their living for centuries. The New England whalers are long gone, having hunted their prey nearly to extinction, and have been replaced by ecotourists. But for landlubbers like me, it's a chance not only to see these huge beasts but also to smell the salt air, to experience the power and immensity of the ocean, and to get just a tiny glimpse of a life that I've only read about.

The ocean has played a critical role in the life of New Englanders ever since the Pilgrims landed at Plymouth Rock. From *Moby Dick*, Melville's nineteenth-century whaling epic, to *The Perfect Storm*, Sebastian Junger's nonfiction story of a 1991 Gloucester fishing disaster, stories of the seafaring life—the danger, exultation, and heroism—have comprised an important part of American literature. Fishing is one of the world's most challenging and dangerous professions. It's a singular way of life that was little known even in Melville's day and is now all but gone. Says Melville in *Moby Dick*, "So ignorant are most landsmen of some of the plainest and most palpable wonders of the world that without some hints touching the plain fact, historical and otherwise of the fishery, they might scout at Moby Dick as a monstrous fable, or still worse and more detestable, a hideous and intolerable allegory." According to Melville, the true stories of the sea, the "tide beating heart of the earth," are beyond what even he could invent.

Don't let *Moby Dick*'s sheer size—as big as the tale it tells—intimidate you. I'll admit it sat on my bookshelf, unread, for years. It looked impressive on the shelf but always seemed like one of those books that are "good for you" and no fun to read. But before our trip to Boston, I rolled up my sleeves and set out to sea with the *Pequod*, and I have to tell you, I love this book. Melville digresses; you learn a lot about everything, from the benefits of sleeping in a cold room to the wonders of chowder to facts about different kinds of ropes. He serves up every gory detail you might ever need about killing a whale and disassembling its parts, *all* of its parts, if you know what I mean. But you can't beat the characters—the narrator, Ishmael; the tattooed cannibal Queequeg, who becomes his best friend; and the maniacal Captain Ahab. *Moby Dick* requires more patience and concentration from its readers than the average bestseller, but it rewards you with humor, wit, poetic prose, enduring symbolism, and a gripping story as pertinent today as it was when Melville wrote it. Author Nathaniel Philbrick, a man who truly loves this book, has read it at least a dozen times. In *Why Read Moby-Dick?* he declares, "Contained in the pages of *Moby-Dick* is nothing less than the genetic code of America: All the promises, problems, conflicts, and ideals that contributed to the outbreak of a revolution in 1775 as well as a civil war in 1861 and continue to drive this country's ever-contentious march into the future." Even if you only read it in spurts, give it a go.

The men of the fictional *Pequod* share many characteristics of their modern-day counterparts, the swordfishermen of Gloucester, a city about thirty-five miles up the coast from Boston. The dangers persist. Today's fishermen, like the whalers of old, must travel increasingly longer distances to find fewer fish, they battle the weather, work in constant danger of falling overboard, and risk being cut, tangled, and drowned by their equipment. It's such a dangerous and unique job that in *The Last Fish Tale: The Fate of the Atlantic and Survival in Gloucester, America's Oldest Fishing Port and Most Original Town*, Mark Kurlansky compares fishermen to combat veterans "who feel understood only by their comrades who have survived the same battles." They love the work despite the danger, drawn to the independent nature of the business, the adventure, and the satisfaction of pulling fish from the water, a singular thrill that even someone who has only caught sunfish from the dock can appreciate. In *The Perfect Storm: A True Story of Men Against the Sea*, Jodi Tyne, the wife of sword boat captain Billy Tyne, says, "The men don't know anything else once they do it; they love it and it takes over and that's the bottom line. People get possessed with church or God and fishing's just another thing they're possessed with. It's something inside of them that nobody can take away and if they're not doin' it they're not gonna be happy."

I reread *The Perfect Storm* for this trip and was more impressed than ever with Junger's portrayal of the swordfishing life (unlike Melville, Junger was never a seaman) and his intricate construction of what might have happened to the crew of the *Andrea Gail* during the historic storm. The book also weaves in the lives of the friends and families who wait for their fishermen to return home from the sea and the Coast Guard personnel who rescue vacationers, fishermen, and merchantmen alike. On the Gloucester waterfront, the famous *Fisherman's Memorial*, an eight-foot statue of a fisherman at the ship's wheel, and its nearby companion, *The Widow of the Fisherman,* offer a melancholy tribute.

The whalers and the swordfishers have another thing in common: overfishing. Back in the 1800s, Melville asked in *Moby Dick* "whether Leviathan can long endure so wide a chase, and so remorseless a havoc; whether he must . . . like the last man, smoke his last pipe and then himself evaporate in the final puff." Later in the chapter he concludes that that won't happen, but Melville wasn't around to see the "remorseless havoc" of industrial whaling that followed in the twentieth century, nearly driving many whale species to extinction. Like whalers, swordfishermen originally hunted with harpoons, killing one fish at a time. But technology helped sword boats bring in tons of fish with each trip, eventually decimating the population the way the whalers had their prey. Other towns on Cape Ann that used to be fishing villages—Rockport, for example—have made the switch to tourism. Gloucester, however, remains steadfastly and proudly a commercial fishing port. After reading *The Perfect Storm*, you'll have a new perspective on all that goes into catching the fillet on your plate—the danger and the hard work. You'll never look at fish the same way again.

BOSTON AND CAPE ANN ITINERARY

Day One

2:00 PM

Whale watching
Travel aboard a whale-watching vessel to Stellwagen Bank

to smell the salt air and see humpback whales. Book tours
through the New England Aquarium.
Central Wharf, 617-973-5200
www.neaq.org/visit_planning/tickets_and_hours/index.php
   Afterward, wander the wharves near the aquarium.

7:00 PM

Dinner at Legal Sea Foods on Long Wharf
255 State Street, 617-742-5300
www.legalseafoods.com/restaurants/boston-long-wharf

Day Two

8:30 AM

Breakfast at your hotel

10:00 AM

A day on Cape Ann
Spend the day touring Gloucester, Rockport, and the Cape
Ann coastline, north of Boston. It's easy and affordable
to rent a minivan or a couple of cars for a day to make the
relatively short trip up the coast. We used Enterprise Rent-
A-Car (1 Congress Street, Boston, 617-723-8077, www
.enterprise.com/car_rental/home.do). In Gloucester, stop
at the visitor's center at Stage Fort Park to pick up a map of
the city, a map of sites featured in *The Perfect Storm*, and the
Rockport Visitors Map that has a number of walking tours
in it. While you're at the visitor's center, be sure to check
out the giant rock on the site where the first settlers arrived
in 1623. Along the waterfront of Gloucester, the country's
oldest fishing port, look for the famous *Man at the Wheel*
statue of the fisherman on Stacy Boulevard and the Wall
of Remembrance adjacent to it, which lists the names of
approximately 5,400 Gloucester fishermen who were lost at

sea, including those on the *Andrea Gail*. From here, you can also watch the fishing boats come and go. Wander Main Street for a bit of shopping and to visit The Bookstore of Gloucester (61 Main) and the Dogtown Book Shop (132 Main).

Cape Ann Museum

A gem of a small museum that covers the art, history, and culture of the region. Look for works by painter Marsden Hartley, who is prominently featured in Elyssa East's *Dogtown: Death and Enchantment in a New England Ghost Town*.
27 Pleasant Street, Gloucester, 978-283-0455
www.capeannmuseum.org

Make the scenic drive to Rockport, which, in contrast to Gloucester, is primarily a tourist town with quaint shops and galleries. It is also the scene of Anita Diamant's *The Last Days of Dogtown* and *Good Harbor*, as well as Elyssa East's book about Dogtown.

1:00 PM

Lunch at the Red Skiff

A tiny, charming, family-owned restaurant with awesome chowder and sub sandwiches.
15 Mt. Pleasant Street, Rockport, 978-546-7647
www.udine4less.com/redskiff

After lunch, be sure to visit the town's übercharming Bearskin Neck section and the shops along Main Street, including Toad Hall Book Store (47 Main). Then choose a walking tour for a short hike before heading back to Boston.

4:00 PM

Return to Boston

Boston Public Library events

When planning your evening's activities in Boston, be sure to check the Boston Public Library's schedule of events for

author readings, movies, concerts, and special lectures that may be happening during your group's time in the city; then tailor your schedule accordingly.
www.bpl.org

7:30 PM

Dinner at Al Dente
Italian food in Boston's charming North End.
109 Salem Street, 617-523-0990
www.aldenteboston.com

9:30 PM

Black Rose Irish Pub
Live Irish music every night.
160 State Street, 617-742-2286
www.blackroseboston.com

Day Three

9:00 AM

Breakfast at your hotel or L'Aroma Café
For great coffee and baked goods.
85 Newbury Street, 617-412-4001
www.laromacafe.com

10:00 AM

Boston by Foot Literary Tour
Walking tour that highlights the great figures of Boston's literary heyday including Alcott, Thoreau, Hawthorne, and others. Tours are regularly scheduled on Saturdays at 10:00 am, but if you have a group, call in advance to arrange a tour to suit your schedule.
617-367-2345
www.bostonbyfoot.org

12:30 PM

Lunch at Boston Public Library
Take a quick look at the country's oldest public library and grab lunch at the MapRoom Café to eat in the courtyard. Or book a table in the Courtyard Restaurant.
700 Boylston Street, 617-859-2251
www.bpl.org

ADD-ON: NANTUCKET

It takes some effort to get there, but whaling aficionados and fans of Herman Melville may want to take a couple of extra days to visit Nantucket, which is off the coast of Cape Cod. To get there, your group can fly directly from Boston to Nantucket. The direct flight takes about forty-five minutes. Or drive or take a shuttle bus to Hyannis on Cape Cod and take the ferry to Nantucket. Once you're there, you can travel around on foot or by bike, moped, taxi, or the island's shuttle, the Wave, so no need for a car.

The island is the place from which the *Pequod* set sail in *Moby Dick*. Visit the island's Whaling Museum, take a walking tour with the Nantucket Historical Association, and enjoy the beaches and New England charm galore. Contact Nantucket Visitors Services and Information (508-228-0925, www. nantucket-ma.gov/Pages/NantucketMA_Visitor/index).

David McCullough: He Made History Popular
The Library of Congress called David McCullough "the citizen chronicler." He is the author of *John Adams, 1776, The Johnstown Flood, The Great Bridge, The Path Between the Seas, Mornings on Horseback, Truman,* and many other works of American history. In recognition of his work, he has won two Pulitzer

Prizes, two National Book awards, and the Presidential Medal of Freedom. His latest book is *The Greater Journey: Americans in Paris* about artists, writers, doctors, politicians, and others who went to Paris between 1830 and 1900 to perfect their skills at a time when the United States was still mostly a rural backwater.

He's known for his intense research, immersing himself in his subjects, even reading the books they read. But what makes his books popular is their readability. In the words of the citation accompanying his honorary doctorate from Yale, "As an historian, he paints with words, giving us pictures of the American people that live, breath, and above all, confront the fundamental issues of courage, achievement, and moral character."

You might assume he was a history major, but McCullough graduated from Yale with honors in English literature and began his career working at *Sports Illustrated*. He then worked at the United States Information Agency and *American Heritage*. In addition, even if you haven't read McCullough's books, you would probably recognize his voice, because he has been the host of several public television series, including *Smithsonian World* and *American Experience*, and the narrator of numerous documentaries, including *The Civil War* and *Napoleon*.

McCullough frequently travels the country lecturing about his books and the inspiring qualities of the people he writes about and advocating for history education and its importance for an informed citizenry. He lives with his wife, Rosalee, in West Tisbury on the island of Martha's Vineyard.

BOSTON READING

FICTION

Louisa May Alcott, *Little Women*. Romance and adventure with a feisty family of women who tend the home fires while their father fights in the Civil War. *Jo's Boys* continues the story of the central character.

Geraldine Brooks, *Caleb's Crossing: A Novel.* Set in the 1600s, the story of a young woman from Martha's Vineyard and her friendship with a young man who became the first Native American graduate of Harvard.

Phillip R. Craig, *The Woman Who Walked into the Sea, Off Season, A Beautiful Place to Die,* and other Martha's Vineyard mysteries.

Anita Diamant, *Good Harbor* and *The Last Days of Dogtown* both take place on Cape Ann, where the author "summers." Diamant is best known for her book *The Red Tent.*

Nathaniel Hawthorne, *The Scarlet Letter,* a story of adultery and redemption in early Massachusetts, and *The House of the Seven Gables,* about the characters living in a house cursed during their ancestors' witch hunt.

George Higgins, *The Friends of Eddie Coyle.* A classic crime novel set on the mean streets of Boston.

William Dean Howells, *The Rise of Silas Lapham.* A young man from Vermont tries to break into Boston society. Set in the 1880s.

Henry James, *The Bostonians.* Suffragists and reformers in post–Civil War Boston.

Deborah Copaken Kogan, *The Red Book.* By their twentieth reunion, life has turned out differently than expected for former Harvard roommates.

Dennis Lehane, *Mystic River.* The tale of three men who grew up in a blue-collar South Boston neighborhood who come together when one man's daughter is murdered.

John P. Marquand, *The Late George Apley.* A Pulitzer Prize–winning novel about the fortunes of a Beacon Hill "Brahmin" family at the turn of the last century.

William Martin, *Back Bay, Harvard Yard,* and *Cape Cod.* Martin's novels typically weave together history and mystery.

Robert McCloskey, *Make Way for Ducklings.* A classic children's book about a duck family's travels around Boston; always worth revisiting just for fun.

Arthur Miller, *The Crucible.* The famous play about the Salem witch trials.

Edwin O'Connor, *The Last Hurrah.* A classic tale of Boston politics, patterned after the life of mayor James M. Curley.

Matthew Pearl, *The Dante Club.* America's first Dante scholars—Henry Wadsworth Longfellow, Oliver Wendell Holmes, James Russell Lowell, and J. T. Fields—solve a murder mystery.

Sylvia Plath, *The Bell Jar.* A college woman from Massachusetts grapples with mental illness.

Jeff Shaara, *Rise to Rebellion: A Novel of the American Revolution.* An exciting refresher on the story of the country's founding.

Zadie Smith, *On Beauty.* This story of two families in Boston and London weaves together issues of class, race, gender, and politics.

David Foster Wallace, *Infinite Jest.* Described as a "philosophical quest and screwball comedy," set in a halfway house and a tennis academy, this is Wallace's magnum opus.

Edith Wharton, *Ethan Frome.* A classic story of a hopeless marriage and star-crossed love, set on a bleak New England farm.

Nancy Zaroulis, *Massachusetts: A Novel.* The saga of a Massachusetts family, spanning 350 years of history.

FOUNDING MOTHERS AND FATHERS

Carol Berkin, *Revolutionary Mothers: Women in the Struggle for America's Independence.* A look at women during the Revolution, from generals' wives to camp followers.

Melissa Lukeman Bohrer, *Glory, Passion, and Principle: The Story of Eight Remarkable Women at the Core of the American Revolution.* About the revolution's women warriors, writers, and thinkers.

Joseph Ellis, *Founding Brothers*. How the Revolutionary generation created the practical workings of government after the Revolution.

David Hackett Fischer, *Paul Revere's Ride*. A serious analysis of the events that led up to Revere's famous ride and what happened after.

Esther Forbes, *Johnny Tremain*, a young-adult novel of the Revolutionary era, and *Paul Revere and the World He Lived In*, a Pulitzer Prize–winning account of Revere's life and times.

Woody Holton, *Abigail Adams: A Life*. A look at her life with a feminist emphasis.

Walter Isaacson, *Benjamin Franklin: An American Life*. A critically acclaimed biography of a Founding Father, diplomat, businessman, and political leader.

David McCullough, *John Adams* and *1776*. Stories of early America from the man who made history popular.

Cokie Roberts, *Ladies of Liberty: The Women Who Shaped Our Nation*. Biographies and vignettes about women such as Martha Jefferson, Theodosia Burr, and Dolly Madison.

Lynne Withey, *Dearest Friend: A Life of Abigail Adams*. Another excellent biography of a founding mother.

Phillis Wheatley, *Complete Writings*. Her poetry and letters. See also Vincent Caretta, *Phillis Wheatley: Biography of a Genius in Bondage*, and Henry Louis Gates Jr., *The Trials of Phillis Wheatley: America's First Black Poet and Her Encounter with the Founding Fathers*, an excellent look at Wheatley in an expanded version of one of Gates's lectures.

OTHER NONFICTION AND MEMOIRS

Henry Beston, *The Outermost House: A Year of Life on the Great Beach of Cape Cod*. A classic of nature writing.

Elyssa East, *Dogtown: Death and Enchantment in a New England Ghost Town*. Covers the investigation of a murder in Dogtown, set against the Gloucester area's history and many colorful characters.

Nat Hentoff, *Boston Boy: Growing Up with Jazz and Other Rebellious Passions.* Growing up Jewish in Boston's Roxbury section during the 1930s and 1940s.

John F. Kennedy, *Profiles in Courage.* The stories of eight famous US senators by one of Massachusetts's most famous native sons.

Michael MacDonald, *All Souls: A Family Story from Southie.* A memoir about growing up in Boston's impoverished Irish Catholic enclave.

Nathaniel Philbrick, *Mayflower: A Story of Courage, Community, and War.* A more contemporary take on the idealized story of the *Mayflower.*

Henry David Thoreau, *Walden.* Daily life on the shores of Walden Pond, near Concord, Massachusetts, with Thoreau's thoughts on individual freedom, self-reliance, politics, and more.

Sarah Vowell, *The Wordy Shipmates.* With great humor, Vowell explores America's Puritan roots.

Susan Wilson, *Literary Trail of Greater Boston.* A literary history of the area along with specific places to visit.

FISH AND FISHERMEN

John Hersey, *Blues.* Fishing for bluefish off Martha's Vineyard.

Sebastian Junger, *The Perfect Storm: A True Story of Men Against the Sea.* Junger's portrayal of the life of Gloucester fishermen and the horrible storm in which a fishing boat was lost.

Rudyard Kipling, *Captains Courageous.* Cod fishing from Gloucester to Newfoundland.

Mark Kurlansky, *The Last Fish Tale: The Fate of the Atlantic and Survival in Gloucester, America's Oldest Fishing Port and Most Original Town.* An excellent explanation of Gloucester's history and continuing role as a fishing port.

WHALE TALES

Eric Jay Dolin, *Leviathan: The History of Whaling in America.*
Whaling from its heyday to modern day.

Herman Melville, *Moby Dick.* The classic story of whaling and
so much more, considered the greatest American novel. *Billy
Budd* and *Typee* are Melville's other tales of the sea.

Sena Jeter Nasland, *Ahab's Wife.* An imagining of what life was
like for the woman Captain Ahab left behind.

Nathaniel Philbrick, *Why Read Moby-Dick?* (he'll tell you why)
and *In the Heart of the Sea: The Tragedy of the Whaleship* Essex,
a true story of a whale ship disaster in the 1800s.

5

Newport, Rhode Island

POSTCARDS FROM THE GILDED AGE

They danced and they drove and they rode, they dined and wined and dressed and flirted and yachted and polo'd and Casino'd, responding to the subtlest inventions of their age; on the old lawns and verandahs I saw them gather, on the old shining sands I saw them gallop, past the low headlands I saw their white sails verily flash, and through the dusky old shrubberies came the light and sound of their feasts.

—**Henry James,** "The Sense of Newport,"
Harper's Magazine

I've always had a thing for the aristocracy. Maybe it was all those Disney movies I grew up watching—*Cinderella, Snow White, Sleeping Beauty*—that captivated my imagination with the idea of dancing at a ball, wearing a fabulous gown, and marrying a handsome prince. Even now, I'll stay up all night to watch all the pomp and romance of royal weddings. I'm totally hooked on *Downton Abbey* on PBS. If, like me, you ever wonder what your life might have been like as a baroness, a doyenne, or just someone who is plain filthy rich, you don't have to go all the way to England to visit the homes of the aristocracy. The lords and ladies of America's Gilded Age—the Astors, the Vanderbilts, and others at the height of American society—flocked to Newport, Rhode Island, every summer like migratory birds and built "cottages" that are essentially palaces. In present-day Newport, you can visit the mansions of the people who were America's answer to the British aristocracy and glimpse a regal lifestyle that few today can imagine.

Newport's history stretches back to its founding in 1639. By the 1750s, it was one of colonial America's five largest ports. Though its role as a top commercial port declined during the Revolutionary War, by the mid-1880s Newport ascended to new heights as the playground of the country's elite. Wealthy southern planters, who had begun to travel north to Newport to escape the summer heat, built homes there. Yankee tycoons followed suit, and in short order "The Kingdom by the Sea" became the summer hot spot for the nation's wealthiest, arriving from Chicago, New York, Washington, and Philadelphia each summer for a season of sun, sailing, and society. Never content simply to relax and enjoy the cool ocean breeze, these American barons of commerce competed nightly with each other in the extravagance of their parties and the over-the-top opulence of the homes they built along Bellevue Avenue and Ocean Drive. Cornelius Vanderbilt II, grandson of Commodore Cornelius Vanderbilt, founder of a steamship line and the New York Central Railroad, became the undisputed king of one-upmanship when he built his palace of ostentation, The Breakers. Unconstrained by cost, Vanderbilt plowed a chunk of the family fortune into a seventy-room, sixty-five-thousand-square-foot Italian Renaissance–style palazzo crammed with enough gold, velvet, and marble to impress any European monarch. Covering more than twenty-four-hundred square feet, the dining room alone is larger than many people's homes. Upon seeing The Breakers, author Bill Bryson quipped, "You can't look at it without thinking that nobody, with the possible exception of oneself, deserves to be that rich." By comparison, Highclere Castle, the setting of *Downton Abbey*, is much larger, with a couple hundred rooms, but remember—the Newport mansions are just "cottages," used only a few weeks each year.

Before you enter the breathtaking Breakers and many other Newport mansions on a tour, you'll want to enter the *life* of America's Gilded Age aristocracy through Edith Wharton's books *The Age of Innocence*, *The House of Mirth*, and *The Buccaneers*, as well as through her short stories. Wharton drew the world of her novels from her personal experience. She grew up in this social milieu, and you'll pass by her Newport homes Pencraig and Land's End on your tour of the area. Some speculate that her parents were models for Newland and May Archer in *The Age of Innocence* and that the mother of her first fiancé inspired that book's nouveau riche and "common" character, Mrs. Lemual Struthers. Wharton takes us to the glittering ballrooms and parties on the lawns that "stretched away smoothly to the big bright sea," where young women played the new sport of lawn tennis but preferred archery because it was more amenable to showing off pretty dresses and graceful attitudes.

For both Newport's real world and its fictional characters, the story wasn't always a fairy-tale romance with a happy ending. Wharton reveals the emotionally suppressed life beneath all the glamour, a life as rigidly constructed, suffocating, and layered as the Victorian clothes her characters wear. For example, in *The Age of Innocence*, she writes that May Archer's life had been as "closely girt as her figure." And of Lily Bart in *The House of Mirth*, Wharton describes the links on her bracelet as "manacles chaining her to her fate." Lacking any real monarchy or aristocratic ranking, these self-made blue bloods created their own. Over time, they took social striving and competition to the level of a blood sport, with a set of rigid societal mores and protocol to uphold their exclusive but fragile social ladder.

It's not all grim, though. She was a creature of her time and place, but I suspect Wharton had quite a sense of humor about it all. Your book club might especially enjoy her short story "Xingu," about members of a pretentious Gilded Age book group whom Wharton calls "indomitable huntresses of erudition." "Amusement," declares the overbearing Mrs. Plinth, "is hardly what I look for in my choice of books." One member never reads the books, one always wants to have the meeting at her house, and none of them really know what they're talking about.

As you travel along Bellevue Avenue in Newport, Wharton's descriptions of the pageantry that took place there each afternoon will bring your trip to life. Wharton notes in her autobiography, *A Backward Glance*, that the regular afternoon diversion in Newport was "coaching," which involved taking horse-drawn carriage rides along Bellevue Avenue and Ocean Drive. For this activity, she says, "it was customary to dress as elegantly as for a race-meeting at Auteuil or Ascot. . . . Carriages, horse, harnesses and grooms were all of the latest and most irreproachable cut, and Bellevue Avenue was a pretty scene when the double line of glittering vehicles and showy horse-flesh paraded between green lawns and scarlet geranium-borders."

Wharton also describes the custom of "calling" on other women in their homes, a daily duty in Newport. It was improper at the time to simply invite a person to one's home without first making an exchange of formal visits. Through this custom, "calling" newcomers could test the social waters and, perhaps more importantly, the socially established could avoid becoming entangled with undesirable new acquaintances. Says Wharton, "the onerous and endless business of 'calling' took up every spare hour. Calling was then a formidable affair, since many ladies had weekly 'days' from which there was no possible escape, and others cultivated an exasperating habit of being at home on the very afternoon when, according to every reasonable calculation, one might have expected them to be at polo, or at Mrs. Belmont's archery party, or abroad on their own sempiternal card-leaving."

If the target of a "call" wasn't home—or, more likely, was on the premises but wished to avoid the caller—visitors left calling cards, often with a corner of the card bent, which had a variety of meanings. In his book *The Gilded Age*, by which this era became known, Mark Twain comments on this card-leaving protocol in his inimitable fashion: "If Mrs. A.'s daughter marries, or a child is born to the family, Mrs. B. calls, sends in her card with the upper left hand corner turned down, and then goes along about her affairs—for that inverted corner means 'Congratulations.' If Mrs. B.'s husband falls downstairs and breaks his neck, Mrs. A. calls, leaves her card with the upper right hand corner turned down, and then takes her departure; this corner means 'Condolence.' It is very necessary to get the corners right, else one may unintentionally condole with a friend on a wedding or congratulate her upon a funeral."

This intricate framework of exclusion and pretense was intended as a barrier to keep the less desirable new rich, "the swells" as they were called, from entering the upper echelons of society. Wharton's posthumously published novel, *The Buccaneers*, tells the story of several young American women whose families possessed newfound wealth but lacked the social currency to crack the many barriers to high society's inner sanctum. Subsequently, they set sail not for a leisurely afternoon on Newport's Narragansett Bay but for England, where they sought social acceptance and, ideally, marriage. Many young British aristocrats who either weren't in line to inherit the family estate or were unable to maintain their vast holdings without an outside infusion of money welcomed these wealthy American status cravers with open arms. *To Marry an English Lord*, by Carol Wallace and Gail MacColl, offers an excellent nonfiction look at these buccaneers who inspired the *Downton Abbey* television series in which Cora, the beautiful daughter of a dry-goods multimillionaire from Cincinnati, becomes Lady Crawley.

Lacking any fortune, dry goods or otherwise, my only entrance into any of the Newport mansions of Wharton's era would have been through the servants' entrance. Nor would I have had the patience to put up with the restricted life of calling, coaching, and casting about for a husband. Even Edith Wharton found the New York and Newport scenes stifling and eventually decamped for Europe and, later, her Lenox, Massachusetts, home, the Mount. But who needs Mrs. Astor or an English lord when you can visit modern Newport with your friends? Or, for me, a Newport weekend made a great mother-daughter visit to the Gilded Age. Once you've hit your limit of "Oh my gosh" and "Can you believe this?" exclamations as you tour the mansions and hike the Cliff Walk, you'll find plenty of other action in Newport, especially in summer—laid-back activities that are a far cry from the aristocratic life that Wharton lived. Yes, today's Newport is a haven for hot-pink and lime-green plaid shorts, deck shoes, and other preppie paraphernalia; a visit to Newport may feel a bit like parachuting into a Ralph Lauren ad. (And, yes, they really do play polo here. You can attend a match.) But we proletarians can enjoy a multitude of activities, too, including the world-famous Newport Jazz Festival, tennis tournaments, sailing regattas, and opportunities to go sailing yourself, plus lively restaurants, bars, and shopping. You don't have to be a Vanderbilt to have fun here.

Ann Hood: Writing from Personal Experience

A native Rhode Islander, Ann Hood began her writing career while also working as a flight attendant for TWA. On a furlough from the airline, she wrote her first novel, *Somewhere off the Coast of Maine*, and continued to pursue her writing on subway trains to JFK and in the galleys of 747s. During a strike, when TWA "replaced" all the flight attendants, she became a full-time writer. Along with short stories and magazine articles, she is the author of the bestselling novel *The Knitting Circle*, which was made into a movie for HBO.

In 2002, her five-year-old daughter, Grace, died suddenly from a virulent form of strep, and her death had an enormous impact on Hood. Many of her subsequent works, including *The Knitting Circle*, draw on that experience. Her memoir *Comfort: A Journey Through Grief*, was named one of the top ten nonfiction books of 2008 by *Entertainment Weekly* and was a *New York Times* Editor's Choice. Hood has won a Best American Spiritual Writing Award, the Paul Bowles Prize for Short Fiction, and two Pushcart Prizes. She now lives in Providence, Rhode Island, with her husband and their children. Her latest novel is *The Red Thread*, inspired by her experience adopting a baby in China.

NEWPORT READING

NEWPORT FICTION

Louis Auchincloss, *The House of Five Talents*. A seventy-five-year-old heiress tells of life through two world wars.

Mary Higgins Clark, *Moonlight Becomes You*. A suspense novel.

James Fenimore Cooper, *The Red Rover*. Newport's Old Stone Mill is used as a setting for a chapter in this story, which is essentially a pirate novel.

John Dandola, *Wind of Time*. A mystery novel revolving around the Norse origins of the Old Stone Mill.

Marie J. Gale, *Alice Brenton*. Newport during Revolutionary days.

Daisy Goodwin, *The American Heiress*. A wealthy young American woman and her life in the world of the English aristocracy.

John Jakes, *The Gods of Newport*. Life in Gilded Age Newport.

Henry James, *The Ivory Tower*. James's critique of life in the Gilded Age as seen through the eyes of two elderly businessmen.

Mary Kruger, *Death on the Cliff Walk*. A murder mystery set in the 1890s.

Antoinette Stockenberg, *Time After Time*. A Newport working girl falls in love with a rich man.

Mark Twain and Charles Dudley Warner, *The Gilded Age*. Takes place in Washington, DC, but a good look at the era by the men who gave it a name.

Edith Wharton, *The Age of Innocence*, *The Buccaneers*, *The House of Mirth*, and *The Selected Short Stories of Edith Wharton* (edited by R. W. B. Lewis). See also two biographies of Wharton: Hermione Lee, *Edith Wharton*, and R. W. B. Lewis, *Edith Wharton: A Biography*.

Thornton Wilder, *Theophilus North*. Set in 1926, the adventures of a young man who finds work in the Newport mansions.

CONTEMPORARY RHODE ISLAND WRITERS

Adam Braver, *Divine Sarah*, *Misfit*, *Mr. Lincoln's Wars*, *November 22, 1963*, and other works of historical fiction.

Ann Hood, *The Knitting Circle*, *An Ornithologist's Guide to Life*, *The Red Thread*, and others.

Laura Moore, *Night Swimming*, *Remember Me*, *Ride a Dark Horse*, contemporary romance.

NONFICTION

Lucius Beebe, *The Big Spenders: The Epic Story of the Rich Rich, the Grandees of America and the Magnificoes, and How They Spent Their Fortunes*.

Deborah Davis, *Gilded: How Newport Became America's Richest Resort*.

Ed Morris, *A Guide to Newport's Cliff Walk: Tales of Seaside Mansions and the Gilded Age Elite*.

Bettie Bearden Pardee, *Private Newport: At Home and in the Garden*. A look at the privately owned Newport mansions of today.

Larry Stanford, *Wicked Newport: Sordid Stories from the City by the Sea*.

Amanda Mackenzie Stuart, *Consuelo and Alva Vanderbilt: The Story of a Daughter and a Mother in the Gilded Age.*

Arthur T. Vanderbilt, *Fortune's Children: The Fall of the House of Vanderbilt.*

Carol Wallace and Gail MacColl, *To Marry an English Lord.*

SERVANT LIFE

Margaret Lynch-Brennan, *The Irish Bridget: Irish Immigrant Women in Domestic Service in America, 1840–1930.* A scholarly look at the many Irish women who found jobs as servants when they came to America.

Elizabeth O'Leary, *From Morning to Night: Domestic Service in Maymont and the Gilded Age South* (set in Virginia, but you get the idea).

Robert Roberts, *Roberts' Guide for Butlers and Other Household Staff: The House Servant's Directory.* An interesting look at the actual rules and protocol.

NEWPORT ITINERARY

More than any other destination in this book, a visit to Newport depends on "the season," June through September. During that period, there are tons of activities and festivals, and the crowds to go with them—everything from the jazz and folk festivals to a kite festival, and sometimes even a chance to watch a portion of the America's Cup yacht race. Other times of year, it's important to check websites for schedules because times for tours, restaurants, and events are much more limited.

Day One

2:00 PM

On the waterfront

Wander Bannister's Wharf, Bowen's Wharf, and Thames
Street in the heart of Newport's historic waterfront. All offer a
variety of classic New England preppy/yachty shopping and a
chance to check out some of the fabulous boats moored here.
1 Bannister's Wharf, 401-846-4500
www.bannistersnewport.com
13 Bowens Wharf, 401-849-3478
www.bowenswharf.com

4:00 PM

Snacks and drinks at the Black Pearl

Relax in the tavern or at the waterside patio and bar.
Bannister's Wharf, 401-846-5264
www.blackpearlnewport.com

6:30 PM (depends on the time of year)

Get your sea legs

Sunset sail on Narragansett Bay aboard the *Madeleine*, a
seventy-two-foot schooner. From the bay you'll see the
oceanfront estate Hammersmith Farm, where, in 1953,
1,200 people attended John and Jackie Kennedy's wedding
reception, the beginning of their modern-day "Camelot."
Departs from Bannister's Wharf, 401-847-0298
www.cruisenewport.com

8:30 PM

Dinner at the Red Parrot

348 Thames Street, 401-847-3800
www.redparrotrestaurant.com

Day Two

8:30 AM

Breakfast at your hotel or at Benjamin's Raw Bar
254 Thames Street, 401-846-8768
www.benjaminsrawbar.com

10:30 AM

Land ho!
Get the lay of the land and plenty of Newport history with a
tour that covers the town's colonial area, Ocean Drive, and
the mansion district. You'll pass by Pencraig, where Edith
Wharton spent her childhood summers.
Tours leave from the Newport Visitor Center, 23 America's
Cup Avenue
401-847-6921
www.vikingtoursnewport.com/sightseeing

12:30 PM

Lunch on the lawn at La Forge Casino Restaurant
Located in the old Newport Casino, this restaurant sits next
to the International Tennis Hall of Fame. You might see
a croquet game or people dressed in old-fashioned tennis
clothes as they play lawn tennis.
186 Bellevue Avenue, 401-847-0418
www.laforgenewport.com

1:30 PM

Go "calling" on Bellevue Avenue
The Preservation Society of Newport County runs eleven
historic properties in this area. Below are two of my favorites.
If you plan to see several, be sure to check on multiple home
package tickets.

401-847-1000
www.newportmansions.org

The Elms, 367 Bellevue Avenue
I especially enjoy the Elms (www.newportmansions.org
/explore/the-elms), the former home of Mr. and Mrs. Edward
Julius Berwind of Philadelphia and New York (Berwind made
his fortune in the Pennsylvania coal industry). You can see
not only the fabulous mansion that the Berwinds' guests saw
but also, through their Servant Life tour, the behind-the-
scenes lives of the people who made it run.

The Breakers, 44 Ochre Point Avenue
You won't want to miss the grandest of the summer cottages,
the home of the Cornelius Vanderbilt II family (www
.newportmansions.org/explore/the-breakers). Every room
is a "wow."

While you're in the neighborhood—and if you still
have enough energy—you may want to walk part of the
stunning Cliff Walk (www.cliffwalk.com) that passes on the
ocean side of the mansions. Or take in one more fabulous
mansion, Rough Point, the home of the twentieth-century
tobacco heiress Doris Duke. (Rough Point is not a Newport
Preservation Society property, so their tickets don't work
here.) Duke's home is a tad smaller and more modern than
others in the neighborhood, but it houses a breathtaking
collection of art, not to mention plenty of stories about
the heiress who is known for her jet-setting lifestyle, her
philanthropy, and the camels she kept on the front lawn.
680 Bellevue Avenue, 401-849-7300
www.newportrestoration.org/visit/rough_point

7:30 PM

Dinner at Christie's
Enjoy small-plate food in this fun and very trendy and

modern spot that provides a refreshing contrast to the New England colonial style.

At the Forty 1° North Marina Resort

351 Thames Street, 401-846-8018

www.41north.com/dining-christies.aspx

9:30 PM

Jazz and more at Newport Blues Cafe

286 Thames Street, 401-841-5510

www.newportblues.com

Day Three

9:00 AM

Breakfast at your hotel or at the Corner Cafe

110 Broadway, 401-846-0606

www.cornercafenewport.com

10:30 AM

Newport's great outdoors

Pick up food for a picnic at A Market.

181 Bellevue Avenue, 401-846-8137

www.myamarket.com

Great places abound along Ocean Drive for hiking, history, or to just hang out and enjoy the spectacular view and maybe even some sailboat races. Check out Brenton Point State Park (on weekends they sell kites to fly here) or Fort Adams State Park.

www.riparks.com

Where to Stay

Newport is full of charming B&Bs, but if you're going with a group, you'll probably want to opt for a larger hotel or inn. Off-season rates are dramatically discounted.

Newport Marriott
25 America's Cup Avenue, 401-849-1000
www.marriott.com/hotels/travel/pvdlw-newport-marriott

Hotel Viking
One Bellevue Avenue, 401-847-3300
www.hotelviking.com

6

New York City

IF I CAN MAKE IT THERE...

Look across the water at the statue of liberty or Ellis Island,
the place to which so many of the New York tribe came in
order to truly live. Learn the tale of our tribe, because it's
your tribe too, no matter where you were born.
—**Pete Hamill,** *Downtown: My Manhattan*

Colson Whitehead says in his book *The Colossus of New York*,
"You start building your private New York the first time you
lay eyes on it." But I'd say you start building your own vision of the
city even before you go there, the first time you read about it or
the first time you see it in a movie. You keep accumulating images, ideas, and scenes in your mind, which is what makes it such a
thrill to go to New York City and actually see those scenes, hear
the accents, ride on the subway, crane your neck at the skyscrapers, and feel the electric energy of Times Square and Broadway, no
matter how many times you've been there.

If you started building your own New York, say, twenty years ago, your city is very different from what a newcomer sees now. Some of the poorest and more dangerous parts of the city have become gentrified. The epicenter for bohemians and artists has moved over the years from Greenwich Village, to Soho, to Chelsea and beyond. Little Italy has shrunk while Chinatown has grown. The World Trade Center towers are gone; a memorial and new tower have risen in their place. An inventive new park, The High Line, has taken root on an old elevated railroad bed on the West Side. This is a place of constant shifting and change.

Yet several aspects of New York City remain constant—the city is a hub for newcomers to this country, and it is America's literary, business, and cultural mecca. It remains the place of dreams, aspirations, glamour, and disappointment for people like Holly Golightly, the heroine of *Breakfast at Tiffany's*, who yearn for a place where they can belong. As Frank Sinatra described in his love song to the city, "New York, New York," "If I can make it there, I'll make it anywhere." All of that makes pretty dramatic material for literature. It's no wonder that countless classics have been written in and about the city, and just about every famous writer has spent time here, creating tales of New York that will be part of the city you build in your mind. A traveler could wander New York's literary places for days, but three popular books—Jane Ziegelman's *97 Orchard: An Edible History of Five Immigrant Families in One New York Tenement*, Patti Smith's *Just Kids*, and Capote's *Breakfast at Tiffany's*—offer the perfect way to understand the challenge of "making it" in New York City, from basic survival to finding acceptance and one's place in the world.

The Big Apple, especially the Lower East Side, is one of the best places in the country to taste (quite literally) the immigrant experience, particularly that of the great wave of newcomers who arrived in America at the turn of the last century. Ziegelman's *97 Orchard* leads readers through a culinary and social history of families from their arrival, usually at Ellis Island, across lower

Manhattan to their home at 97 Orchard, which is preserved pretty much as it was then as the remarkable Tenement Museum. This is the neighborhood where German, Irish, Lithuanian, and Italian immigrant families began to build their new American lives. Here they learned a new language and customs, built congregations and businesses, and educated their children, and from this mean environment they eventually moved up in the world.

I find the Tenement Museum one of the places in New York City that most captures my imagination. When you trudge up the creaky steps of 97 Orchard and tour the tiny, dimly lit rooms, you'll understand just how much these families must have wanted to come to America and how bad things must have been where they came from. You can imagine how it must have smelled, the scents of steamy stuffed cabbage wafting through the building and mingling with the odor of horses and the privies out back. This is where immigrants learned to be Americans. It's also the neighborhood melting pot, where their culinary traditions and other aspects of their culture blended into the mix of the city, became part of the popular culture, and spread across the country like cream cheese on a bagel. Through Ziegelman's book and a visit to 97 Orchard, their experience of New York becomes yours.

Artists and bohemians have migrated to New York, too, but for reasons very different from those of the residents of 97 Orchard. These were, and continue to be, cultural travelers who seek the bohemian life and a place where they can find connection and meaning through their art. Patti Smith, punk rocker, poet, and visual artist, is one of these. She tells her story in the National Book Award–winning memoir *Just Kids*, the story of her life with the artist and photographer Robert Mapplethorpe, a life dedicated to art and to each other. Smith and Mapplethorpe met in New York in the late 1960s, while they were in their early twenties, and through most of their journey together they lived like stereotypical starving artists—homeless, jobless, hungry, and itching from various vermin. The book offers not only a fascinating and tender look at their relationship but also a tour of Manhattan in the last period of twentieth-century artistic ferment. Smith offers a view of Greenwich Village, Chelsea, and other bohemian neighborhoods of the 1960s and 1970s, when artists sought this community as a place where they felt they could be among like-minded comrades. She weaves together fascinating encounters with the most iconic artists of the day, including Jimi Hendrix, Janis Joplin, William Burroughs, Andy Warhol, and Allen Ginsberg.

Many of those 1960s hot spots, such as Max's Kansas City, are long gone, and gentrification has pushed the art scene into Chelsea, the Meatpacking District, Brooklyn, and beyond. Smith and Mapplethorpe lived in one of the most famous bastions of the artistic and countercultural scene, the Chelsea Hotel, which has been purchased by a real estate developer. But present-day visitors can still find plenty of places in which to experience the same New York that lured Smith and previous generations of bohemians. The old "artsy" neighborhoods, like most parts of the city, are cleaner, nicer, and more expensive than in the sixties. That makes it even more fun to wander through the west Village, which contains the tiniest and most charming streets of Manhattan, so unlike the concrete jungle further uptown. These are the haunts of William Faulkner, Dylan Thomas, and Jack Kerouac and his Beat buddies.

Head to Washington Square Park to soak up the sun and do a little people watching. In *Just Kids*, Smith tells the story of a couple of tourists who saw her and Mapplethorpe hanging out there. One asked the other if he thought Smith and Mapplethorpe were artists and hence people they should photograph. The other said no, they're "just kids." The park, with its famous mini Arc de Triomphe, was completely refurbished a couple of years ago, and you're far more likely to see famed chef Mario Batali walking by in his orange Crocs than to witness a drug deal. But don't worry, you'll find enough wacky entertainers and strange behavior there to give you a little feel of the old days.

Further uptown, you move from grit to the glamour of Fifth Avenue and the fictional haunts of "Miss Holiday Golightly, Traveling." Holly, whose real name is Lula Mae Barnes, travels because, as she says, "Home is where you feel at home. I'm still looking." That statement resonates throughout the book as Holly struggles to reinvent herself and to find her place in New York and in life. She's searching for a place a little like Tiffany's, where she goes when she gets the blues, or what she calls the "mean reds." She says, "What I've found does the most good is just to get into a taxi and go to Tiffany's. It calms me down right away, the quietness and the proud look of it; nothing very bad could happen to you there, not with those kind men in their nice suits, and that lovely smell of silver and alligator wallets." I've often seen groups of young women posing outside the store in sunglasses and black dresses, mimicking Audrey Hepburn in the 1961 *Breakfast at Tiffany's* movie. They were undoubtedly building their own New York in the process.

According to Capote biographers, Holly shared many traits with the author's mother, which meant he had a rather unhappy childhood. Holly's story was personal but also universal, drawn from the dreams, aspirations, and struggles of real people transplanted to the city and striving to achieve the American dream. It's a classic theme of our country's literature as well as the story of generations of New Yorkers. In a November 2011 discussion of *Breakfast at Tiffany's* on the *New York Times*'s "Big City Book Club" forum, it was a Korean immigrant who rather poetically summarized it all: "Thanks for Truman's miserable life, which enabled him to write *Breakfast at Tiffany's* that has made me belong to this city, New York, consisting of splendor and melancholy."

Colum McCann: Another Immigrant Makes It in New York

Born in Dublin, Ireland, in 1965, Colum McCann is the award-winning author of five novels and two collections of short stories. His novel *Let the Great World Spin* won worldwide acclaim, including the 2009 National Book Award and, in 2010, a literary award from the American Academy of Arts and Letters. The book takes place in the 1970s but parallels the present day and the events of 9/11.

McCann began his career as a journalist in Ireland. In the early 1980s, he took a bicycle trip across North America and later worked as a wilderness guide in a program for juvenile delinquents in Texas. Now a dual citizen, he lives in New York with his wife and their three children and teaches creative writing at Hunter College. McCann said, in a Radio OpenSource interview, "I do think there's still something at the core of the experience of coming here and being an immigrant here that's unlike anywhere on earth. It makes American literature as far as I'm concerned one of the most muscular, elastic, and brilliant of anywhere, and I still think it's at the forefront."

NEW YORK READING

New York is the literary capital of the United States. Just about every famous writer has either written about New York or lived there for some period of time. Here are a few of the classics, old and new. In addition, for an anthology of great New York writers, see Phillip Lopate's *Writing New York*.

Kevin Baker, *Dreamland*, the story of Lower East Side immigrants at Coney Island, and *Paradise Alley*, which takes place during the Civil War draft riots.

James Baldwin, *Go Tell It on the Mountain*. A semiautobiographical story of a young African American boy in 1930s Harlem.

Truman Capote, *Breakfast at Tiffany's*. A novella about the unforgettable Holly Golightly, made even more famous by the film. See also Sam Wasson, *Fifth Avenue, 5 A.M.: Audrey Hepburn, Breakfast at Tiffany's, and the Dawn of the Modern Woman*.

E. L. Doctorow, *World's Fair*, the story of a boy's life in 1930s New York, and *Ragtime*, in which fact and fiction weave together in early 1900s New York. *Ragtime* became a Broadway musical.

Ralph Ellison, *Invisible Man*. The complex life of a young African American man in the South and later in Harlem. Winner of the National Book Award.

Jack Finney, *Time and Again*. Time travel to 1880s New York. Finney also wrote *The Body Snatchers*, as in "invasion of."

Mark Helprin, *In Sunlight and in Shadow*. About a love affair that takes place in post–World War II New York.

Langston Hughes, *The Collected Poems of Langston Hughes* and *Not Without Laughter*. Classic works from one of the most famous figures of the Harlem Renaissance.

Henry James, *Washington Square*. A plain but wealthy young woman must choose between a manipulative father and a handsome but penniless suitor.

Jonathan Lethem, *Motherless Brooklyn*. A riff on detective novels, set in Brooklyn.

David Lewis, ed., *The Portable Harlem Renaissance Reader*. An anthology.

Colum McCann, *This Side of Brightness*, a family saga that starts with a worker building the tunnels under New York, and *Let the Great World Spin*, the stories of a tightrope walk between the World Trade Center Towers and people who witness it.

Jay McInerney, *Bright Lights, Big City*. A tale of hedonism in 1980s New York.

Steven Millhauer, *Martin Dressler: The Tale of an American Dreamer.* Historical fiction about the son of a cigar merchant who becomes a great hotelier.

Dorothy Parker, *The Portable Dorothy Parker.* Stories from one of New York's most famous humorists. See also James R. Gaines, *Wit's End: Days and Nights of the Algonquin Round Table.*

Betty Smith, *A Tree Grows in Brooklyn.* A classic story of an Irish family in New York.

Haley Tanner, *Vaclav and Lena.* The love story of two Russian immigrants in Brighton Beach.

Edith Wharton, *The Age of Innocence, The House of Mirth, Old New York.* Life among the city's wealthy in the late 1800s. (For more on Wharton, see chapter 5.)

Colson Whitehead. This inventive author's work ranges from *Sag Harbor*, a coming-of-age story set in Manhattan and the Hamptons; to *Zone One*, about zombies; to essay collections such as *The Colossus of New York*, his musings on various sections of the city.

Tom Wolfe, *The Bonfire of the Vanities.* A classic portrait of New York City in the 1980s.

HISTORY

Herbert Asbury, *The Gangs of New York: An Informal History of the Underworld.* The dirty underbelly of New York City in the nineteenth and early twentieth centuries, made into a film by Martin Scorsese.

Robert Caro, *The Power Broker: Robert Moses and the Fall of New York.* Praised and vilified, Moses was the master builder of New York in the mid-twentieth century and one of the most powerful men in the history of the city. This book won the Pulitzer Prize.

H. Paul Jeffers, *The Napoleon of New York: Mayor Fiorello LaGuardia.* A biography of one of New York's most influential mayors.

David McCullough, *The Great Bridge*. The drama, politics, and science behind building the Brooklyn Bridge.

Jacob Riis, *How the Other Half Lives*. A groundbreaking exposé of tenement life.

Jane Ziegelman, *97 Orchard: An Edible History of Five Immigrant Families in One New York Tenement*. The culinary and social life of families who lived in what is now the Tenement Museum.

MEMOIRS

Mary Cantwell, *Manhattan, When I Was Young*. The author's life, set in five New York apartments.

Pete Hamill, *Downtown: My Manhattan*. A personal and historical portrait of the Big Apple.

Marjorie Hart, *Summer at Tiffany*. Two Iowa girls become shop girls in 1945.

Patti Smith, *Just Kids*. A memoir of Smith's early life in New York and her relationship with photographer Robert Mapplethorpe.

NEW YORK ITINERARY

Working from the immigrant experience of Ellis Island and Lower Manhattan north to the bohemian life of Greenwich Village in the 1960s and 1970s and on to the glamour of Fifth Avenue and the Upper East Side, this three-day itinerary offers glimpses at the lives of real and fictional people in some of New York's most iconic places. Break out the little black dress.

Day One

A Booklover's tour of Midtown

For most visitors to New York, Midtown means the theater district and shopping. But it also offers great strolling opportunities that will make the hearts of lit lovers beat a little faster, plus the thrill of live theater.

2:00 PM

The New York Public Library

Say hello to Patience and Fortitude, the lions that guard the entrance. They've had several names since the library was dedicated in 1911, but Mayor Fiorello LaGuardia gave them these names in the 1930s because these were the qualities he felt New Yorkers needed during the Great Depression. The building's colossal Beaux Arts architecture and majestic ceiling frescoes make the library worth the trip. Yet, for book lovers, the sheer size and solidity of the place, with its grand staircases and the giant Rose Reading Room, give a feeling that books—in whatever form—will never go away. The library also offers exhibitions of its collection of original manuscripts and a great gift shop.

Fifth Avenue at Forty-Second, adjacent to Bryant Park, 917-275-6975.

www.nypl.org/locations/schwarzman

Morgan Library & Museum

Financier and book/manuscript collector Pierpont Morgan built this palatial library to house his collection. If this was his library, I'd love to see his house! The library has been adding to the collection ever since Morgan's day, resulting in one of the world's greatest collections of artistic, literary, and musical works from ancient times to the medieval and Renaissance periods to the present day.

225 Madison Avenue at Thirty-Sixth Street, 212-685-0008

www.themorgan.org

Hello to Holly and Eloise

Hike and window-shop your way up Fifth Avenue. Even if it's not the holiday season, the store windows along Fifth Avenue are worth the exercise. Pay homage to Holly Golightly at Tiffany (Fifth Avenue at Fifty-Seventh). There's no better cure for the "mean reds" than something in a little blue box or just looking in Tiffany's windows. Then wander over to the luxurious Plaza Hotel (Fifth Avenue at Central Park South), the residence of Kay Thompson's spunky character, Eloise. If you're feeling wealthy, stop in the hotel's Palm Court for a snack or afternoon tea (including a Tea with Eloise menu). If not, looking around is free.

Also in Midtown, fans of *The Catcher in the Rye* can find the sites of Holden Caulfield's New York activities: Rockefeller Center skating rink, Central Park carousel and zoo, Grand Central Station, the Dakota, the Metropolitan Museum, the American Museum of Natural History, and Radio City Music Hall.

6:00 PM

Dinner at PizzArte

Neapolitan pizza served in an art gallery.
69 West Fifty-Fifth Street (near Sixth Avenue), 212-247-3936
www.pizzarteny.com

8:00 PM

On Broadway

Take in a Broadway show or simply sit on the red steps at Forty-Seventh and Broadway to watch the people, the gigantic electronic billboards, and the bright lights of the Great White Way.

11:00 PM

Drinks with Dorothy at the Algonquin Hotel

Channel the literati with a postshow drink at the famous watering hole of Dorothy Parker, Robert Benchley, and other members of their "Vicious Circle," also known as the Algonquin Round Table.
59 West Forty-Fourth Street, between Fifth and Sixth Avenues

212-840-6800
www.algonquinhotel.com

Day Two

Immigrant Life

9:00 AM

Breakfast at Le Pain Quotidien
It's a chain but very cozy, especially on a blustery New York day, and they offer great bread, pastries, fresh OJ, and killer oatmeal. If it's warm, get coffee and croissants to go and eat across the street in Bryant Park.
70 West Fortieth Street (Fortieth and Sixth), 212-354-5224
www.lepainquotidien.us/#/en_US

10:30 AM

Ellis Island
Plan to start on Lower Manhattan's west side at Battery Park, where you will board a Statue Cruises ferry (operating out of Battery Park) for a trip to Ellis Island, and turn on your imagination. The Statue Cruises ferry stops at Liberty Island first. From there, the boat stops at Ellis Island and then returns to New York City. You can choose to stop both places or just go to Ellis Island.
Statue Cruises
1 Battery Place, 201-604-2800
www.statuecruises.com
Ellis Island
212-363-3200
www.nps.gov/elis/index.htm

1:00 PM

Lunch at Katz's Deli
Katz's Deli is one of the last of the delis that used to fill the

neighborhood. It was also the location of Meg Ryan's famous "faking it" scene in *When Harry Met Sally*.
205 East Houston, 212-254-2246
katzsdelicatessen.com

2:30 PM

The Tenement Museum

Experience the lives of newcomers to America at the turn of the last century. Located on the corner of Delancey and Orchard Streets, the Visitor Center and Museum Shop is where tours start and end and where tickets are sold. Don't look for a big museum. These are real buildings that were formerly tenements. The office where you purchase tickets is at 108 Orchard. You can only see the museum with a tour, so book tickets ahead because groups are small! Your tour group will walk to the actual tenement building at 97 Orchard. They have a terrific gift shop, with items ranging from literary to funky.
103 Orchard Street, 212-982-8420
www.tenement.org

5:00 PM

Kick back at your hotel

7:30 PM

Dinner at DBGB Kitchen & Bar

French brasserie meets American tavern at DBGB, where Chef Daniel Boulud's favorite culinary quotations cover the mirrors in the bar.
299 Bowery (between Houston and First Street),
212-933-5300
www.danielnyc.com/dbgb.html

9:30 PM

Upright Citizens Brigade Theatre

Improv, stand-up, and sketch comedy. Check locations (they have two) for times.

153 East Third Street, 212-366-9231

307 West Twenty-Sixth Street, 212-366-9176

www.ucbtheatre.com

Day Three

Artists and Bohemians

9:00 AM

Breakfast at your hotel

10:30 AM

I walk the (High)line

The High Line is an elevated park that was originally an elevated railroad line, built in the 1930s. Now it's a very long and narrow park with landscaping, art installations, and impressive views of the New York skyline, especially the Empire State Building and the Hudson River. Get on at Thirtieth Street and Tenth Avenue and walk south to Fourteenth. www.thehighline.org

Running below the High Line in the same neighborhood is one of New York's largest concentrations of art galleries. (See Steve Martin's take on the New York art world in *An Object of Beauty*.)

chelseagallerymap.com

11:30 AM

Lunch at Chelsea Market

The former home of Nabisco, this space has evolved from the home of the Oreo to a mouthwatering gourmet-food concourse and shops.

75 Ninth Avenue (near Fifteenth), 212-243-6005

www.chelseamarket.com

1:00 PM

Big Onion Walking Tour of Greenwich Village

This tour takes in the sights of New York's literary and artistic mecca, Greenwich Village, the former home of writers and artists such as Edna St. Vincent Millay, Hart Crane, Eugene O'Neill, Dylan Thomas, Bob Dylan, and Jimi Hendrix. End your tour at Washington Square Park. All tours are available for private walks and group bookings.
Call 212-439-1090 ext. 5 or e-mail info@bigonion.com.
www.bigonion.com (or see their book of walks)

Grey Dog Coffee Shop

Top off your walking tour with a latte and a giant cookie. I love that they serve my latte with the froth in the form of a dog's paw print. Clearly I don't have what it takes to be a starving artist.
90 University Place, 212-414-4739
www.thegreydog.com

Strand Bookstore

With "eighteen miles of books," Strand is the sole survivor of New York's legendary Book Row—forty-eight bookstores that used to run from Union Square to Astor Place. A great place for book lovers to buy a few souvenirs from New York.
828 Broadway (Twelfth and Broadway), 212-473-1452
www.strandbooks.com

ADD-ON:

Got extra time to spend in New York City? There's so much more for literary travelers! You may want to take a tour of Harlem (David Lewis, ed., *The Portable Harlem Renaissance Reader*), walk the Brooklyn Bridge (David McCullough, *The Great Bridge*) or visit the 9/11 memorial in the financial district (Colum McCann, *Let the Great World Spin*, or Jonathan Safran Foer, *Extremely Loud and Incredibly Close*).

Where to Stay

Library Hotel

Each of the ten guest-room floors honors one of the ten categories of the Dewey Decimal System, and each of the sixty rooms are uniquely adorned with a collection of books and art exploring a distinctive topic within the category it belongs to. Located on "Library Walk," (which runs on Forty-First between Madison and Park) not far from the New York Public Library and the Morgan Library.
299 Madison Avenue at Forty-First Street, 212-983-4500
www.libraryhotel.com

Residence Inn New York Manhattan/Times Square

Spacious studio suites. Also has large sitting and gathering areas, great for groups and families.
1033 Avenue of the Americas, 212-768-0007 or
888-236-2427.
www.marriott.com/hotels/travel/nycri-residence-inn-new
-york-manhattan-times-square

7

Charleston

A NEW LOOK AT THE OLD SOUTH

You can forsake the Lowcountry, renounce it for other climates, but you can never completely escape the sensuous, semitropical pull of Charleston and her marshes.

—Pat Conroy, *The Lords of Discipline*

On my first visit to Charleston, I couldn't have been any more of an outsider. I didn't know that a front porch is called a "piazza," I didn't know a "she crab" from any other, and I thought hush puppies were a type of footwear. My midwestern accent prompted a carriage driver to quip, "We just love the way ya'll talk." Yet everyone from cabdrivers to innkeepers to soft-spoken folks who serve as volunteer guides at historic sites made me feel totally at home and relaxed in this most southern and traditional of American cities. That air of hospitality is one of Charleston's trademarks, and it leaves a visitor feeling that the city still holds the same appeal it did for Rhett Butler in the closing lines of *Gone with the Wind*. He tells Scarlett O'Hara that he's going back home to Charleston, where he can find "the calm dignity life can have when it's lived by gentle folks, the genial grace of days that are gone. When I lived those days, I didn't realize the slow charm of them."

Charleston is one of the country's oldest cities, and many of its old guard trace their roots to the early English colonists, who laid out its series of broad, elegant boulevards. It's also one of the most active cities for historic preservation. Most of the grand houses, built by slaves in a dizzying array of pastel colors and architectural styles—Colonial, Federal, Georgian, Italianate, Victorian—still stand, protected by law since the early 1930s. They're on display as you walk down Charleston's East Bay Street past the iconic palmetto trees and secluded gardens. Looking out from the Battery here at the southern tip of the city, Fort Sumter looms on the horizon, and the breeze that blows in from the Cooper River feels like the wind of history swirling around you. This is the city where Confederate soldiers fired the first shots of the Civil War. Cannonballs are embedded in the walls of its mansions, just the way the war is embedded in the city's history.

That was more than 150 years ago, but so much has been preserved in Charleston that, even now, it's easy for visitors to view Charleston through the lens of the white aristocracy, the old South that Margaret Mitchell glorified in *Gone with the Wind*. OK, most of the book takes place in Georgia, but there's not a better book to get an understanding of the old South frame of mind. Pat Conroy, the quintessential South Carolina writer, says in his book *My Reading Life*, "*Gone with the Wind* is as controversial a novel as it is magnificent. . . . Margaret Mitchell was a partisan of the first rank and there never has been a defense of the plantation South so implacable in its cold righteousness or its resolute belief that the wrong side had surrendered at Appomattox Court House."

Until relatively recently, that was the predominant story that visitors heard, told largely in terms of the lovely lost plantation days and of the honor of "the boys in gray" who died on the battle-field. But the discussion of local history skimmed over a major plotline: the story of the African Americans who built the city. Enslaved Africans and free blacks comprised the majority of people in South Carolina at the time of the war, and Charleston was the major entry point to the continent for Africans. Yet just as the winds of change blew through Tara, they've also blown through Charleston, literally and figuratively. A number of hurricanes, notably Hurricane Hugo in 1989, changed the face of Charleston. Actually, Hugo resulted in a face*lift* for the city, bringing insurance money that restored the buildings to a condition better than before the hurricane. And though the city is still steeped in history—some people here still talk about the Civil War as the "war of Northern aggression"—fresh voices are adding to the city's collective story, making a richer and more accurate narrative than one solely from Margaret Mitchell's perspective.

For example, in 1998 author Edward Ball, who descended from a dynasty of Charleston rice planters, broke the taboo against talking about the city's slave heritage. His *Slaves in the Family*, which won the National Book Award, chronicles the Ball family's history as slaveholders and his discovery of his black relatives, the descendants of relationships between his plantation-owning forebears and their slaves. The Old Slave Mart Museum, which opened in 2007, recounts the story of Charleston's role in the interstate slave trade; the museum focuses on the history of the building, which served as a hub for the sale of human beings.

And the former plantations that tourists visit near Charleston have begun to offer programs about the slaves who resided there, making clear who made the bricks, forged the stunning ironwork, cultivated the rice, and raised the children in the area's magnificent homes and plantations. Many plantation tours now feature the slave cabins on their grounds in addition to the masters' homes. One of the chief proponents of telling the slaves' story is Joseph McGill, a program officer for the National Trust for Historic Preservation and a Civil War reenactor who plays the role of a soldier in the Fifty-Fourth Massachusetts, a black Union regiment known for its assault on Fort Wagner in Charleston (which was depicted in the movie *Glory*). As part of what he calls the Slave Cabin Project, he works to bring attention to the slave cabins— the need both to preserve them and to honor the memory of the people who lived in them. He has slept in slave cabins across the South in order to call attention to the fact that for years tourists have visited the "big house" at plantations and were lulled into a false sense of history. Without the cabins out back and the people who lived in them, the big house and all that supported that life could not have existed.

So much history, along with Charleston's tradition of hospitality, has made Charleston one of the country's top tourist destinations. Still, without a little break, the past can begin to feel as confining as a corset and hoop skirt. No problem, says local artist Amelia Whaley. "This is a very arty city. There's almost always some sort of art festival going on." Chief among these, she says, is Charleston's Spoleto Festival, which runs for seventeen days each spring. During the festival, historic theaters, churches, and outdoor spaces fill with performances by an international list of renowned artists in opera, theater, dance, and chamber, symphonic, choral, and jazz music. She particularly recommends the festival's counterpart, Piccolo Spoleto, which focuses primarily on artists of the Southeast region and offers performances and events either free of charge or at prices that are more affordable than Spoleto.

Charleston dining is equally hip. The cuisine adheres to its southern and seaside roots, but the city has a huge array of inventive restaurants where chefs offer their own creative twists on tradition and local ingredients. The *New York Times* recently called it "one of the great eating towns of the south." But what about she-crab soup? According to Whaley, the story goes that this classic crab bisque got its name around the turn of the last century, when a member of the aristocratic Rhett family asked their butler to "dress up" the pale crab soup they usually served. The butler added orange-hued crab eggs to give color and improve the flavor, thus inventing the Charleston delicacy.

Whaley says that, whatever your interest, it's important to experience Charleston from the water, the most enduring feature of the Low Country (as opposed to the state's higher elevation Upcountry.) "A visit to Fort Sumter is worth it just for the boat ride," she says. "And then there are the beaches, or just walk or bike out on the Ravenal Bridge." The lovely suspension bridge opened in 2005 and spans the Cooper River between Charleston and Mt. Pleasant. She sees the bridge as the perfect symbol of Charleston, straddling the old and new. Ironically, the new bridge is named for Congressman Arthur Ravenal Jr., a member of one of Charleston's oldest families. Ultimately, despite all the changes, Charleston has retained enough of its tradition and charm that Rhett Butler would still feel at home here.

Pat Conroy: Tales of Family and the Low Country

Born in Atlanta, Pat Conroy was the son of a Marine Corps officer. The Corps transferred his family nearly every year of his childhood, always to southern towns close to swamps and the sea. He later attended the Citadel Military Academy in Charleston. Conroy's family life was tumultuous, to say the least, and his books are based on fictionalized versions of those experiences. While still a student, he published his first book, *The Boo*, a tribute to a beloved teacher. After teaching for a year at a school for underprivileged children in a one-room schoolhouse on Daufuskie Island off the South Carolina shore, he wrote a book about that experience, *The Water Is Wide*, published in 1972. The book was made into the feature film *Conrack*, starring Jon Voight. He has written several other semiautobiographical books. *The Great Santini* is set in a fictional town modeled after

Beaufort, South Carolina, and was made into a film with Robert Duvall. *The Lords of Discipline* takes place in a Charleston military school that is the Citadel, thinly disguised. He published his most successful novel, *The Prince of Tides*, in 1986, and it was later made into a movie that Barbra Streisand directed. In 2009, Conroy published *South of Broad*, which takes place in Charleston, a city that he says is "enchanting enough to charm cobras out of baskets."

In his memoir, *My Reading Life*, Conroy examines the authors and reading experiences that influenced his own literary career. His mother was probably the reason he began writing. He says, "My mother, southern to the bone, once told me, 'All southern literature can be summed up in these words: On the night the hogs ate Willie, Mama died when she heard what Daddy did to Sister.'" She constantly took him to the library and they read everything, but the biggest influence was *Gone with the Wind*. He says, "My mother saw in *Gone with the Wind* the text of liberating herself. She took *Gone with the Wind* as the central book in her life and made it the central book in her family. As a result, he says, "My mother raised me up to be a 'Southern' novelist, with a strong emphasis on the word 'Southern,' because *Gone with the Wind* set my mother's imagination ablaze when she was a young girl in Atlanta." Conroy was in negotiations with St. Martin's Press, which had asked him to write a *Gone with the Wind* sequel from the perspective of Rhett Butler, but he eventually pulled out of talks because he did not believe he would be given true editorial freedom.

He now lives on Fripp Island, a barrier island off the South Carolina coast, not far from Charleston.

CHARLESTON READING

LOCAL HISTORY

Edward Ball, *Slaves in the Family* and *Sweet Hell Inside: The Rise of an Elite Black Family in the Segregated South*. Ball details his shame over the Ball family's control of some four thousand slaves and tells the story of the Harleston family of Charleston, who are related to the author.

Alphonso Brown, *A Gullah Guide to Charleston: Walking Through Black History*. The owner and operator of Gullah Tours, Inc., offers walking tours and a driving tour through the places, history, and lore relevant to the rich and varied contributions of black Charlestonians.

Mary Boykin Chesnut, C. Vann Woodward, ed., *Mary Chesnut's Civil War*. The diary of the wife of Confederate General James Chestnut Jr., who was also an aide to President Jefferson Davis, provides an eyewitness narrative of all the years of the war.

David Detzer and Gene Smith, *Allegiance: Fort Sumter, Charleston, and the Beginning of the Civil War*.

Belinda Humence, ed., *Before Freedom, When I Just Can Remember*. A compilation of narratives of South Carolina ex-slaves.

And the movie *Glory*, the story of the US Civil War's first all-black Union regiment and their battle for Fort Wagner near Charleston.

CIVIL WAR FICTION

E. L. Doctorow, *The March*. The tale of Sherman's March to the Sea, which veered north from Savannah through the Carolinas.

Charles Frazier, *Cold Mountain*. This book takes place in North Carolina, but the heroine, Ada, comes from Charleston, and the book gives a great view of the South's misery at the end of the Civil War.

DuBose Heyward, *Peter Ashley*. Set in Charleston on the eve of secession. Heyward also wrote *Porgy and Bess*.

Margaret Mitchell, *Gone with the Wind*. The classic novel and movie of the Civil War and the old South.

Alexandra Ripley, *Charleston* and *On Leaving Charleston*. Ripley gained acclaim for her historical fiction but was panned for her sequel to *Gone with the Wind*, entitled *Scarlett*.

LIFE IN THE LOW COUNTRY

Hamilton Basso, *The View from Pompey's Head*. Set in the 1950s, a story about a Manhattan lawyer who returns to his hometown in South Carolina.

Gwen Bristow, *Celia Garth*. A story about a young dressmaker living in Charleston during the American Revolution.

Pat Conroy, *Beach Music*, *The Prince of Tides* (and the movie which Conroy cowrote), *The Water Is Wide*, and many others. Conroy's books paint a portrait of the Low Country environment and its people.

Mamie Garvin Fields, *Lemon Swamp and Other Places: A Carolina Memoir*. Fields, born in 1888, relates her story of African-American life in early-twentieth-century South Carolina.

Dorothea Benton Frank, *Bulls Island*, *Folly Beach*, *Lowcountry Summer*. Frank bases her stories in the South Carolina Low Country, where she grew up.

Josephine Humphreys, *Rich in Love*. Set in modern-day Mount Pleasant.

Sue Monk Kidd, *The Secret Life of Bees*, *The Mermaid Chair*. The former book is set in South Carolina farm country, the latter on a South Carolina barrier island.

Gloria Naylor, *Mama Day*. A generational saga of former slaves set on a sea island centered off the coast between the South Carolina and Georgia border.

Julia Peterkin, *Scarlet Sister Mary*. Peterkin, a white former plantation mistress, won a Pulitzer Prize for this work, set among the Gullah people of the Low Country.

Padgett Powell, *Edisto*. A coming-of-age novel set off the Carolina coast.

Anne Rivers Siddons, *Sweetwater Creek, Lowcountry*. Siddons is known for her descriptions of the Low Country landscape of oak groves and tidal rivers.

Karen White, *The House on Tradd Street, The Girl on Legare Street*. This series combines romance and the supernatural in a Charleston setting.

Curtis Worthington, ed., *Literary Charleston: A Lowcountry Reader*. An anthology of works by writers who have lived in Charleston or based stories there.

CHARLESTON ITINERARY

The historic section of Charleston sits at the southern tip of a peninsula, where the Ashley River on the west side and the Cooper River on the east come together. It's a terrific area for walking, with historic sites, inns, shops, and restaurants, not to mention beautiful views of the waterfront, all within close proximity to each other.

Day One

3:00 PM

> **Tour time**
> A tour of Charleston's historic sites is the absolute best way to gain an orientation to the city and a look at Charleston's most famous homes, government buildings, and the churches and synagogues that have led to the nickname The Holy City. Charleston Walks' Freedom and Slavery Tour provides an excellent complement to Edward Ball's *Slaves in the Family*. Fans of Pat Conroy's books, *South of Broad* in particular, should ask them to tailor a tour that emphasizes some sites from his books. Keep your camera ready for shots of stunning homes, gardens, and the waterfront to add to your post-trip scrapbook.

Charleston Walks
843-408-0010
www.charlestonwalks.com

7:30 PM

Heirloom southern food

In a restored 1893 Queen Anne home in the town center,
Husk charms you before you even taste the food. *Southern
Living* magazine named it the Best New Restaurant in 2011,
and its chef Sean Brock has received numerous other awards,
including being named the James Beard Foundation best
chef in the Southeast. Dinner at Husk is a distillation of all
that is Southern with a capital "S," and the restaurant grows
much of its own produce in the restaurant's garden. Brock
uses heirloom grains and vegetables that once flourished
in the region but were lost to twentieth-century industrial
agriculture. His motto is "If it doesn't come from the South,
it's not coming through the door."
Husk Restaurant
76 Queen Street, 843-577-2500
www.huskrestaurant.com

9:30 PM

Evening scene(ry)

For a scenic nightcap, head to the popular rooftop Pavilion
Bar at the Market Pavilion Hotel. Sip your drink with a view
of the Holy City's steeples, the Ashley River, and the Ravenal
Bridge.
225 East Bay Street, 843-440-2250
www.marketpavilion.com

Day Two

7:00 AM

Breakfast at your inn

9:00 AM

Kayak the marshes
A kayak trip from Shem Creek or Folly Beach will give you an up-close view of Low Country marshes and the Charleston waterfront that is the backdrop for so many local literary works. These trips combine history, bird watching, and a chance to see dolphins and other marine animals. While you're here, you'll experience the unique landscape that forms the backdrop for the works of authors such as Pat Conroy, Anne Rivers Siddons, and Dorothea Benton Frank. See especially Frank's books, aptly titled *Shem Creek* and *Folly Beach*.
Coastal Expeditions
2223 Folly Road, 843-884-7684
www.coastalexpeditions.com

1:00 PM

Wholly Cow Ice Cream
Grab a salad and smoothie for a quick lunch or an ice cream for a snack.
159 Church Street, 843-722-6665
www.whollycowicecream.com

1:30 PM

Antiques and cool crafts
Stroll Upper King Street for hip shops and galleries and Blue Bicycle Books (420 King Street), lower King Street and Broad Street for antiques and more art galleries. Be sure to check the Charleston Preservation Society (www.

preservationsociety.org) at 147 King for a great selection of
gifts and Charleston-related books and Low Country Artists
(www.lowcountryartists.com) at 148 East Bay Street.

5:30 PM

Dinner at Hanks Seafood

Classic Charleston seafood in a renovated warehouse
overlooking the market.
Corner of Church and Hayne Street, 843-723-3474
hanksseafoodrestaurant.com

7:30 PM

Old theater made new

The Dock Street Theater originally opened in 1736, but
after a couple of hundred years of varying uses, the City of
Charleston updated it and reopened the theater in 2010.
It now offers performances each season ranging from
Shakespeare to contemporary plays.
Dock Street Theatre
135 Church Street, 843-577-7183
www.charlestonstage.com

Day Three

8:00 AM

Breakfast at your inn

9:30 AM

Pack a picnic

Drayton Hall Plantation is a perfect place for a post-tour
picnic, so gather some goodies before you leave.
Bull Street Gourmet & Market
120 King Street, 843-722-6464
bullstreetgourmetandmarket.com

Plantation Road

A tour of one or more of the plantations along Ashley River Road will give you an authentic and somewhat haunting experience of the plantation life you've read about in books such as *Slaves in the Family* or any of the other books on the reading list that relate to the Civil War. Begin your trip with a visit to Drayton Hall. It's the first of the big three plantations on the Ashley River Road, if you're driving from Charleston. Tickets are $14. Drayton Hall is different from its counterparts down the road because it is bound by its mission to preserve the property—that is, to keep it in near-original condition just as the National Trust received it from the Drayton family in 1974. The buildings are "stabilized," meaning they are protected but not restored or altered. There is no furniture or electricity, all of which enhances the experience of life as it truly was at Drayton Hall. The home remains empty and echoes with footsteps of former inhabitants.

3380 Ashley River Road, 843-769-2600
www.draytonhall.org

Visiting multiple plantations can take several hours, so if you want to visit more than one, you may want to spread the visits across at least a couple of days. The other plantations include Magnolia Plantation and Gardens, which is next along the road at 3550 Ashley River Road, 800-367-3517, www.magnoliaplantation.com, and Middleton Place, several miles farther down the road at 4300 Ashley River Road, 843-556-6020, www.middletonplace.org

Where to Stay

John Rutledge House Inn

John Rutledge, one of the fifty-five signers of the US Constitution, built this home in 1763. Breakfast and afternoon tea and much personal service included, with a living room (the former ballroom) and a courtyard for gathering.

116 Broad Street, 800-476-9741

www.johnrutledgehouseinn.com

Meeting Street Inn

Across from the city market, built in the style of the Charleston single house. All rooms have four-poster rice beds. Has expanded continental breakfast and afternoon wine reception.

173 Meeting Street, 800-842-8022

www.meetingstreetinn.com

8

Miami

BEACH READING

Florida was to Americans what America had always been to the rest of the world—a fresh, free, unspoiled start.
—**Susan Orlean,** *The Orchid Thief*

You don't always have to hunker down with a hefty classic like *Moby Dick* (see chapter 4) to get the feel of a place. To the contrary, "beach reading," that guilty pleasure of highbrow book lovers, can take sunburned and sandy readers to some fascinating places, and South Beach, the southern portion of the sandbar that is Miami Beach, is one of the best. So along with your bathing suit and sunscreen, toss *Tourist Season, Skinny Dip,* or any of Carl Hiaasen's other zany environmental thrillers into your suitcase. Sure, they're fun to read, but along the way they satirize Florida politics and culture and also make a clear point about Florida real estate development and its effect on the delicate and diminishing wild areas of Florida. Or pack along something by humorist Dave

Barry. You won't necessarily learn a lot about Florida, but Barry will have you laughing into your frozen tropical drink and reading passages to your friends. In fact, most of the books on this chapter's list of "beach reading" are fun and don't require much deep thinking, but they do capture the essence of South Florida culture and all its eccentricities. You might call them "high-quality beach reading"—not so trashy that you'll have to hide them inside a copy of *War and Peace*.

However, because you may lose all of your ambition once the sun and surf do their work, you'll want to read up a bit *before* you go to Miami. You may want to tackle Tom Wolfe's book *Back to Blood*, which takes a look at Miami's "blood lines," with a cast of characters that make up each segment of Miami's immigrant culture. You also won't want to miss reading up about the real backstory of South Beach—you won't believe it. The antics of Hiaasen's characters pale in comparison to those of the politicians, drug dealers, mobsters, and the glamorous, gaudy, and downright sleazy celebs who have been part of the "SoBe" scene since the turn of the last century. Wealth! Power! Corruption! Scandal! Those ingredients make nonfiction books such as Gerald Posner's *Miami Babylon* a read to rival anything Carl Hiaasen could concoct.

In these books, and in person, South Beach often looks like Las Vegas, only with an ocean and better-looking people. The area is a regular watering hole for some of the richest people in the world. That's especially obvious during Art Basel, an art show that attracts a Who's Who of the international art world and those who flock to South Beach to party with them, the way seagulls follow the fishing fleet. The area has become known for the exclusive clubs and hotels clustered along the shoreline, and at night Ferraris, Lamborghinis, and Bentleys line the curb. Throbbing techno music provides the beat for all-night parties with the likes of the Kardashians and Paris Hilton.

So SoBe is the girl with the "fast" and wild reputation that your mother wanted you to avoid in high school. But if there's any place where reading can give you a greater sense of its personality, dispel the myths, and allow you to see beyond the tight, leopard-print minidress, it's South Beach. Get to know her a little better; you'll find that under the makeup and bling she's a gal with a bit more substance than you thought. You'll realize it's a place of big ideas and dreamers, including people like Henry Flagler, who built a railroad to Key West known as Flagler's Folly. Or Carl Fisher (builder of the nation's first freeways and a founder of the Indianapolis Motor Speedway), who envisioned building Miami Beach into a resort from what was then only a tangle of mangroves, rats, and swamp and thereby unleashed the demon of development. Through hurricanes and the Depression, Fisher lost his fortune; the Miami area continues to experience extreme cycles of boom and bust to this day. Yet the tradition of dreamers lives on with the ever-changing waves of immigrants—Cubans, Columbians, Venezuelans—who have come to find a better life and made the Miami area the capital of Latin culture in the United States. Says Charles Kropke, operator of Dragonfly Expeditions and author of *South Beach: Tales of a Renaissance*, "They're the next wave of up-and-coming artists, musicians, and entrepreneurs."

Take off your sunglasses for a minute and take a closer look at SoBe. Notice the crazy-colored lifeguard station you've flopped next to on the beach; there's a story there. While there have been elevated lifeguard stations here almost since the area became a resort, they weren't so interesting until Hurricane Andrew swept most of them away in 1992. They were rebuilt with panache typical of South Beach. And those Necco candy-colored art deco hotels all around you—their tale is a whopper, best told in M. Barron Stofik's *Saving South Beach*. Built mostly in the 1930s, these hotels and the night-life here made a scene straight out of a Busby Berkeley musical. Vacationers dined and danced the night away like Fred Astaire and Ginger Rogers, despite the crushing gloom of the Depression. You'll still find the arrows that pointed visitors to the secret gambling rooms and speakeasies embedded in the hotels' terrazzo floors.

But World War II ended all the fun, and the army transformed the hotels into soldiers' barracks. By the late 1950s and 1960s people with a bit of cash deserted SoBe in favor of newer, bigger, fancier hotels like the Fontainebleu or the Eden Roc up the beach. Gradually the deco area slid into despair and became a dilapidated group of old folks homes with rooms converted to efficiencies or "pullmanettes," with enough room for a bed, a hot plate, and a shared bathroom on each floor—places often called "God's waiting room." It's hard to imagine now, but by the late 1970s the area was one of the poorest in the country, and its residents were a curious combination of drug dealers and old ladies. SoBe had sunk so low that the producers of the 1980s television show *Miami Vice* could shoot scenes with cops chasing drug dealers without having to manufacture a set. South Beach was ripe for the wrecking ball.

In the nick of time, a feisty retired magazine editor, Barbara Baer Capitman, spearheaded a movement to save South Beach. Capitman founded the Miami Design Preservation League, which fought to save the deco district. She jousted with powerful developers who wanted to level the deco district in order to build new modern hotels and convention centers. She fought with city officials and occasionally her fellow preservationists. "She was immovable," says Kropke, "but a revolution has to have a leader who isn't willing to give. I revere her." The Miami Beach Architectural District was listed on the National Register of Historic Places in 1979. Many buildings were lost, but as a result of the efforts of Capitman and many others, you'll be staying amid the largest collection of art deco buildings in the world. Preserving South Beach architecture set it on a course of overwhelming success. "If you love urban space and architecture, it's a dreamland," says Kropke.

The Miami Design Preservation League offers excellent deco tours several times a day. And you can stop in for a look at most of the hotels' public areas any time—for free. In fact, contrary to its expensive reputation, South Beach offers many other opportunities for the bargain minded. There are free yoga classes on the beach at 7:00 AM and 5:30 PM right next to the Third Street life-guard station. For a modest hourly rate, you can grab a bicycle at any of the many Deco Bike stations around South Beach and cruise from South Point Park up the beach or anywhere around town. The gorgeous beach scenery is free, too. Have a seat in South Point Park along the channel into the Port of Miami and take in the sun-set view of downtown Miami as gigantic cargo ships, cruise ships, and yachts pass by. In the evening Ocean Drive abounds with out-door musical entertainment ranging from techno to flamenco, all for the price of a drink, and the people watching is free. At its Frank Gehry–designed home, the New World Symphony, with state-of-the-art visual and audio technology, shows free movies and live concerts on its seven-thousand-square-foot outdoor wall (www.nws.edu).

There's no charge for the beautiful public beaches, either. The beaches are known for scantily clad sunbathers. Once, in one of my more naive and embarrassing moves, I persuaded my husband and two adolescent sons to hit South Beach for lunch and a bit of beach time while we waited to meet up with the friends we were staying with in Coral Gables. We trooped enthusiastically out to the beach, planted ourselves on our towels, and then looked around to find a great many topless women, which my sons decid-ed was one of the highlights of their spring break. But don't let that discourage you. Even for someone like me, who bares winter-white skin in a sturdy black one-piece, there's no better winter tonic than sun and surf.

From crazy nightlife to peaceful yoga, South Beach is a very alive place with an extraordinary history and a culture uniquely its own. But let's not be too serious here. Roll over, put on a little more sunscreen, and have fun. After all, it's just beach reading.

Edwidge Danticat, Creating Dangerously for Those Who Read Dangerously

The storytelling tradition of her homeland, Haiti, has inspired Edwidge Danticat's own storytelling. She delves into the Haitian American experience through fiction, memoir, and essay. Born in 1969, she moved to the United States from Haiti when she was twelve, and she grew up in Brooklyn. She received a BA from Barnard College and an MFA from Brown University. Danticat has been a visiting professor of creative writing at New York University and the University of Miami, and she now lives in Miami with her husband and two daughters.

In a simple prose style, she recounts the stories of Haiti, of both pain and beauty, as well as the experience of an immigrant in a new land. *The Farming of Bones*, told through the eyes of a young domestic servant, covers the 1937 massacre of Haitian workers in the Dominican Republic. In *Brother, I'm Dying*, she recounts the struggles her father and uncle experienced in Haiti and the United States. Her other books include *After the Dance: A Walk Through Carnival in Jacmel*, the novel *Breath, Eyes, Memory*, and a collection of stories called *Krik? Krak!* whose National Book Award nomination made Danticat the youngest nominee ever. In all her works she weaves together the issues of home and exile as well as the power of human resistance and endurance against great obstacles. Danticat says in her 2010 book *Creating Dangerously: The Immigrant Artist at Work*, "Create dangerously, for people who read dangerously. This is what I've always thought it meant to be a writer. Writing, knowing in part that no matter how trivial your words may seem, someday, somewhere, someone may risk his or her life to read them."

BEACH READING

These books go well beyond the confines of South Beach to include stories from the Everglades and Key West. You can't come this far and not include Hemingway.

Russell Banks, *Continental Drift.* The collision between the lives of a New Hampshire man and a Haitian family, both seeking the American dream in Florida.

Dave Barry, *Dave Barry's Only Travel Guide You'll Ever Need, Dave Barry's Complete Guide to Guys,* and many others. A former *Miami Herald* columnist, Barry won the Thurber Prize for American Humor and the Pulitzer Prize for Commentary. Hilarious.

Daina Chaviano, *The Island of Eternal Love.* A Miami journalist discovers a saga of Cuba, with a dose of magical realism.

Susanna Daniel, *Stiltsville.* A romance that begins among the collection of houses built on stilts in Miami's Biscayne Bay.

Stanley Elkin, *Mrs. Ted Bliss.* The story of an eighty-two-year-old widow starting life anew in a Florida retirement community after the death of her husband. She inadvertently becomes involved with a drug kingpin trying to use her as a front for his operations.

Gail Godwin, *Queen of the Underworld.* A more-than-loosely autobiographical novel of life as a young reporter in Miami in the 1950s.

Carl Hiaasen, *Tourist Season, Star Island, Skinny Dip, Nature Girl,* and many others. Sample Hiaasen's frenetic fiction, full of local sights, details, issues, and characters, as well as the nonfiction *Paradise Screwed,* a collection of his columns for the *Miami Herald.*

Caridad Piñero, *South Beach Chicas Catch Their Man* and *Sex and the South Beach Chicas.* The ulimate chick (or *chica*) lit, set in South Beach.

Theodore Pratt, *The Barefoot Mailman.* Historical fiction of delivering the mail by foot from Palm Beach to Miami.

Virgil Suárez and Delia Poey, eds., *Little Havana Blues: A Cuban-American Literature Anthology.*

Ana Veciana-Suarez, *The Chin Kiss King.* A novel about the lives of three generations of Cuban American women sharing a home in Miami.

Tom Wolfe, *Back to Blood.* In his latest novel Wolfe turns his literary lens on Miami, especially its immigrant culture.

Helen Yglesias, *The Girls.* A tale of four elderly sisters living in Miami.

CRIME AND THRILLERS AND DETECTIVE BEACH READING

Edna Buchanan, *Contents Under Pressure, The Corpse Had a Familiar Face,* and *A Dark and Lonely Place.* A Pulitzer Prize–winning crime journalist, Buchanan now writes popular crime fiction.

Elmore Leonard, *LaBrava.* Former Secret Service agent Joe LaBrava gets mixed up in an extortion scheme.

Barbara Parker, *The Dark of Day.* Crime set in South Beach.

MIAMI NONFICTION AND MEMOIR

Ann Armbruster, *The Life and Times of Miami Beach.* Miami Beach in its heyday.

Ann Louise Bardach, *Cuba Confidential: Love and Vengeance in Miami and Havana.* The warring personalities and politics between Cuba and Cuban exiles.

Joann Biondi, *Miami Beach Memories: A Nostalgic Chronicle of Days Gone By.* An oral history of the people and events that shaped this tropical island from the 1920s through the 1960s.

Iris Garnett Chase and Susan Russell, *South Beach Deco: Step by Step.* A walking tour of South Beach and its development.

Joan Didion, *Miami.* A classic investigation of Miami politics and culture.

Carlos Eire, *Waiting for Snow in Havana: Confessions of a Cuban Boy* and *Learning to Die in Miami: Confessions of a Refugee Boy.* Award-winning memoirs.

Mark S. Foster, *Castles in the Sand: The Life and Times of Carl Graham Fisher.* A biography of Fisher, who transformed Miami Beach from swampy island into a luxury resort. A hurricane wiped out much of what he had built in 1926, and he lost most of his fortune in the stock market crash of 1929.

Steven Gaines, *Fool's Paradise: Players, Poseurs, and the Culture of Excess in South Beach.* One of the most scintillating accounts of South Beach history.

Paul Hendrickson, *Hemingway's Boat: Everything He Loved in Life, and Lost, 1934–1961.* A terrific Hemingway biography with an emphasis on his love of the sea and his boat, *Pilar.*

Charles Kropke, *South Beach Tales.* The businesses, institutions, and entrepreneurs who rebuilt SoBe. A great South Beach souvenir with beautiful photos.

Gerald Posner, *Miami Babylon: Crime, Wealth, and Power—A Dispatch from the Beach.* The making of Miami Beach from the very beginning.

Susan Russell, *South Beach Lifeguard Stations: The Fabulous Life and Lifeguard Stands on Miami Beach's Atlantic Seashore.* The story and photos of these South Beach landmarks.

Les Standiford, *Last Train to Paradise: Henry Flagler and the Spectacular Rise and Fall of the Railroad That Crossed an Ocean.* The story of Flagler's Miami to Key West railroad.

M. Barron Stofik, *Saving South Beach.* A chronicle of how South Beach was saved from the wrecking ball.

THE EVERGLADES AND SOUTH FLORIDA

NONFICTION

Marjory Stoneman Douglas, *The Everglades: River of Grass.* With this book, Douglas redefined the popular conception of the

Everglades as a treasured river instead of a worthless swamp. Its impact has been compared to that of Rachel Carson's influential book *Silent Spring* (1962).

Michael Grunwald, *The Swamp: The Everglades, Florida, and the Politics of Paradise*. The natural, social, and political history of this unique area.

Susan Orlean, *The Orchid Thief: A True Story of Beauty and Obsession*. The story of a likeable criminal who smuggles endangered orchids from Florida's Fakahatchee swamp.

SOUTH FLORIDA FICTION

Ernest Hemingway, *To Have and Have Not*. The story of a fishing boat captain who runs contraband between Florida and Cuba. Made into a movie with Bogart and Bacall.

Zora Neale Hurston, *Their Eyes Were Watching God*. Hurston's most famous novel, set in central Florida and the Everglades.

Peter Matthiessen, *Shadow Country*. A fictionalized story of the notorious real-life Everglades sugar planter and outlaw E. J. Watson at the turn of the twentieth century.

Karen Russell, *Swamplandia!* Set in the Ten Thousand Islands of southwest Florida, this is the story of the Bigtree family trying to survive in their impoverished gator-themed amusement park.

SOUTH BEACH ITINERARY

This itinerary is all about options, from what you read to how little you wear on the beach. Stay firmly parked in the sand or sample the other sites of South Beach.

Day One

2:00 PM

> **News Cafe**
> Have a snack and watch the crowd go by at this sidewalk café by the beach.

800 Ocean Drive, 305-538-6397
www.newscafe.com

3:00 PM

Hit the beach
Lummus Park Beach
On Ocean Drive between Sixth and Fourteenth streets.

6:00 PM

Cocktails at Smith & Wollensky
Watch the sun set and the cruise ships set sail with a view of
downtown Miami.
1 Washington Avenue (at South Pointe Park), 305-673-2800
smithandwollensky.com/locations-2/miami-beach

7:30 PM

Stay for dinner at "Smith and Wo"or head to Joe's Stone Crab
Open only during the stone crab season (October to May),
Joe's restaurant is a Miami Beach institution. If you plan to
eat dinner here, stop in to put your name in early because
they don't take reservations. The crabs are pricey, but
you can get a plate to share and order other menu items.
Another alternative: go next door to Joe's take out and grab
everything you need for a picnic at South Point Park.
11 Washington Avenue, 305-673-0365
www.joesstonecrab.com

9:30 PM

Stroll Ocean Drive
There's plenty of entertainment on this strip of art deco
hotels. Skirt around the menu-and-seafood-platter-wielding
hostesses trying to lure you in for dinner and head to the
Hotel Victor (1144 Ocean Drive) for drinks and music outside
or to the Clevelander (1020 Ocean Drive) for disco and drinks.

Day Two

7:00 AM

Free beach yoga

Early risers can enjoy yoga in the sand. Meet at the Third Street lifeguard station.
www.3rdstreetbeachyoga.com

8:30 AM

Breakfast at your hotel

10:00 to 10:15 AM

Art Deco tour of South Beach

Tour starts at 10:30 AM. Learn the story of saving South Beach and see some of its most significant buildings, as portrayed in *Saving South Beach*.
Miami Design Preservation League
1001 Ocean Drive, 305-672-2014
www.mdpl.org

12:00 PM

Lunch at the Front Porch Cafe

1458 Ocean Drive, 305-531-8300
frontporchoceandrive.com

2:00 PM

Back to the beach or . . .
Board a boat on Biscayne

Take a two-hour tour of Biscayne Bay and the mansions of the rich and famous you can read about in Hiaasen's *Star Island*.
Miami Aqua Tours
401 Biscayne Blvd., 786-663-1199
www.miamiaquatours.com

6:00 PM

Shopping at Lincoln Road Mall

Hard-core shoppers may want to go earlier to this pedestrian mall between Alton Road and Washington Avenue. Especially recommended: Romero Britto gallery; Taschen Books, a publisher of glossy "coffee table" books on art, architecture, design, and photography; and Books & Books, a beautiful bookstore with a section devoted to local books. www.lincolnroadmall.com

7:30 PM

Dinner at Books & Books Café

The Café at Books & Books
927 Lincoln Road, 305-695-8898
www.booksandbooks.com

9:00 PM

Jazz music at Van Dyke Café

846 Lincoln Road, 305-534-3600
www.thevandykecafe.com

Day Three

7:00 AM

Beach yoga

For those who aren't exhausted by now.

8:30 AM

Breakfast at your hotel

9:30 AM

Bike the beach

Pick up a Deco Bike from any of the many kiosks near your hotel and hit the trail.

The city is constantly expanding the bike/pedestrian path along the beach. Head to South Point Park and bike to the causeway bridge. Turn back and go north, up the beach as far as the pavement currently allows. You can actually go further on city streets. It's a great way to peek into the "backyards" of some opulent hotels.
www.decobike.com

12:00 PM

Lunch at David's Café and Marketplace
Great Cuban food to eat here, or get a sandwich to take to the beach.
1058 Collins Avenue, 305-534-8736
www.davidscafe.com

ADD-ON

For a different kind of wildlife, fans of Karen Russell's bestseller *Swamplandia!*, Peter Mathiesson's *Shadow Country*, or Susan Orleans' *The Orchid Thief* may want to rent a car and drive to the Ten Thousand Islands section of the Everglades, about two hours from Miami. You'll get a better understanding of the mysterious watery world of these books and see birds and "gators," too. (The area is actually much closer to Naples on Florida's Gulf Coast.) For tours, check out the following:
www.tourtheglades.com
www.shurradventures.net
www.evergladesbackcountryexperience.com (especially for fishing)

Where to Stay

These two hotels are close to the action, with most of the South Beach attractions within walking distance but on the edge of the pounding nightlife, which will allow you to get a good night's sleep.

Park Central Hotel

A restored art deco hotel on the National Historic register, right across from the beach.

640 Ocean Drive, 305-538-1611

www.theparkcentral.com

The Hotel

This hotel used to be called the Tiffany, hence the tower with that name on top, but the jewelry company objected, so now it's simply the Hotel.

801 Collins Avenue, 305-531-2222

www.thehotelofsouthbeach.com

9

Minneapolis and St. Paul

UP TO THE LAKE

"Go faster," she called, "fast as it'll go."

Obediently he jammed the lever forward and the white spray mounted at the bow. When he looked around again the girl was standing up on the rushing board, her arms spread wide, her eyes lifted toward the moon.

"It's awful cold," she shouted. "What's your name?"

He told her.

"Well, why don't you come to dinner to-morrow night?"

His heart turned over like the fly-wheel of the boat, and, for the second time, her casual whim gave a new direction to his life.

—**F. Scott Fitzgerald**, "Winter Dreams"

That's Minnesota for you, all water and romance . . . and, occasionally, the "awful cold" part, too. For F. Scott Fitzgerald and other Minnesota-born writers, lakes and rivers provide the perfect backdrop for a story. The water serves as a symbol and a metaphor, a way to create a feeling of peace or a hair-raising sense of foreboding so strong that the water almost becomes a character in itself. Put on your English-major hat for a minute and consider all the symbolic uses of water in literature (the source of life, washing clean, a barrier between worlds—the list goes on), and you'll see why Minnesota's watery geography ties so well with great storytelling.

Literary travelers to the Land of 10,000 Lakes soon discover that water is never far away in Minnesota life. A man from England told me that the first time he flew into Minneapolis and saw it from the air he thought there had been a flood, but he later realized that's the way it always looks. Water provides the perfect backdrop for Minnesota authors to dive beneath the surface and find the drama and meaning in the lives of ordinary people, whether they're the denizens of Garrison Keillor's Lake Wobegon, the St. Paul family at the center of Jonathan Franzen's *Freedom*, or the Vietnam veterans in Tim O'Brien's books *Northern Lights* and *In the Lake of the Woods*. In her introduction to an anthology, *The North Country Reader*, Jean Ervin says of Minnesota literature, "One does not have to look far to find geography and weather woven into a short story or novel either metaphorically or explicitly. The violence of winter blizzards and summer thunderstorms, the vastness of the prairies, the importance of the lakes and rivers and of the ever-present wilderness in the North—all inform the literature of Minnesota."

Since the beginning, Minnesota's lakes and rivers have been the engine of development and the focus of recreation, not to mention the source of some very large fish. The Twin Cities have their roots on the Mississippi River, which has transported timber and grain from the Midwest to market and powered the flour mills of the Pillsbury family, among others. Those mills are mostly condominiums now, but you can get an idea of what the industry was like at Minneapolis's Mill City Museum. From there, walk out onto the Stone Arch Bridge over the Mississippi. Railroad baron James J. Hill built the gently curving bridge in 1883 for his trains to cross the Mississippi River, but the bridge now offers a serene point for pedestrians to view St. Anthony Falls. It's no Niagara, but it is the only significant waterfall on the entire Mississippi River, and it's big enough to create electricity and power the flour mills on the adjacent riverbanks. Depending on the time of year, you can feel the mist and sense the power of "Old Man River" as it rushes over the falls on its journey all the way to New Orleans.

As it did for Judy Jones and Dexter Green in Fitzgerald's "Winter Dreams," water plays a major role in Minnesota's outdoorsy lifestyle. People go north to summer cabins, "up to the lake," in droves, and you'll see them swimming, paddling, and sailing the Chain of Lakes in the heart of Minneapolis. But the watery pursuits aren't confined to the short Minnesota summer. Even on days so cold that moisture in the air forms "sun dogs," ice crystal rainbows around the sun, Minnesotans play pond hockey and fishermen drag "ice houses" onto the frozen lakes, chop holes in the ice, and enjoy the camaraderie of their fellow half-frozen anglers. And every few years in St. Paul, they harvest ice from a local lake to build a colossal ice palace as part of the Winter Carnival, which Fitzgerald depicts in his short story "The Ice Palace."

About two and a half hours from the Twin Cities lies Lake Superior, Gitche Gumee, the "Big Sea waters" of Longfellow's *Song of Hiawatha*, and gradually the water begins to become intimately entwined with the wilderness. Further on, one reaches the Boundary Waters Canoe Area Wilderness, where trees and water seem to spread endlessly along the border between Minnesota and Canada. Moving west, the international border cuts through Lake of the Woods, the setting of Tim O'Brien's *In the Lake of the Woods*. O'Brien describes it: "Then there were no roads at all. There were no towns and no people. Beyond the dock the big lake opened northward into Canada, where the water was everything, vast and very cold, and where there were secret channels and portages and bays and tangled forests and islands without names. Everywhere, for many thousand square miles, the wilderness was all one thing, like a great curving mirror, infinitely blue and beautiful, always the same." It's both beautiful and ripe for drama and suspense.

Though he's most famous for his portrayals of Jazz Age society, Minnesota's greatest writer, F. Scott Fitzgerald, also embraced water as setting and symbol. Born in St. Paul in 1896, he spent much of his early childhood in Buffalo, New York, but he returned to St. Paul when his father lost his job and, like any Minnesota kid, spent time on the water, notably White Bear Lake (seen as Black Bear Lake, the location of the Sherry Island Yacht Club in his short stories). Expelled from St. Paul Academy, he left for a New Jersey prep school, then Princeton and the army, but returned again to St. Paul to revise what would become his breakthrough novel, *This Side of Paradise*.

"Great fiction is great social history," the late professor Matthew Bruccoli said in his preface to the 1992 edition of Fitzgerald's *The Great Gatsby*. That's clearly on display in the short stories collected in *The St. Paul Stories of F. Scott Fitzgerald*, edited by Patricia Hampl and Dave Page, in which Fitzgerald draws upon his own youth and social milieu, the epitome of 1920s life in the Twin Cities and the larger American society. Says Hampl in her introduction to the *Saint Paul Stories*, "He watched the capital city elite conduct its intense and introverted social life, rounds of parties and dances, as snowbound and fashion-conscious as any provincial capital in a Russian novel."

Both of my book groups have had a great time in St. Paul, where you can walk the streets where the author famously said he lived "in a house below the average on a street above the average," a middle-class kid amid St. Paul's elite society. One time, we were standing outside the house where Fitzgerald was born when one of the tenants (who is probably used to gawkers) came out and gave us a little history of how the neighborhood has been rejuvenated since the 1970s, when the building was almost torn down. If you visit the mansion of the railroad baron James J. Hill just a couple of streets over on Summit Avenue, you'll see why Fitzgerald may have felt the impossibility of truly becoming part of that world. (Hill shows up in *The Great Gatsby* when Gatsby's father says, "If he'd of lived he'd of been a great man. A man like James J. Hill. He'd of helped build up the country.") Fitzgerald was a "poor boy in a rich boy's world," says Hampl—an experience that set in place his own personal striving and became a theme in his greatest novels. Like the young Fitzgerald, and like Jay Gatsby, Dexter Green in "Winter Dreams" "wanted not association with the glittering things and glittering people—he wanted the glittering things themselves. Often he reached out for the best without knowing why he wanted it—and sometimes he ran up against the mysterious denials and prohibitions in which life indulges."

After his success with *This Side of Paradise*, Fitzgerald left St. Paul and went on to become both the chronicler and an icon of the "Lost Generation." However, he did return to his native city, by proxy, through his characters, as he continued to set many of his short stories in St. Paul. He took Sally Carrol to the Winter Carnival in "The Ice Palace" and, as Basil Duke Lee, spent "A Night at the Fair." And he went boating with the beautiful Judy Jones in "Winter Dreams," the precursor to his masterpiece, *The Great Gatsby*. In *Gatsby*, water again plays a role as the playground of the wealthy and as a symbol. Gatsby's parties take place on the water's edge, and Gatsby dies in a swimming pool. Like Fitzgerald, Nick Carraway, the story's narrator, grew up in St. Paul. After Gatsby's death, the East holds nothing but bad memories for Nick, and he returns home to St. Paul. It's a place less tainted than the East, cold and crisp and much more innocent—and where water may wash away guilt and hold the promise of a new life.

Louise Erdrich Fosters Stories of the "Indigirati"

Louise Erdrich is the author of novels, poetry, and children's books featuring Native American heritage, including *The Round House*, *Love Medicine*, *Tracks*, *A Plague of Doves*, and *The Master Butchers Singing Club*. She has garnered a long list of literary awards—most recently a National Book Award for *The Round House*—not to mention being named one of *People* magazine's most beautiful people.

Born in Minnesota, Erdrich grew up in Wahpeton, North Dakota, where her parents taught at the Bureau of Indian Affairs school. She is a tribal descendant of the Turtle Mountain Band of Chippewa Indians. Most of her books take place in North Dakota, although in *Four Souls* one of her continuing characters, Fleur Pillager, travels to Minneapolis to seek revenge on wealthy John James Mauser, who made his fortune by cheating Indians out of their land. *Shadow Tag* takes place in modern-day Minneapolis. Erdrich typically tells her stories through the perspectives of multiple characters in a style similar to William Faulkner in *As I Lay Dying*.

In addition to writing books, she plays a vital role in the Twin Cities' literary scene as the owner of Birchbark Books in Minneapolis. The cozy store carries a wide selection of all sorts of books, many with handwritten notes from Erdrich to recommend them. But the store also works to promote the literary and artistic works of Native Americans, whom she calls the "Indigirati." The store sponsors readings by Native and non-Native writers, journalists, and historians and also features Native American quillwork, traditional basketry, and paintings. In addition, Erdrich and sister Heid Erdrich (a poet and curator of Native·American fine art) run Wiigwaas Press, which publishes books in the Ojibwe language.

TWIN CITIES READING

Minnesota authors are difficult to categorize: memoirists, mystery writers, nature and environmental writers, poets, and humorists. Here's a sampling.

THE MINNESOTA CLASSICS

Jean Ervin, *The North Country Reader: Classic Stories by Minnesota Writers.* An anthology of works by classic and contemporary writers about the city, the prairie, the lakes, and the north woods of Minnesota.

F. Scott Fitzgerald, *The St. Paul Stories of F. Scott Fitzgerald* (Hampl and Page, eds.) contain great stories, and Hampl's introduction gives an excellent background of Fitzgerald's formative years; *This Side of Paradise*; *The Great Gatsby*; and *Tender Is the Night.* See also Arthur Mizener's *The Far Side of Paradise: A Biography of F. Scott Fitzgerald.*

Sinclair Lewis, *Main Street, Babbit.* Lewis was this country's first Nobel laureate for literature.

O. E. Rolvaag, *Giants in the Earth.* Takes place in the Dakotas, but Rolvaag lived in Minnesota.

MEMOIRS

David Carr, *The Night of the Gun.* Now a *New York Times* reporter, Carr tells his story of life as a junkie in Minneapolis and his recovery.

Bob Dylan, *Chronicles, Vol. 1.* This book primarily portrays life in New York, but Dylan is one of Minnesota's most cherished native sons.

Jim Northrup, *Anishinaabe Syndicated: A View from the Rez.* Ojibwe life in Sawyer, Minnesota, with a twist of humor.

Sigurd Olson, *The Singing Wilderness.* A look at the eternal values of the outdoors by Minnesota's greatest nature writer.

Peter Razor, *While the Locust Slept.* An account of Razor's childhood as an abused Native American orphan.

Sarah Stonich, *Shelter.* A memoir about her writing retreat in far northern Minnesota.

Jennifer Vogel, *Flim Flam Man: A True Family History.* Life with a father who is sometimes a criminal, sometimes a doting dad, and always a heartbreaker.

Diane Wilson, *Spirit Car: Journey to a Dakota Past.* In a blend of memoir and carefully researched fiction, Wilson reconstructs the story of her mother's side of the family.

HUMOR

John Louis Anderson, *Scandinavian Humor and Other Myths.* Humor from a stoic group.

Garrison Keillor, *In Search of Lake Wobegon, WLT: A Radio Romance, Leaving Home.* Minnesota stories from writer, essayist, musician, and host of public radio's *A Prairie Home Companion.* Get the audiobook and listen to Keillor read it.

Lorna Landvik, *Patty Jane's House of Curl.* Book groups might especially enjoy *Angry Housewives Eating Bon Bons,* about a suburban Minneapolis book group.

Charles Schulz, *Happiness Is a Warm Puppy.* From the creator of the beloved "Peanuts" comic strip.

HISTORY

Annette Atkins, *Creating Minnesota: A History from the Inside Out.* Readable history about the conflicting interests of native people, traders, politicians, and others in early Minnesota.

Peg Meier, *Bring Warm Clothes.* Photos, diary, and journal entries from Minnesota settlers.

Eric Sevareid, *Canoeing with the Cree.* The radio/TV journalist recounts a Minneapolis–Hudson Bay canoe trip.

Lori Sturdevant and George Pillsbury, *The Pillsburys of Minnesota.* The story of the famous flour-milling family.

Anton Treuer, *Ojibwe in Minnesota, The Assassination of Hole in the Day.* History from the Native American view.

Stanley Gordon West, *Until They Bring the Streetcars Back.* A fabulous fictional account of the demise of the streetcar system in St. Paul.

Laura Ingalls Wilder, *On the Banks of Plum Creek.* A children's fictional account of the life of the Ingalls family's pioneering days in Minnesota.

See also Wendy McClure's *The Wilder Life*, her memoir of trying to live in "Laura World."

OTHER PROMINENT MINNESOTA FICTION WRITERS

Charles Baxter, *Gryphon*, *The Feast of Love*, and *Shadow Play.* This University of Minnesota professor is considered one of America's finest short story writers.

Sandra Benitez, *Bitter Grounds*, *The Weight of All Things*, and *A Place Where the Sea Remembers.* Benitez's fiction illuminates life in Central America and Mexico.

Carol Bly, *Letters from the Country* and *The Tomcat's Wife and Other Stories.* Bly is best known for her stories set in small-town Minnesota.

Peter Bognanni, *The House of Tomorrow.* (He's from Iowa but teaches at Macalester College in St. Paul, so we're claiming him). A funny and poignant story about an orphaned boy growing up with his eccentric grandmother.

Kate DiCamillo, *Because of Winn-Dixie* and *The Tale of Desperaux.* Award-winning bestsellers for children.

Leif Enger, *Peace Like a River* and *So Brave, Young, and Handsome.* Powerful stories of redemption, one set in Minnesota and the Dakotas, the other further west.

Louise Erdrich, *Love Medicine*, *The Master Butcher's Singing Club*, *A Plague of Doves*, and *The Round House.* Erdrich's powerful novels blend history and Native American lore.

Judith Guest, *Ordinary People.* About a family's pain and healing after the death of a son.

Jon Hassler, *Staggerford, North of Hope,* and *The Love Hunter.* Hassler's novels focus on life in small-town Minnesota.

Tim O'Brien, *Northern Lights, The Things They Carried,* and *In the Lake of the Woods.* O'Brien's works revolve around psychologically wounded Vietnam veterans. Great scenes of Minnesota's wild places.

Arthur Phillips, *Prague, The Egyptologist,* and *The Tragedy of Arthur.* They're not about Minnesota, but Phillips grew up in St. Louis Park, Minnesota.

Robert M. Pirsig, *Zen and the Art of Motorcycle Maintenance.* The motorcycle journey from Minneapolis to California is also a classic philosophical exploration.

J. F. Powers, *Morte D'Urban.* A funny story about a priest, Father Urban, and his life in the Minnesota hinterland.

Mary Francois Rockcastle, *Rainy Lake.* A family's idyllic lakefront life converges with the reality of the outside world in the 1960s.

Danielle Sosin, *The Long-Shining Waters.* The stories of an Ojibwe woman in the 1600s, a Norwegian fishing couple in 1902, and a woman who takes a road trip in 2000, all revolving around Lake Superior.

Sarah Stonich, *These Granite Islands.* An elderly woman shares the story of her life in a mining town in northern Minnesota.

Faith Sullivan, *The Cape Ann* and *The Empress of One.* Two stories of family drama set in small-town Minnesota.

David Treuer, *Rez Life* and *The Hiawatha.* Portraits of Native American life in Minnesota.

Will Weaver, *Red Earth, White Earth.* The story of two friends and a "whites versus Native Americans" land conflict in rural Minnesota.

For poetry and poetry-like prose, see the works of the inimitable Bill Holm and Robert Bly.

And for mysteries and thrillers, see Vince Flynn, Thomas Gifford, Elizabeth Gunn, William Kent Kreuger, and John Sandford.

TWIN CITIES ITINERARY

This tour offers a look at literary life on both sides of the Mississippi River.

Day One

2:00 PM

Mill City Museum and the Minneapolis riverfront
Begin your exploration of the Twin Cities here where it all began. The museum is built into the ruins of what was once the world's largest flour mill. From there, explore the riverfront and the historic Stone Arch Bridge.
704 South Second Street, 612-341-7555
www.millcitymuseum.org

4:30 PM

The Minnesota Center for Book Arts at Open Book
Explore the artistic assembly of the pages, covers, and spine, then peruse the shop at MCBA, which is a reader's delight of books, gifts, handmade paper, and journals.
1011 Washington Avenue South
www.openbookmn.org

If you have extra time, rent the green bikes from one of the Nice Ride Minnesota stations (www.niceridemn.org) for a quick ride along the river, or go to the Minneapolis Sculpture Garden at the Walker Art Center (1750 Hennepin Avenue, garden.walkerart.org) for a view of artist Claes Oldenburg's famous sculpture *Spoonbridge and Cherry* against the Minneapolis skyline. You can also ride to the Hennepin County Library's Caesar Pelli–designed downtown library (300 Nicollet Mall, www.hclib.org).

7:30 PM

Dinner at Bachelor Farmer

The name is a play on references from Garrison Keillor's public radio show, *A Prairie Home Companion*. The Bachelor Farmer draws inspiration from Scandinavian cuisine, for which Minnesota has been (in)famous, but this contemporary version goes well beyond the Swedish meatball, with no lutefisk in sight.

50 North Second Avenue, 612-206-3920
www.thebachelorfarmer.com

10:00 PM

Nightcap at Psycho Suzi's Motor Lounge

Head across the river to "nordeast" Minneapolis for some decidedly un-Scandinavian fare at this irreverent Tiki hut on the banks of the Mississippi. Suzi's has a beautiful riverfront patio with, as they say, "a fantastic view of industrial barges." Upstairs there's a cocktail lounge with three theme bars that offer "group drinks" served in smoking volcanoes.

1900 Marshall Street, 612-788-9069
www.psychosuzis.com

Day Two

9:00 AM

Breakfast at your hotel or
Mill City Farmers Market

(Saturdays, May through October 8:00 AM to 1:00 PM)
704 South Second Street, 612-341-7580
www.millcityfarmersmarket.org

10:30 AM

Minnehaha Park and Falls

You know you're in Minnesota when you find yourself at the

intersection of Hiawatha Avenue and Minnehaha Parkway. Overlooking the Mississippi River, Minnehaha Park is one of Minneapolis's oldest and most popular parks. Minnehaha Falls became a tourist destination after the publication of Henry Wadsworth Longfellow's epic poem "The Song of Hiawatha" in 1855. Longfellow never visited the falls in person, and there's not much of historical fact in it; the real Hiawatha lived in New England. Nonetheless, "Hiawatha" became America's most widely read poem of the nineteenth century, spreading the fame of Minnehaha Falls and the uppermost regions of the Mississippi and the "shores of Gitche Gumee by the shining Big Sea waters."

12:30 PM

An afternoon in St. Paul with F. Scott Fitzgerald

Head to the Cathedral Hill neighborhood of St. Paul for a stroll through the charming neighborhood where F. Scott Fitzgerald grew up. (Though they are called the "Twin Cities," it takes about fifteen minutes to get between the downtowns of the two cities.) This is where he made the revisions on his debut novel, *This Side of Paradise*. (If its original, not-so-catchy title, *The Romantic Egoist*, is any indicator, you can see why the publisher suggested revisions.) It also serves as the setting for many of his best short stories. Even if you're not a big Fitzgerald fan and don't know Amory Blaine from Jay Gatsby, this is a great neighborhood for a stroll, especially in summer. With its gorgeous Victorian homes, overarching elm trees, and fun shops nearby, it is—if not this side of paradise—really, really nice.

Start with lunch at W. A. Frost

The restaurant was a pharmacy in Fitzgerald's day. This charming turn-of-the-century setting has great food and one of the best outdoor patios anywhere.

374 Selby Avenue, St. Paul, 651-224-5715
www.wafrost.com

2:30 PM

Fitzgerald's roots

The St. Paul Public Library offers a brochure called *F. Scott Fitzgerald in St. Paul—Homes and Haunts* that you can download for a walking tour (www.sppl.org/sites/default/files/rcl/images/Friends/fitzgeraldbrochure.pdf).

Start the tour at 481 Laurel Avenue, where Fitzgerald was born. Real people still live in this building, and they must be used to people staring at their home. Park there and start the walk. At 593/599 Summit, you'll find the house where his parents later lived and where he finished *This Side of Paradise*. This is the residence he described as "a house below the average on a street above the average."

3:30 PM

James J. Hill House

Home of James J. Hill, builder of the Great Northern Railway. Guides lead tours that help you imagine family and servant life in this Gilded Age mansion. Completed in 1891, five years before Fitzgerald was born, the red sandstone residence was the largest and most expensive home in Minnesota. In *The Great Gatsby*, Gatsby's father says his son would have been like James J. Hill if he had lived long enough.
240 Summit Avenue, St. Paul, 651-297-2555
www.mnhs.org/places/sites/jjhh

5:00 PM

Head back to Minneapolis

6:00 PM

Dinner at Spoonriver

A great spot for sustainably produced and beautifully prepared food—on the river and across the plaza from the Guthrie Theater.

750 South Second Street, 612-436-2236

www.spoonriver.com

7:30 PM

The curtain rises by the river

Take in a show at the Guthrie Theater, called a "21st century dream factory" by *Time* magazine. Be sure to walk out on the theater's "sky bridge," which offers a prime view of the riverfront. Also check the calendar of the Penumbra Theater, a forum for African American theater in the Twin Cities, which occasionally presents its performances at the Guthrie.

818 South Second Street, Minneapolis, 612-377-2224

www.guthrietheater.org

Day Three

8:30 AM

Breakfast at Hell's Kitchen

This fun restaurant was slinging hash years before Gordon Ramsay's TV show of the same name.

80 South Ninth Street, Minneapolis, 612-332-4700

www.hellskitcheninc.com

10:00 AM

A bikes and books tour of Minneapolis

The Twin Cities are regularly rated among the most literary cities in the country. And more than 120 miles of bikeways, many bike amenities, and a strong, vibrant bicycling community have prompted *Bicycling* magazine to name

Minneapolis America's best bike city. So it makes sense
to put the two together for a two-wheel tour of some of
Minneapolis's outstanding independent bookstores as well
as its famous Chain of Lakes. It's also a great way to see some
of the area's most beautiful homes and neighborhoods. (For
anyone not familiar with this area of Minneapolis, we're
talking flat, paved, bikes-only paths, great for groups, kids,
and anyone who may not be Tour de France fit.) Start at
Magers and Quinn with stops thereafter.

Magers and Quinn
This is the city's largest independent bookseller, which bills
itself as "A bounty of the world's best books assembled by
biblioholic booksellers." It will make even the most dedicated
e-book reader want to stock up on print volumes.
3038 Hennepin Avenue, Minneapolis, 612-822-4611
www.magersandquinn.com

Calhoun Bike Rental
If you haven't come equipped, trot around the corner from
Magers and Quinn and rent bikes for the rest of your journey.
They also offer bike tours of some of the most interesting
areas of Minneapolis.
1622 West Lake Street, Minneapolis, 612-827-8231
www.calhounbikerental.com

The Chain of Lakes
The Chain of Lakes is part of the Grand Rounds National
Scenic Byway. Head south along the east side of Lake Calhoun
and on down and around Lake Harriet.
http://minneapolisparks.org/grandrounds/dist_CL.htm

Wild Rumpus
A short side trip from Lake Harriett, Wild Rumpus is a
fantastic children's bookstore that features, in addition to
books, live animals and a tiny front door for children to enter.

2720 West 43rd Street, Minneapolis, 612-920-5005
www.wildrumpusbooks.com

Head back to Lake Harriet and north again to Lake
Calhoun, around Lake of the Isles, and on to . . .

Birchbark Books and Native Arts

In the lovely, leafy Kenwood neighborhood, Birchbark puts a
special emphasis on Native American literature. The staff and
owner, novelist Louise Erdrich, carefully choose the books
here, and handwritten notes offer insight into books for
browsers. Books aside, any store with a confessional and dogs
on the premises is good for the soul.

2115 West Twenty-First Street, 612-374-4023
www.birchbarkbooks.com

You'll need a little nosh to sustain you as you retrace your
path back to Uptown. Stop next door at the . . .

Kenwood Café

2115 West 21st Street, 612-377-6876
www.kenwoodcafe.com

ADD-ON: WALNUT GROVE

Fans of the Laura Ingalls Wilder *Little House on the Prairie*
series may want to add a pilgrimage to Walnut Grove to their
itinerary. About three hours from Minneapolis, the town is
one of the many places the family lived and is the location of
the book *On the Banks of Plum Creek.* Walnut Grove offers a
Laura Ingalls Wilder Museum, the site of the dugout where
the family lived (open May through October) and, in July, a
pageant based on her story.
www.walnutgrove.org

Where to Stay

Grand Hotel

615 Second Avenue South, Minneapolis, 866-843-4726 or
612-288-8888
www.grandhotelminneapolis.com

The Depot Renaissance Hotel

Retrofitted in a historic train depot.
225 South Third Avenue, Minneapolis, 612-375-1700
www.thedepotminneapolis.com

10

Chicago

THE TALES OF TWO ARCHITECTS

Eventually, I think Chicago will be the most beautiful great city left in the world.

—Frank Lloyd Wright

Clicking along on the El train or driving in on the freeway, there it is, *BOOM*, Chicago, bursting up out of the prairie. That skyline—with some of the tallest buildings in the world rising from the surrounding flatlands next to Lake Michigan—delivers a thrill of anticipation every time.

Chicago—it's a Toddlin' Town. It's the "stormy, husky, brawling, City of the Big Shoulders." It's the home of the blues, rabid sports fans, and ethically challenged politicians, home of the Second City comedy troupe, Oprah, and Barack Obama.

Yet it's those buildings that strike me when I first arrive, and they stay with me whether I'm doing business in the Loop, shopping on the Magnificent Mile, or enjoying a concert in Millennium Park.

Pulitzer Prize–winning architecture critic Paul Goldberger says, "Architecture is one area in which we in New York truly do have a second city complex toward Chicago—not the other way around, as it is in so many other realms. And for all that has happened over the years, little has changed in the sense that those of us in New York, as well as the rest of the country, still have of Chicago as being the essential city of American architecture. . . . It is everywhere present—here in the Michigan Avenue area, down in the Loop, but also all through the North Side, down on the South Side, out at Oak Park and River Forest and Highland Park and Evanston. You cannot escape Chicago's architectural history—Louis Sullivan, Frank Lloyd Wright, Daniel Burnham, John Wellborn Root, Mies van der Rohe, Myron Goldsmith, Skidmore, Owings & Merrill, Helmut Jahn. . . ."

Fortunately, you don't have to be a connoisseur of skyscrapers and their designers to understand Chicago's pivotal place in architectural history and the innovative, risk-taking outlook that continues to make Chicago "America's City." Two books have generated sky-high interest in Chicago by combining the stories of the city's architectural lions with juicy plots. The first, Erik Larson's *The Devil in the White City: Murder, Magic, and Madness at the Fair That Changed America*, is the story of the incredible events surrounding the 1893 World's Columbian Exposition in Chicago. Larson weaves together the stories of Daniel H. Burnham, the legendary architect responsible for the fair's construction (and later the Plan of Chicago) and H. H. Holmes, a serial killer masquerading as a charming doctor. He crafts the story so dramatically that readers often wonder if the book is a true story or a gripping work of fiction. The other book, Nancy Horan's *Loving Frank*, which *is* a novel of historical fiction, tells the tale of architectural genius Frank Lloyd Wright's scandalous relationship with his client, Mamah Borthwick Cheney. Their relationship began in the Chicago suburb of Oak Park and shocked Chicago society. Both books have sent their readers packing off to Chicago to see firsthand where the plots thickened.

"When I finished *The Devil in the White City* I got in my car and drove to Jackson Park," says Mary Jo Hoag, who is now tour director for the Chicago Architecture Foundation's (CAF) *Devil in the White City* tours. "I just wanted to see where it all took place." She's not the only one to feel the urge. So many readers have come in search of the White City that a host of tours have sprung up. Depending on the time of year, you can go on foot or via kayak, bike, Segway, the El, or a "ghost trolley" for a White City tour with the CAF, the Chicago History Museum, the Art Institute, and other organizations.

So it's a little surprising to realize that almost nothing remains of the famed White City, though it was the greatest tourist attraction in American history, hosting twenty-seven million visitors. Burnham and Frederick Law Olmsted (who also designed Central Park, the US Capitol grounds, and Stanford University) began to lay out the fairgrounds in 1890. It took three years and forty thousand workers to construct the fabulous Beaux Arts–style fair buildings and monuments . . . out of plaster. The historic fair opened to visitors on May 1, 1893. It closed six months later, and within a year almost every structure from the fair was destroyed by fire, demolished, or moved elsewhere. Only the Palace of Fine Arts, on the north end of Jackson Park, remains. Fortunately, that building, which is now the Museum of Science and Industry, provides a reference point for what the buildings that surrounded it must have looked like. In addition, a small reproduction of the fair's symbol, the sixty-five-foot-high statue of the *Republic*, can be found in Jackson Park.

Yet strolling through modern-day Jackson Park with Hoag, it's not hard to conjure an image of the park as it was then, its white buildings surrounding the Court of Honor illuminated at night with that amazing new technology, electric lighting, as one fairgoer said, "like a sudden vision of heaven." The fair also introduced the world to the Ferris Wheel, the telephone, mass production, musical broadcasts, the zipper, belly dancing, and the Pledge of Allegiance, among many other things.

According to Hoag, the headlong energy, the spirit of progress, and the creativity that made the extravaganza possible took root in Chicago long before the fair. She says, "After the great Chicago Fire in 1871, the city needed rebuilding. The population boomed and some of the most innovative architects in the world came to Chicago to get their start. They were willing to try new types of design and construction techniques that many of the old and staid architects in the east were not." Rebuilding Chicago, they developed and refined the basic structural system of the modern steel and glass skyscraper, this time with sturdy construction and fireproof materials. Among the aspiring Chicago newcomers was Frank Lloyd Wright, who arrived from Wisconsin in 1887.

To Wright, the fair's architecture was a disappointment, more a look back at Old World classical architecture than a vision of America's own architectural future. At this point, Wright was beginning to create a new architectural sensibility grounded in the natural colors and forms that grew from the prairie landscape. The only place at the fair he found inspiring was the Wooded Island, which featured the traditional ho-o-den buildings that served as the government of Japan's pavilion at the fair. His interest in Japanese architecture endured throughout his career. It's no surprise that the young upstart, Wright, and Chicago's most prominent architect, Burnham, didn't exactly see eye to eye. At one point, Burnham told Wright that his concepts of open space and horizontal lines would never succeed and tried to persuade Wright to study architecture at the École des Beaux-Arts in Paris. Wright declined. Unlike the White City, the work of Frank Lloyd Wright's early career survives in the Chicago suburb of Oak Park, where visitors can tour the neighborhood and see the many Wright-designed homes, including the former Mamah Cheney residence.

But it wasn't just architects who flocked to the city. At the time, Chicago was the fastest-growing city in the world. As the city rose like a phoenix from the ashes of the great fire, it attracted a critical mass of artists, writers, and reformers, particularly from the Midwest, who saw opportunity there, who viewed it as a place where they could join a community of people who thought with innovation and daring. Among the first wave of the Chicago literary renaissance, writers such as Henry Blake Fuller, Theodore Dreiser, Frank Norris, Carl Sandburg, and many others established their reputations and that of the city as a cultural hub. By the 1910s, the writer H. L. Mencken had declared that Chicago, formerly the hinterland, had become, for a time, the literary capital of the United States. Over the following decades, Chicago literary heavyweights such as Saul Bellow, Gwendolyn Brooks, and Nelson Algren added to the city's literary tradition.

So the story of Chicago and its fair didn't really end with the demise of the White City. What lives on is the fair's energy and sense of possibility and the city's ability to take chances, as well as the cultural and economic development it inspired. "This is one of the few Rust Belt cities that hasn't fallen by the wayside," says Hoag. "That's because of that same attitude and adaptability, always asking 'What can we do to embrace change?'"

The White City is long gone, yet its spirit prevails. As we stand outside its last surviving building, the Museum of Science and Industry, and look north along the lakefront, we can see what is probably Burnham's greatest legacy, the Chicago skyline. It's flanked by miles of open lakefront parks that my book group enjoyed scooting through on Segways. Among the newest additions to the skyline, Millennium Park, with its striking sculptures and architecture, serves as a modern-day "bookend" to the architectural innovation that started with Daniel Burnham, Louis Sullivan, and other early Chicago architectural visionaries. From this viewpoint, it's clear that Chicago's story rolls on, told not only through its writers but also through its architects.

Gritty Realism: Scott Turow Carries On the Chicago Tradition

❧ Chicago attorney Scott Turow came on the literary scene in 1987 with his first bestseller, *Presumed Innocent*, one of the most acclaimed and bestselling crime novels ever. Eight bestsellers later, he still practices white-collar criminal defense law, though, he says, "I spend more time writing than lawyering." For Turow, the two intertwine perfectly.

Influenced by the works of Charles Dickens and fellow Chicagoan Saul Bellow, Turow always wanted to be a writer. After graduating from Amherst College in 1970, he studied and later taught creative writing at Stanford. In 1975, he decided on a career change and entered Harvard Law School, which he jokingly says was the greatest break of his literary career. Turow later became an assistant US attorney in Chicago, serving in that position until 1986. There he prosecuted several high-profile corruption cases, including the tax fraud case of State Attorney General William Scott. Turow was also lead counsel in Operation Greylord, the federal prosecution of Illinois judicial corruption cases. So his legal career in Chicago (which appears as Kindle County in his books) has given him abundant subject matter for his novels. "It gave me a subject that I was passionate about, that, you know, I still find as interesting as I did the day I entered law school."

Turow portrays his characters and their world with what he calls a "meat and potatoes realism," a tradition in the Chicago literary scene that dates back to Theodore Dreiser and, later, Saul Bellow. "There's an urban grittiness that's always been characteristic of fiction coming out of this city," he says.

CHICAGO READING

Ever since the Chicago literary renaissance, which blossomed soon after the World's Columbian Exposition in 1893, Chicago writers have been known for their realism, with an emphasis on working people and the rougher side of urban life.

THE MOST FABULOUS FAIR

James Gilbert, *Perfect Cities: Chicago's Utopias of 1893.* About the Exposition and also the "workers' paradise" in Pullman, Illinois.

Erik Larson, *The Devil in the White City.* Based on true events, the book tells the twin stories of Daniel Burnham, architect of the 1893 Chicago world's fair, and H. H. Holmes, a serial killer, depicting the beauty and the horror of Chicago in the late nineteenth century.

Donald L. Miller, *City of the Century: The Epic of Chicago and the Making of America.* See also the terrific PBS *American Experience* episode of the same name. It's based on this book, and you can obtain it from many public libraries.

FRANK LLOYD WRIGHT

T. C. Boyle, *The Women.* A fictional account of Wright's life, viewed through his tumultuous relationships with four women.

Brendan Gill, *Many Masks: A Life of Frank Lloyd Wright.* A well-regarded Wright biography covering his turbulent career and private life.

Nancy Horan, *Loving Frank.* Historically accurate fiction about Frank Lloyd Wright and his scandalous relationship with Mamah Borthwick Cheney. Hold on to your hat for the ending.

ABOUT ARCHITECTURE

Paul Goldberger, *Why Architecture Matters*. Offers a basic understanding of architecture.

CHICAGO CLASSICS

Nelson Algren, *The Man with the Golden Arm*. This story of the downward spiral of Chicago card dealer Frankie Machine was the first winner of the National Book Award when it was first published in 1949. It was made into a movie with Frank Sinatra. See also Algren's *Chicago: City on the Make*, a prose poem about the alleys, El tracks, neon lights, and dive bars, the best and worst of Chicago.

Theodore Dreiser, *Sister Carrie*. A cornerstone of the turn of the twentieth-century Chicago literary renaissance, this is the sad story of a small-town midwestern girl in the immoral big city. Also see his entrepreneurial epic, *The Titan*.

James. T. Farrell, *Studs Lonigan*. A trilogy of the youth, early manhood, and death of Studs Lonigan in Chicago's Irish South Side.

Henry Blake Fuller, *The Cliff-Dwellers*. A critique of skyscrapers and the life of the people in them. Fuller has been called the "father of urban literature."

Frank Norris, *The Pit: A Story of Chicago*. About the Chicago wheat market in the early 1900s. Corruption, greed, and redemption!

Upton Sinclair, *The Jungle*. Socialist author Sinclair exposed the brutality and the working conditions of the meatpacking industry in this classic. The stockyards are gone, but Sinclair's descriptions will still make you lose your appetite.

LEGENDARY CHICAGO OBSERVERS

Alex Kotlowitz, *Never a City So Real* and *There Are No Children Here*. A keen observer of the city and of racial issues.

Ring Lardner, *You Know Me Al*. Lardner began his career as a sportswriter. His ear for the American vernacular endeared him to readers and he is now considered one of the great American short story writers.

Mike Royko, *Boss*. The definitive biography of Mayor Richard J. Daley and politics in Chicago, written by the beloved late *Tribune* columnist.

Carl Sandburg, *Chicago Poems*. The most famous collection of poems about Chicago by its own "bard of the working class."

Studs Terkel, *Division Street: America* and *Chicago*. Terkel is known for his interviews with ordinary people and pioneered oral histories as a literary form.

CHICAGO'S IMMIGRANT AND ETHNIC CULTURE

Saul Bellow, *The Adventures of Augie March*. Widely viewed as *the* Chicago epic, this work charts the life of a Jewish Chicagoan and the eccentric characters he encounters all around the city. Bellow won the Nobel Prize "for the human understanding and subtle analysis of contemporary culture that are combined in his work."

Gwendolyn Brooks, *Selected Poems*. Her poetry focused on the 1940s Bronzeville neighborhood.

Sandra Cisneros, *The House on Mango Street*. A Mexican American coming-of-age novel, dealing with a young Latina girl, Esperanza Cordero, growing up in the Chicago Chicano ghetto.

Stuart Dybek, *Childhood and Other Neighborhoods* and *The Coast of Chicago*. In these two critically acclaimed collections of short stories, Dybek depicts Chicago with a strong sense of place and ethnic tradition.

John Guzlowski, *Lightning and Ashes*. Chronicles the author's experiences growing up in the neighborhoods around Humboldt Park in Chicago.

Tony Romano, *If You Eat, You Never Die: Chicago Tales*. Different members of an Italian immigrant family tell their stories of Chicago in the 1950s.

Richard Wright, *Native Son*. A classic Chicago neighborhood novel, set in Bronzeville and Hyde Park, about a young, doomed, black boy hopelessly warped by the racism and poverty that defined his surroundings.

COPS, CRIMINALS, AND QUESTIONABLE MORALS

Karen Abbott, *Sin in the Second City*. A nonfiction bestseller about Chicago's vice district, the Levee, and some of the personalities involved: gangsters, corrupt politicians, and two sisters who ran the most elite brothel in town.

Sara Paretsky, *Tunnel Vision*, *Hard Time*, and many others. The adventures of Chicago private investigator V. I. Warshawski have made Paretsky one of the mystery world's most popular authors.

Scott Simon, *Windy City*. The Chicago native and host of National Public Radio's "Weekend Edition" offers a fictional portrait of Chicago politics, with some very strong similarities to real events and people. Also see *Home and Away*, his memoir of growing up in Chicago.

Scott Turow, *Presumed Innocent*, *The Burden of Proof*, and *Innocent*. Dividing his time between the courtroom and the typewriter, Turow has become the king of the legal thriller. Most of his stories take place in the fictional Kindle County, which bears a striking resemblance to Cook County.

AND MORE

Other local kids who made good in the literary world include Michael Crichton, John Dos Passos, Langston Hughes, Lorraine Hansberry, Edgar Rice Burroughs, Ernest Hemingway, Edgar Lee Masters, Sidney Sheldon, and Audrey Niffenegger. And see *Literary Chicago: A Book Lover's Tour of the Windy City* by local author Greg Holden.

CHICAGO ITINERARY

As famed architect Daniel Burnham said, "Make no small plans, dream no small dreams." This itinerary's "big plan" starts with Frank Lloyd Wright's studio and the family homes he designed in Oak Park, just a short ride from the Loop on the CTA "Green Line." You'll spend the rest of the time in the midst of Chicago's fabulous architecture and along the waterfront that is Burnham's legacy, so keep looking up.

Day One

2:00 PM

Loving Frank in Oak Park

Oak Park is home to the world's largest collection of Wright-designed buildings, and in a visit to this Chicago suburb, you'll discover the development of Wright's style between 1889 and 1909 and trace the evolution of American residential architecture. If your group arranges ahead, the Frank Lloyd Wright Preservation Trust provides a unique tour experience for lovers of Nancy Horan's popular novel, *Loving Frank*. At the Frank Lloyd Wright Home and Studio you'll see Wright's own drafting room, where so many ideas took shape, and explore the truth and fiction of the novel with a discussion facilitated by the Preservation Trust's education staff and volunteers. The collection of historic photographs and artifacts will enrich your appreciation of the history behind the book.

951 Chicago Avenue, Oak Park, 312-994-4000
http://gowright.org

(The Edward H. Cheney House featured in *Loving Frank* is a private residence, but you can walk by at 520 North East Avenue.)

6:30 PM

Regroup for cocktails at your hotel

8:00 PM

Dinner at Frontera Grill

This is the casual restaurant of award-winning chef, cookbook author, and television personality Rick Bayless, who has changed the image of Mexican food in America.
45 North Clark Street, 312-661-1434
www.rickbayless.com/restaurants/grill.html

Day Two

9:00 AM

A walk in the park

Take a morning wander through Millennium Park to discover the Frank Gehry–designed Jay Pritzker Pavilion, the most sophisticated outdoor concert venue of its kind in the United States. See yourself and a reflection of the city skyline in artist Anish Kapoor's interactive sculpture *Cloud Gate* (aka the Bean) that sits in the center of the park. Walk south on Michigan Avenue and take in artist Jaume Plensa's fifty-foot glass-block towers of flowing water that project the video images of a thousand different Chicagoans.

10:00 AM

Late breakfast at Heaven on Seven

Hearty Cajun cuisine that will tide you over until an early dinner.
111 North Wabash, Seventh Floor, 312-263-6443
www.heavenonseven.com

11:30 AM

On the waterfront

Start at Oak Street Beach and stroll north through Lake Michigan's waterfront parks. Cross under Lake Shore Drive at North Avenue and return through the Gold Coast neighborhood. Stop by the Newberry Library in the heart of Chicago's Gold Coast neighborhood. In Audrey Niffenegger's *The Time Traveler's Wife*, Henry DeTamble works as a librarian at the Newberry, and it's the scene of many of his fictional comings and goings. In real life the library is the scene of a huge number of literary events, symposia, and presentations by the Shakespeare Project of Chicago, among others. Call ahead for events and tour times.

60 West Walton Street, 312-943-9090
www.newberry.org

2:00 PM

City Segway tours

Once you get the hang of it, a Segway tour is the perfect way to cover a lot of territory in Chicago's lakefront parks and to get an orientation to the city's sites seen in movies, postcards, and history books.

400 East Randolph Street, 1-877-734-8686 or 312-819-0186
www.citysegwaytours.com/chicago

5:15 PM

Pre-theater dinner at Petterino's

Caricatures of actors and Chicago celebrities adorn the walls of this upbeat steakhouse, reminiscent of New York's Sardi's, in the heart of Chicago's theater district. A speakeasy-type variety of specialty drinks.

150 North Dearborn (at Randolph), 312-422-0150
www.petterinos.com

7:30 PM

The curtain rises

Head to one of the theaters located within a block or two of the restaurant. Or take a seat at one of Chicago's many literary events. Check out the Chicago Poetry Center's calendar (www.poetrycenter.org/scene_events), which may include an evening activity such as the Chicago Poetry Brothel (www.chicagopoetrybrothel.com), an occasional gathering that features evenings of poetry and "intemperance" with a Victorian/Steampunk flair.

10:00 PM

After the curtain, drinks at the Top

After the theater curtain, enjoy post-theater cocktails at the luxurious Trump Hotel Chicago. The view of the river makes up for the cost of the drinks.

401 North Wabash Avenue, 312-588-8000

www.trumphotelcollection.com/chicago

Or sample the nightlife on Lincoln Avenue, where Chicago blues was born.

Day Three

Breakfast at the hotel

10:00 AM

Chicago Architecture Foundation *Devil in the White City* Tour

This tour explores the places and the story that Erik Larson tells in his bestselling book *The Devil in the White City*, about two simultaneous events in Chicago history: the World's Columbian Exposition of 1893 and the emergence of serial murderer Dr. Henry H. Holmes. CAF will arrange special tours for groups of ten or more. Check the website to verify tour times and details and to explore the many other tours CAF offers.

224 South Michigan Avenue, 312-922-3432
www.architecture.org

1:30 PM

Lunch with Lauren—RL

Located adjacent to the world's largest Polo store, the Chicago
flagship on Michigan Avenue, RL Restaurant represents Ralph
Lauren's debut into the restaurant industry. Opened in 1999,
the restaurant features the vision and decor of Ralph Lauren
and modern city-club cuisine. The ultimate "ladies who lunch"
location and the perfect spot to recap your trip and toast to
your next adventure.
115 East Chicago Avenue, 312-425-1100
www.rlrestaurant.com

3:00 PM

Shopping on the Magnificent Mile

Where to Stay

Palmer House

Stay the way fair visitors stayed, at Potter Palmer's iconic,
historic downtown Chicago hotel. Palmer and his wife,
Bertha, played a prominent role in the world's fair and appear
in Larson's *Devil in the White City*. The hotel's fabulous lobby
makes a great place to gather. Don't miss the Tiffany brass
peacock doors. (The CAF also has a Palmer House tour for an
insider's look at the hotel.)
17 East Monroe Street, 312-726-7500
www.palmerhousehiltonhotel.com

Omni Hotel

An all-suite hotel on the Magnificent Mile, a perfect location.
676 North Michigan Avenue, 312-944-6664
www.omnihotels.com/Chicago

ADD-ONS

Art Institute of Chicago

One block south of Millennium Park on Michigan Avenue. Even for frequent Chicago visitors, there's always something new here, especially since the museum added its new modern wing. Check out the Impressionist collection donated by the "queen of Chicago," Bertha Palmer of Palmer House fame, and look for the Edward Hopper paintings mentioned in Saul Bellow's *The Actual*.

111 South Michigan Avenue, 312-443-3600
www.artic.edu/aic

Combine a museum visit with lunch in Millennium Park at the Millennium Park Grill.

11 North Michigan (at Madison), 312-521-7275
www.parkgrillchicago.com/millennium-park

Or eat outdoors at the Park Café (outside the Grill), which also offers picnic baskets.

Chicago Neighborhoods

Check out Explore Chicago (www.explorechicago.org) to find an ever-changing array of organized tours of many Chicago neighborhoods, some with a literary flair, such as the Augie March tour based on the Saul Bellow classic. They also offer free tour "apps" to download for your phone so you can find a tour to fit your time frame and interest. For example, take a look at the tour of the Bronzeville neighborhood, which was the home of African American literary greats such as author Richard Wright, playwright Lorraine Hansberry, and poet Gwendolyn Brooks.

www.explorechicago.org/city/en/things_see_do/tours
/tourism/mobile_neighborhood.html

After hours at Frank Lloyd Wright's Robie House
Depending on the time of year, the Robie House is open after hours. You and your friends can wander the celebrated spaces of this icon of modernism while enjoying live music, drinks, light hors d'oeuvres, and a festive, casual atmosphere. Call the Frank Lloyd Wright Preservation Trust for availability.
5757 South Woodlawn Avenue, 312-994-4000
www.gowright.org

Hemingway Home and Museum
Fans of Ernest Hemingway may want to venture a bit outside Chicago and visit the Hemingway Museum, his birthplace, and his boyhood home in Oak Park. Start at the museum on Oak Park Avenue. The home where Hemingway was born is one block north and open to the public. If you wander through the beautiful Frank Lloyd Wright Historic District, you will also see the outside of the house later planned, built, and occupied by the Hemingways at 600 North Kenilworth. It's now privately owned, but the new owners plan to open it to the public occasionally for viewing.
200 North Oak Park Avenue, Oak Park, 708-524-5383
www.ehfop.org

11

Memphis

ROLLIN' ON THE RIVER

No city has had more of an impact on modern culture.
—**Robert Gordon**, *It Came from Memphis*

It's hard to stand still in Memphis. Even the most reserved person will look down and find her feet tapping and fingers seemingly snapping by their own volition. Soon a little shimmy sneaks in, but as Elvis sang, "That's all right, mama," because in Memphis they encourage a whole lot of free-spirited enthusiasm. The melody of Memphis is as complex as its history—sometimes happy and harmonious, sometimes discordant and mournful—a blend of river, race, and rhythm. But by the time you hit the dance floor at the Stax Museum, surrounded by life-size videos of performers including Sly and the Family Stone and the Jackson Five, you will, indeed, "dance to the music."

Memphis and Memphis music owe their existence to the Mississippi River. Like its ancient Egyptian namesake on the Nile,

Memphis is perched at the top of a river delta, where the land is flooded and fertilized seasonally by the river. Its location made Memphis both the gateway to bountiful farmland and the perfect port from which to ship the crops, most notably cotton. Because the cotton trade depended on slave labor, Memphis became the site of one of the South's biggest slave markets. Here in the delta, enslaved Africans cultivated not just cotton but also a unique form of music based on spirituals and the call-and-repeat chanting that made their work bearable, planting the seeds of music that would someday rock the world.

America's beloved author Mark Twain owes his existence to the river, too. It was on the Mississippi that the cub riverboat pilot Samuel Clemens heard the riverboat leadsman call out, "mark twain" (indicating a depth of two fathoms or twelve feet) and adopted that call as his pen name. Because of Twain, when you stand on the levee in Memphis for the first time, it may seem strangely familiar. People around the world have some notion of the Mighty Mississippi, even though they've never seen it. For them, it's a river of the imagination, a ship's locker full of tall tales and the place where Huckleberry Finn and the slave Jim launched their adventures. It's the ultimate symbol of hope and freedom. Just get on your raft and go.

Growing up in the river town of Hannibal, Missouri, Twain felt the same pull and yearned to be a riverboat pilot. In his autobiography-cum-travelogue, *Life on the Mississippi*, Twain peppers the first and, in my view, most entertaining part of the book with hair-raising and hilarious stories about learning to navigate the river's ever-changing waters as a cub pilot. Over his lifetime, Twain traveled every portion of the Mississippi's journey between St. Paul and New Orleans, so there's no better guide than Twain to connect you to the river's dangerous meanderings or to the quirks of the people along its banks. University of Memphis professor Eric Carl Link says in his introduction to *Life on the Mississippi*, "Twain viewed the Mississippi River as a defining feature of his life, culture and country."

In the second part of *Life on the Mississippi*, Twain returns to the river in 1882 as an established author rather than a pilot and offers a travelogue of his tour both up and down the river. Yet of all the great cities on the Mississippi, it's Memphis that offers book groups the best opportunity to actually *experience* the Mississippi and ride the river that runs through the literal and the symbolic heart of America. Here in the South, the Mississippi is an entirely different beast from the narrow waterway flowing near my Minnesota home. Here it's four-dimensional: it boasts not just length, breadth, and depth but also a sense of place all its own. It may look placid, but its calm surface belies the tumultuous current below. Aboard a paddlewheel boat, you'll see the river's power as it rushes under the Hernando de Soto Bridge, and you'll understand Twain's dismay at trying to learn the river's ever-changing channels and hazards. Even modern-day river pilots find themselves challenged by the Mississippi's ability to constantly carve out new islands, spawn new sand bars, and uproot mammoth trees. No matter how much the Army Corps of Engineers tries to tame it with locks, dams, and levees, the Mighty Mississippi always seems to win.

When Twain wrote the second part of *Life on the Mississippi*, post–Civil War Memphis had become the economic crossroads of a changing nation. "It is a beautiful city," he says, "nobly situated on a commanding bluff overlooking the river. The streets are straight and spacious, though not paved in a way to incite distempered admiration. No, the admiration must be reserved for the town's sewerage system." While that may seem a rather backhanded compliment, Twain explains that the sewers were part of the city's plan to prevent yellow fever, which, in one 1878 epidemic, killed at least five thousand Memphians. Though bankrupted by the epidemic and loss of trade, Memphis recovered. Twain says, "A thriving place is the Good Samaritan City of the Mississippi: has a great wholesale jobbing trade; foundries, machine shops; and manufactories of wagons, carriages, and cotton-seed oil; and is shortly to have cotton-mills and elevators. . . . Her cotton receipts reached five hundred thousand bales last year—an increase of sixty thousand over the year before. Out from her healthy commercial heart issue five trunk-lines of railway; and a sixth is being added."

But all that prosperity was built on the backs of enslaved Africans. Even after emancipation, the free black sharecroppers who toiled in the cotton fields didn't find life much improved, but at least they could leave the fields and set out for "greener pastures." Twain's stories, especially *Huckleberry Finn* and *Pudd'nhead Wilson*, touch on the racial issues festering in American society and give context for what was to come in the 1950s and 1960s. In *Life on the Mississippi*, Twain writes of encountering groups of free blacks just south of Memphis who were leaving the fields. Says Twain, "These poor people could never travel when they were slaves; so they make up for the privation now. They stay on a plantation till the desire to travel seizes them; then they pack up, hail a steamboat, and clear out. Not for any particular place; no, nearly any place will answer; they only want to be moving."

This became known as the Great Migration. Former field hands came up the river to the closest city, Memphis. As a result, Memphis became the place where broad musical streams came together—spirituals and hymns from the slave tradition mingled with regional folk music. From that confluence emerged a new and groundbreaking form of music; by the 1890s, with the help of W. C. Handy, Memphis became the capital of Delta Blues. It's been one of the city's defining features ever since, even as blues musicians continued to migrate north and leave their musical mark on cities such as St. Louis and Chicago. Over the ensuing decades, white musicians fell under the spell of the blues and began to play along, blending in some old-time gospel and country licks of their own. Then one local musician, Elvis Presley, combined these genres to put his own spin on a new musical form, rock and roll, and the world was forever changed. Sam Phillips recorded Elvis's first song, "That's All Right, Mama," in Memphis, and his Sun Studios went on to be the musical home of Johnny Cash, Carl Perkins, and many others. Races and musical genres mixed over at Stax Records, too, particularly in the music of Booker T. & the M.G.'s. That company eventually emerged as the home of R&B, funk, and soul artists such as Otis Redding, Wilson Pickett, and Isaac Hayes, among many greats.

Memphis's color line may have blurred in the world of music, but that was about the only place. Jim Crow was the law of the land throughout the South. The civil rights movement took hold in Memphis, a city founded on inequality. The Reverend Martin Luther King Jr. came to Memphis to support and draw attention to the sanitation workers' strike and gave his famous "I've Been to the Mountaintop" speech here on April 3, 1968. The next day, James Earl Ray shot and killed King as he stood on the balcony of the Lorraine Motel, and Memphis was forever changed. (Hampton Sides's book *Hellhound on His Trail* does a masterful job of telling the story.) Talk to any longtime Memphians, and they'll all tell you the same thing—after April 4, 1968, the city was never the same again, and it began to slide.

Yet like the river on which it resides, Memphis just keeps rollin' along. Over the last twenty years, the city has worked tirelessly and successfully to change course. The city values the arts and culture that have emerged from its struggles and attempts not to forget but to place its history in context. For example, the Lorraine Motel has become the National Civil Rights Museum, an emotionally stirring place where exhibits trace the civil rights struggle from abolitionism to Dr. King's death. Simultaneously, Memphis is working to blend in an increasing dose of modern vibrancy and economic development. A Memphian friend of mine told me, "If anyone's going to get it right this time, we will, because now we're all in this together and we have to."

It's not as pretty a place as, for example, its southern sister Charleston, with its antebellum elegance, or its closer cousin Nashville. People often describe Memphis as "real" and "gritty." That's why I like Memphis, and so will your book club. It epitomizes the extremes and contrasts, the peaks and valleys, that typify much of American history, and it has emerged singing a hopeful tune. As Robert Gordon writes in *It Came from Memphis*, "The forces of cultural collision struck thrice in the Memphis area, first with the Delta blues, then with Sun, then Stax. These sounds touched the soul of society; unlike passing fads, these sounds have remained with us. By definition, most of popular culture is disposable, but Memphis music has refused to disappear. In electrified civilization, even when stripped from the particular racial and social context in which it was born, what happened in Memphis remains the soundtrack to cultural liberation."

Memphis is a city that will move you in more ways than one.

Robert Gordon: The Memphis Beat Is His Beat

Author, music historian, film producer, and director—it's difficult to find just one label for Memphian Robert Gordon. Brought up on the blues and living in Memphis, he's an insider, at the hub of the musical subject matter he covers. He's the author of *Can't Be Satisfied: The Life and Times of Muddy Waters*, and he produced and directed, with filmmaker Morgan Neville, a documentary based on that book. He was the writer and producer of *The Road to Memphis*, an episode in Martin Scorsese's seven-part series *The Blues*, and he directed *Respect Yourself: The Stax Records Story*. He has also produced documentaries and music videos. Gordon is the author of *It Came from Memphis*, a book about the evolution of the Memphis sound with a focus on the musicians behind the scenes, and he produced the book's two companion CDs. His other books include *The King on the Road* and *Jerry Lee Lewis: Last Rocker Standing*. Gordon lives in Memphis with his wife and two children.

MEMPHIS READING

HISTORY

Molly Caldwell Crosby, *The American Plague.* About the yellow fever epidemic of 1878, which wiped out much of New Orleans and Memphis.

Mike Freeman, *Clarence Saunders and the Founding of Piggly Wiggly: The Rise & Fall of a Memphis Maverick.* The flamboyant Saunders worked his way out of poverty to found Piggly Wiggly, invent the concept of the self-service grocery store, and lose a couple of fortunes along the way.

Stanley Hamilton, *Machine Gun Kelly's Last Stand.* A vivid portrait of the Memphis native who became America's most wanted man.

Jack Hurst, *Nathan Bedford Forrest.* The story of a murderous racist who General Sherman said must be "hunted down and killed if it costs 10,000 lives and bankrupts the [national] treasury" and who later became a racial moderate.

Wanda Rushing, *Memphis and the Paradox of Place: Globalization in the American South.* This is a scholarly but readable work for anyone who truly wants to understand the role of Memphis today.

MARK TWAIN AND THE MISSISSIPPI

Stephen E. Ambrose, *The Mississippi and the Making of a Nation.* Especially read chapter 6 on Memphis.

John Barry, *Rising Tide: The Great Mississippi Flood of 1927 and How It Changed America.* The story of one of America's biggest natural disasters.

Jerry O. Potter, *The Sultana Tragedy: America's Greatest Maritime Disaster.* The story of the 1864 sinking of a ship loaded with Union soldiers.

Jonathan Raban, *Old Glory: A Voyage Down the Mississippi.* In the early 1980s, Raban, a longtime fan of the river and Twain's stories, went down the river in a motorboat. It's somewhat dated now, but his descriptions of navigating the river and its perils echo many of Twain's.

Mark Twain, *Life on the Mississippi, The Adventures of Huckleberry Finn, The Adventures of Tom Sawyer.* See also Fred Kaplan, *The Singular Mark Twain.*

CIVIL RIGHTS

Joan Turner Beifuss, *At the River I Stand.* A narrative history of the Memphis 1968 sanitation-workers strike.

Taylor Branch, *Parting the Water, Pillar of Fire,* and *At Canaan's Edge.* Branch's masterful trilogy of America during the Martin Luther King years.

Vincent Harding, *There Is a River: The Black Struggle for Freedom in America.* Covers the quest for freedom from the beginnings of slavery to Reconstruction.

Michael K. Honey, *Going Down Jericho Road: The Memphis Strike, Martin Luther King's Last Campaign.* A moving account that combines labor history and civil rights history by a University of Washington professor.

Gerald Posner, *Killing the Dream.* Posner tracks the path of two-bit hood James Earl Ray as he stalked Martin Luther King.

Hampton Sides, *Hellhound on His Trail: The Stalking of Martin Luther King, Jr., and the International Hunt for His Assassin.* A well-researched and tautly written work that reads like fiction.

MEMOIRS

James Conaway, *Memphis Afternoons: A Memoir.* Growing up in Memphis in the 1950s.

W. C. Handy, *Father of the Blues: An Autobiography.* The life and career of the man who brought blues to the world's attention.

Ida B. Wells, *The Memphis Diary of Ida B. Wells.* Born into slavery, Wells became a respected journalist, anti-lynching activist, and proponent of women's suffrage.

Richard Wright, *Black Boy.* The novelistic memoir of a literary giant who spent his formative years in Memphis.

MUSIC

Robert M. J. Bowman and Rob Bowman, *Soulsville, U.S.A.: The Story of Stax Records.* A history of one of the country's iconic recording studios, where the likes of Ike and Tina Turner, Otis Redding, and Booker T. and the M.G.'s made it big.

Robert Gordon, *It Came from Memphis.* A popular history of the development of the Memphis sound, told from the perspective of its behind-the-scenes players. Also *Jerry Lee Lewis: Last Rocker Standing, Can't Be Satisfied: The Life and Times of Muddy Waters, The Elvis Treasures,* and *The King on the Road.*

Peter Guralnick, *Last Train to Memphis* and *Careless Love: The Unmaking of Elvis Presley.* The two combined offer a complete biography of Elvis Presley. Also *Sweet Soul Music: Rhythm and Blues and the Southern Dream of Freedom.*

MEMPHIS FICTION

Mark Childress, *Tender.* A fictionalized story of Elvis.

William Faulkner, *The Reivers.* One of Faulkner's comic masterpieces; three car thieves from rural Mississippi head for Memphis and Miss Reba's bordello.

Edna Ferber, *Showboat.* Not Memphis-specific, but the story takes place on one of the showboats that ran up and down the Mississippi.

Arthur Flowers, *Another Good Loving Blues.* A turn-of-the-last-century tale of a Memphis bluesman and the woman he loves, written by a native Memphis blues singer.

Shelby Foote, *September, September.* Takes place in Memphis, where Foote lived from 1953 until his death in 2005. His other novels of the South include *Shiloh: A Novel, Tournament, Follow Me Down, Love in a Dry Season,* and *Jordan County.* He is also famous for his nonfiction historical works about the Civil War.

John Grisham, *The Firm*, *The Client*, *The Rainmaker*. Thrillers from the South's favorite attorney/author, all set in Memphis.

Alan Lightman, *Ghost*, *Einstein's Dreams*, *The Diagnosis*, and many others. His books aren't set in Memphis, but Lightman is one of the city's most accomplished native sons (author, physicist, and MIT professor) and a prolific author of many critically acclaimed works.

Tova Mirvis, *The Ladies Auxiliary*. A novel focusing on Memphis's tightly knit Orthodox Jewish community.

Nora Roberts, *Blue Dahlia*, *Red Lily*, and *Black Rose*. Roberts's "Garden Trilogy" of ghostly romance novels is set in Memphis.

Fergus Ryan, *The Redneck Bride*. A southern farce with characters that might have inspired comedians such as Jeff Foxworthy.

Peter Taylor, *A Summons to Memphis* and *The Old Forest and Other Stories*. Taylor received the Pulitzer Prize for *A Summons*, the story of the narrator's family and his attempt to reconcile his family's past. *The Old Forest* stories are set in Memphis's lovely, leafy Overton Park neighborhood.

William Watkins, *Cassina Gambrel Was Missing*. A coming-of-age story set in 1970s Memphis.

James Williamson, *The Architect*. A look at the natives of Memphis and the city's social scene.

MEMPHIS ITINERARY

Day One

2:00 PM

Backbeat Tours "Big Mojo Tour"
Hop aboard an old Memphis city bus for a tour that provides a great orientation to the city. Guides are Memphis musicians who play and sing selections from the city's rich musical heritage, while also including generous amounts of comedy

and audience interaction. Seriously, I saw my guide playing in a Beale Street club the night before. (The schedule for this tour depends on the time of year.) The Big Mojo Tour includes a tour of Sun Studio, where Elvis recorded his first record and where Sam Phillips surreptitiously recorded an informal and impromptu session of what was later called "The Million Dollar Quartet"—Elvis, Johnny Cash, Jerry Lee Lewis, and Carl Perkins.

140 Beale Street, 901-272-2328

www.backbeattours.com

Or you can tour Sun Studio on your own.

706 Union Avenue, 800-441-6249

www.sunstudio.com

6:30 PM

Dinner at B. B. King's Blues Club

Itta Bena (named after B. B. King's birthplace), located on the third floor of B. B. King's Blues Club in Memphis, is tucked away and worlds apart from Beale Street. If you're looking for a sophisticated getaway where the lights are low and the jazz music is low-key, come to Itta Bena. The menu focuses on contemporary southern cuisine with a Delta influence. Or, for more casual fare in a bar-like setting, dine downstairs and listen to blues music.

143 Beale Street, 901-524-KING (5464)

www.bbkingclubs.com/index.php?page=memhome

8:30 PM

Boogie on Beale Street

Beale can be a madhouse of crowds and loud music. Check local listings and plan ahead to hear the best music and avoid hearing bland cover bands of the type you could hear at home. As of this writing, look for rockabilly music at the Blues City Café (138 Beale), Rum Boogie (182 Beale) for soul and blues, and Mr. Handy's Blues Hall (174 Beale) for delta blues in the last real Beale Street "juke joint."

Day Two

8:00 AM

Walk or run the riverfront

If you weren't out too late the previous night, take an early-morning walk or run along the Mississippi Riverfront in Tom Lee Park, on Riverside Drive from Beale Street to South Bluff.

9:00 AM

Memphis trolleys

The city operates trolleys on either the Main Street Line or the Riverfront Line. Buy a day pass if you plan to get on and off the line more than twice. (You can take a brief tour of downtown Memphis on the Riverfront Line, which loops from one end of downtown to the other.) Hop on the Main Street Line going south and hop off near G. E. Patterson Street to find the Arcade Restaurant.

Arcade Restaurant

Memphis's oldest café, founded in 1919. Offers traditional southern breakfasts (grits, sweet-potato pancakes) that have been featured on the Food Network and the Travel Channel; the restaurant is a frequent location for movies filmed in Memphis.

540 South Main Street, 901-526-5757

www.arcaderestaurant.com

10:00 AM

The National Civil Rights Museum

Housed in the Lorraine Motel, where Dr. Martin Luther King Jr. was assassinated, and another building across the street, the museum traces the key episodes in the civil rights movement from slavery to the movement's present-day

legacy and, above all, the efforts of Dr. King. This is a mecca for anyone interested in the civil rights movement.
450 Mulberry Street, 901-521-9699
www.civilrightsmuseum.org

12:00 PM

Lunch at the Majestic Grille

Hop back on the trolley and get off near Peabody Place to nab a table on the sidewalk patio or dine inside this restored movie theater.
145 South Main Street, 901-522-8555
www.majesticgrille.com

1:00 PM

The Cotton Museum

The old Memphis Cotton Exchange has been turned into a museum devoted to sharing the story of King Cotton, the crop that defined the culture of the South, including music and the literature of authors such as William Faulkner, Walker Percy, and Richard Wright.
65 Union Avenue, 901-531-7826
www.memphiscottonmuseum.org

2:00 PM

On the Big Muddy

Head straight down Monroe Street to the riverfront and purchase your ticket for a 2:30 tour aboard a riverboat. A fun-loving narrator will share information about the Mighty Mississippi and its history. The river looks placid on the surface, but check out the speed at which the water rushes past the pilings of the bridges that cross the river and you'll see why Mark Twain had such a hard time learning the river's ways when he was a riverboat pilot. Wave hello to Arkansas on the other side of the river.

Memphis Riverboats
45 South Riverside Drive (Monroe Avenue and the
riverfront), 901-527-2628
www.memphisriverboats.net

4:30 PM

Just ducky

This is the craziest gimmick ever, but even if you're not
staying at the grand Peabody Hotel, you just have to take
a peek at the live ducks in the lobby fountain. The "Duck
Master" leads their entry from the elevator at 11:00 AM and
their departure at 5:00 PM, but it's fine to avoid the crowd and
peek in to see them (and the palatial hotel lobby) any time in
between. You may want to stay for a cocktail.
149 Union Avenue, 901-529-4000
www.peabodymemphis.com/peabody-ducks

6:00 PM

A big choice—wet or dry?

As one tour guide reminded me, there's a lot of food in
Memphis other than barbeque. Nevertheless, it would be a
shame not to treat yourself to the city's most famous food.
Some barbeque fans tout the virtues of the dry rub version of
BBQ found at . . .

Charles Vergo's Rendezvous

Located in the alley, downstairs, behind 52 South Second,
901-523-2746
www.hogsfly.com

For the "wet" version, look no further than . . .

Cozy Corner
Just a short distance from downtown, this is truly a hole-in-the-wall restaurant, known for its barbequed Cornish hens, but every other thing on the menu is also awesome.
745 North Parkway, 901-527-9158
www.cozycornerbbq.com
In the wet-versus-dry rivalry, the Rendezvous has the nicest atmosphere and is a bit more convenient, but the Cozy Corner gets my vote for best barbeque. These places don't take reservations, so prepare to wait a bit.

8:00 PM

Musical encore
Head back to Beale, or check out the musical offering at the . . .

Southern Folklore Center
This nonprofit organization is dedicated to documenting and celebrating the people, music, and traditions of the region. The center combines a colorful and funky shop; folklore hall and gallery; food, including amazing peach cobbler; and music on certain evenings. This group is behind the Memphis Music and Heritage Festival on Labor Day Weekend.
119 South Main Street, 901-525-3655
www.southernfolklore.com

Day Three

8:30 AM

**Breakfast at your hotel or head down to
Bluff City Coffee**
The café offers coffee, smoothies, fresh-baked pastries, and breakfast sandwiches.
505 South Main Street, 901-405-4399
www.bluffcitycoffee.com

10:00 AM

Graceland

South of downtown is the home of "the king," Elvis Presley. You'll see his amazing decor, frozen in time as it was at the time of his death in 1977, and learn more about the life and the legend of one of the most important entertainers in history. Depending on the type of tour you purchase, see his automobile and airplane collections. Go in the morning and try to skip Saturdays in order to avoid the crowd, which will be *un*avoidable if you go during the annual Elvis Week in August.

3765 Elvis Presley Boulevard, 800-238-2000
www.elvis.com/graceland

1:00 PM

Laid-back lunch at Flying Fish

If catfish isn't your thing, the Flying Fish also offers an abundance of other seafood, po'boy sandwiches, and burgers.

105 South Second Street, 901-522-8CAT (8228)
http://flyingfishinthe.net/Memphis.php

2:30 PM

Finish with some soul: Stax Museum of American Soul Music

You'll be dancing through your entire visit to Stax. With interactive exhibits, films, artifacts (including a tiny church), items of memorabilia, and galleries, this museum traces the history of soul music from its roots in the Delta to its heyday with the likes of Otis Redding, Isaac Hayes, Booker T. and the M.G.'s, Ike and Tina Turner, and many others. A portion of the admission supports the Stax Music Academy next door.

926 East McLemore Avenue, 901-946-2535
www.staxmuseum.com

ADD-ON

There are two big things missing from the above itinerary, so depending on your interests and the time available, you'll want to visit the following:

Mud Island River Park and Museum

The museum offers historical information about the river (you'll find Mark Twain there in wax form) and a replica of an 1870s steamship. There's also a five-block-long scale replica of the entire Mississippi River. You can also rent canoes for paddling the calm waters near Mud Island.

Open from mid-April to the end of October, 10:00 AM to 5:00 PM, Tuesday through Sunday (closed Mondays)

125 North Front Street, 901-576-7241

www.mudisland.com

The green and leafy side of Memphis

You wouldn't guess it from downtown or South Memphis, but the city also has stately homes and lush tree-filled avenues and parks. Head to Midtown in the Cooper-Young neighborhood and pop in at Burke's Book Store, Memphis's great little indie bookstore.

936 South Cooper Street, 901-278-7484

www.burkesbooks.com

Proceed to Overton Park to see the area featured in Peter Taylor's acclaimed books, *A Summons to Memphis* and *The Old Forest*. From there, visit the Dixon Gallery and Gardens. The wealthy Memphian Dixon family bequeathed their home, gardens, and collection of French Impressionist paintings for the enjoyment and education of the public. You'll have a chance to stroll beautiful formal, shade, and cutting gardens and tour the art collection.

4339 Park Avenue, 901-761-5250

www.dixon.org

Where to Stay

The Peabody Hotel
Memphis's grandest hotel, in the heart of downtown, famous for its ducks.
149 Union Avenue, 901-529-4000
www.peabodymemphis.com

Holiday Inn Select
Located across the street from the Peabody Hotel in downtown Memphis, a short walk from Beale Street.
160 Union Avenue, 901-525-5491
www.hisdowntownmemphis.com

12

New Orleans

WHERE PIETY RUNS PARALLEL WITH DESIRE

New Orleans isn't like other cities.
—Stella Kowalski in Tennessee Williams's
A Streetcar Named Desire

Stella dahlin', truer words were never spoken. "The Big Easy" is a cultural gumbo of French, Spanish, African, and dozens of other traditions that have swirled together in this port city the way spices meld in chef Paul Prudhomme's stockpot. For me, New Orleans is a tasty but confusing concoction. Take, for example, that quintessential New Orleans event, Mardi Gras, which with its secret societies (krewes), formal balls, costumes, floats, and bead throwing poses a special mystery for nonnatives. But also in New Orleans they "bury" their dead above ground, drink beer in Saks Fifth Avenue, and follow a legal code slightly different from the rest of the country. I'm stumped by the whole concept of living in a city below sea level, too, barely kept dry with the complex system of levees, drainage canals, pumps, and flood walls that always seems precarious. Another conundrum: you never know when a parade of second-line marchers will arrive heralded by the thump of a base drum, the blare of a trombone, and a few dancers twirling with parasols and handkerchiefs. It's enough to make you run off to a local watering hole for a Sazerac or seek comfort in muffulettas, po' boys, mudbugs, and all sorts of other food you've never heard of.

The general meandering pace of life here is equally mysterious if you're a fast-paced northerner. There's a bohemian, laissez-faire attitude toward behavior that left "quirky" in the dust. There's also a feeling of camaraderie among residents brought together by their affection for their football team (for whom they yell out "Who dat?" for some reason) and by living below sea level in a place where hurricanes of enormous proportions are prone to visit. It's a city of "oddnicity," says one of my favorite New Orleans writers, Andrei Codrescu, in his collection of essays, *New Orleans Mon Amour*.

Despite—or perhaps because of—all that cultural complexity, it's easy for visitors to pass off New Orleans with the simplest and most hackneyed idea of what the city is about—just one big drunken party on Bourbon Street. "But under all that is the real story," New Orleans author Chris Wiltz told me, "and it's hard to get a grasp of it. New Orleans has a great history, but that's not the whole picture. It's a city of amazing contradictions," she says. "People in New Orleans will party until dawn on Fat Tuesday, but it's a city of extremely devout Catholics who show up with ashes on their foreheads the next day. This is a city where Desire Street runs parallel to Piety Street."

The city's quirkiness and contrasts make New Orleans loveable, like your crazy Uncle Jacques. They also make it a place where writers find stories ripe for the picking and an atmosphere just right for dreaming. With its crumbling facades, shadowy courtyards, and hazy humidity, the French Quarter is practically a living, breathing collection of metaphors and allegories. That's why so many great writers have flocked to New Orleans, including William Faulkner, Sherwood Anderson, and F. Scott Fitzgerald. In their day, the city wasn't the fixed-up version it is today but rather a rundown city in the throes of the Great Depression. Like Paris's Left Bank, writers found in New Orleans cheap rooms, balconies, and buildings with a European flair, and an environment full of kindred spirits, artists, and misfits.

Says Codrescu, "There are certain cities and certain areas of certain cities where the official language is dreams. Venice is one. And Paris. North Beach in San Francisco. Wenceslaus Square in Prague. And New Orleans, the city that dreams stories. Writers come and eavesdrop and take some of those stories with them, but these are just a few drops from a Mississippi River of stories. The Mississippi brings all its stories here from the rest of the country and can barely contain itself from bursting when New Orleans adds its own stories."

No other writer has captured so elegantly the essence of New Orleans and what it stands for as Tennessee Williams did in *A Streetcar Named Desire*. The city's beauty, party life, and its shadowy bohemian side fit Williams like a glove. In a personal journal entry written on December 28, 1938, the playwright wrote, "I am delighted, in fact, enchanted with this glamorous, fabulous old town. I've been here about three hours but have already wandered about the Vieux Carré and noted many exciting possibilities. Here surely is the place that I was made for if any place on this funny old world." Today you can walk past the places where he lived in the "Vieux Carré": 623 St. Peters Street, where he finished *Streetcar*; 722 Toulouse Street; and 1014 Dumaine, the house he purchased in the 1960s. You can also visit other places he loved to hang out—the Hotel Monteleone, Lafitte's Blacksmith Shop, and the elegant Galatoire's.

The real New Orleans things and places that Williams employed in *A Streetcar Named Desire* hold obvious metaphorical value. He really could hear a streetcar named Desire clanging in his neighborhood as he finished the play. Elysian Fields Avenue, the Kowalskis' street that runs just outside the French Quarter, is named for the land of the dead in Greek mythology. New Orleans itself bears a resemblance to Blanche Dubois, an aging beauty and relic of the old South who tries to keep up the appearance of refined gentility while hiding her promiscuous behavior. She struggles to cope with the brutality and vitality of newcomers like Stanley Kowalski, her sister Stella's husband. No southern gentleman, he's the type of guy who provocatively throws meat to his wife and, in what is one of the all-time great theatrical scenes, stands below the window of their apartment screaming for Stella to forgive him and let him in after he has beaten her—and she does.

Countless writers have added to the flow of stories after Williams, attempting to explain the city and its characters. For many New Orleanians the job was done best by a NOLA native, John Kennedy Toole, who captures the city and its oddnicity to a T in *A Confederacy of Dunces* with characters such as Ignatius J. Reilly, a modern-day Don Quixote. Another New Orleans native, Anne Rice, saw in the city's aging facades and amazingly creepy cemeteries the perfect place for vampires like Lestat and witches like the Mayfair family. But it's interesting that so many authors who work to decipher New Orleans are transplants to whom the city is as mystifying as it is irresistible. Wisconsin native Sara Roahen offers one of my favorite efforts in *Gumbo Tales*, which is part memoir, part guide to New Orleans food and all that it stands for, especially gumbo. She says, "It's not unthinkable that a person would decide to pack up and head south based on a single transcendent bowl of it."

Nothing in recent history has added to the flow of New Orleans stories as the cataclysm of Hurricane Katrina. "It brought the city to its knees," says Chris Wiltz. "The French Quarter wasn't flooded, but 80 percent of the city was. The entire infrastructure of the city crumbled." Wiltz and her husband rode out the hurricane itself just fine, but "when we saw the water coming we knew we'd have to leave." While many of the New Orleans residents have not returned, many have, and while there's still much to repair, I'm happy to say that the city is back in gear, with tourism levels as high as they were before the double whammy of 9/11 and Katrina. You can tie much of the city's resurrection to the same bohemian community of artists, writers, musicians, bar owners, and restaurateurs who exemplify New Orleans culture. As the waters receded, bookstores opened, writers wrote, and musicians played. Cooks and bartenders served burgers and beer to emergency workers. Says Wiltz, "It brought the community together like never before."

I love walking through the French Quarter early in the morning, before the tourists pack the streets. People are washing sidewalks in front of their restaurants and shops. The hazy sunlight filters through the Spanish moss–draped live oaks in the parks and courtyards. I feel enveloped in the dreamy atmosphere of this enigmatic city and begin to understand what Blanche Dubois means when she says, "Don't you just love those long rainy afternoons in New Orleans, when an hour isn't just an hour, but a little piece of eternity dropped into your hands and who knows what to do with it?"

Some things even a hurricane can't change.

Tom Piazza: His Stories Flow in New Orleans

A Long Island, New York, native, Tom Piazza has been one of his adopted city's most passionate spokespersons since Katrina. He began his career as a music writer in New York, with a focus on jazz. He later enrolled in the prestigious Iowa Writers' Workshop to hone his skills. But what better place to write about jazz than New Orleans, where he finally moved in 1994?

His books include nonfiction, such as *The Guide to Classic*

Recorded Jazz, Blues Up and Down: Jazz in Our Time, and *True Adventures with the King of Bluegrass*, along with fiction works, a short story collection called *Blues and Trouble*, and his first novel, *My Cold War*. But after Hurricane Katrina, Piazza really got rolling. His impassioned book *Why New Orleans Matters* responds to House Speaker Dennis Hastert's question about whether there was a need to rebuild New Orleans. His subsequent novel, *City of Refuge*, came out in 2009. The book looks at the Katrina experience through the lives of two families: a white family from a prosperous neighborhood and a less affluent African American family from the city's Ninth Ward. The book transcends the Katrina experience and reveals the distinctive cultures of the city, the choices people make, and the price they pay for their decisions.

Several characters in the book bear a striking resemblance to real-life New Orleans characters. Piazza told the *New Orleans Times-Picayune*, "I think to some degree it is hard for people to understand that a fiction writer turns everything in a book—no matter how closely it might seem to resemble actual fact, actual persons, actual places—into something imaginary. Even if a writer is writing a novel about his or her best friend, in the course of that writing, the friend turns into something else—a character," he said. "It can be a fun parlor game to look for possible models for people and places in a novel, but that's all it is. If the novel is any good, the people and places take on a special, fictional, life of their own."

NEW ORLEANS READING

FICTION

John Biguenet, *Oyster*. The murderous story of two Louisiana families, set on the coast in 1957.

John Gregory Brown, *Decorations in a Ruined Cemetery.* The saga of a mixed-race New Orleans family.

James Lee Burke, *A Morning for Flamingos* and *Creole Belle.* These and other titles in Burke's Dave Robicheaux detective series take place in New Orleans and other Louisiana settings.

Kate Chopin, *The Awakening.* A classic about a woman who goes from a stifling marriage to a "spirited" relationship with another man and the fate that befalls her.

Joshua Clark, ed., *French Quarter Fiction: The Newest Stories of America's Oldest Bohemia.* Some of the best works by New Orleans's living writers.

William Faulkner, *Mosquitoes, Pylon, The Wild Palms,* and *Absalom! Absalom!* were all inspired by New Orleans. Faulkner wrote his first novel, *Soldier's Pay,* in New Orleans. See also his collection of essays, *New Orleans Sketches.*

Shirley Ann Grau, *The Keepers of the House.* The story of a Louisiana family and its racial secrets; winner of the Pulitzer Prize.

Barbara Hambly, *A Free Man of Color.* A thriller set in 1833.

Frances Parkinson Keyes, *Dinner at Antoine's.* A 1948 mystery that commences in the famous restaurant.

Nancy Lemann, *Lives of the Saints.* A humorous look at "wastrel youth" in New Orleans.

Judy Long, ed., *Literary New Orleans.* An anthology of fiction, essays, memoirs, and poetry.

James Nolan, *Higher Ground.* A comic noir novel set in post-Katrina New Orleans.

Walker Percy, *The Moviegoer.* A young New Orleans dandy searches for meaning in life. This is a National Book Award winner.

Tom Piazza, *City of Refuge.* About the impact of Katrina on two very different New Orleans families.

Anne Rice, the Vampire Chronicles, *The Witching Hour,* and *Lasher.* Though she's best known for her vampires and witches, Anne Rice has also written outstanding historical fiction, such as *The Feast of All Saints*, about New Orleans's free people of color.

John Kennedy Toole, *A Confederacy of Dunces.* The famous comic story of Ignatius J. Reilly, the Don Quixote of the French Quarter.

Robert Penn Warren, *All the King's Men.* A tale of the rise and fall of a man who closely resembles Louisiana governor Huey Long, not to mention other Louisiana politicians who were corrupted by power.

Tennessee Williams, *A Streetcar Named Desire* in *Tennessee Williams: Plays 1937–1955.* Also watch the classic film version of *Streetcar* with Vivien Leigh and Marlon Brando, and read Williams's *Memoirs* and *Tennessee Williams and the South* by Kenneth Holditch and Richard Freeman Leavitt.

Chris Wiltz, *The Killing Circle, The Emerald Lizard,* and *A Diamond Before You Die.* Wiltz sets her series of Neal Rafferty mysteries in New Orleans.

The list of New Orleans fiction goes on and on. Be sure to see **Susan Larson**'s *The Booklover's Guide to New Orleans* for a complete picture.

HISTORY AND ANALYSIS

Herbert Asbury, *The French Quarter: An Informal History of the New Orleans Underworld.* The historic underbelly of the Big Easy.

Dave Eggers, *Zeitoun.* About Hurricane Katrina and the outrageous events of its aftermath as experienced by Syrian American Abdulrahman Zeitoun and his family.

Joan Garvey, *Beautiful Crescent.* A good overview of the city's history.

James Gill, *Lords of Misrule: Mardi Gras and the Politics of Race in New Orleans.* An in-depth look at Mardi Gras beneath the masks.

Arnold R. Hirsch and Joseph Logsdon, eds., *Creole New Orleans: Race and Americanization.* Essays on the city's racial heritage.

Errol Laborde, *Krewe: The Early New Orleans Carnival Comus to Zulu.* An explanation of Mardi Gras traditions.

A. J. Liebling, *The Earl of Louisiana.* The story of Louisiana governor Huey Long's final year in politics.

Tom Piazza, *Why New Orleans Matters, Devil Sent the Rain: Music and Writing in Desperate America, Understanding Jazz: Ways to Listen,* and other nonfiction books.

Ned Sublette, *The World That Made New Orleans.* About the Crescent City's colonial years. Recently selected for the city's One Book, One New Orleans city-wide reading program.

John Swenson, *New Atlantis: Musicians Battle for the City of New Orleans.* New Orleans music guru John Swenson examines the impact of the city's jazz culture on its survival.

Robert Tallant and Lyle Saxon, *Gumbo Ya-Ya: A Collection of Louisiana Folk Tales.* Stories and legends from the Bayou State.

Christine Wiltz, *The Last Madam: A Life in the New Orleans Underworld.* The story of the famous madam Norma Wallace.

MEMOIRS AND ESSAYS

Roy Blount, *Feet on the Street: Rambles Around New Orleans.* Eight rambles through the city with Blount's humorous insights on food, literature, and politics.

Andrei Codrescu, *New Orleans Mon Amour.* Poetic essays about Codrescu's adopted home.

Julia Reed, *The House on First Street: My New Orleans Story.* The author recounts her experience with Katrina and rehabbing her Garden District house.

Sara Roahen, *Gumbo Tales: Finding My Place at the New Orleans Table.* An entertaining investigation of New Orleans's amazing food culture.

Ned Sublette, *The Year Before the Flood: A Story of New Orleans.* About growing up in 1950s Louisiana, in which parties and festivals contrast with poverty and racism.

NEW ORLEANS ITINERARY

On this trip your group will travel the city that has inspired so many writers, while spending time eating, sightseeing, shopping, and cooking, all seasoned with a dash of jazz. You'll see how New Orleans, though changed, has emerged from the ravages of Katrina, partly with the help of its vibrant arts community.

Day One

2:00 PM

Literary walking tour

These tours, created by author and professor Kenneth Holditch, stop at spots where great New Orleans writers lived, played, wrote, and caroused. Tours can be designed around a specific author, such as John Kennedy Toole, Tennessee Williams, and others. Group tours (three people minimum) are scheduled by appointment only.
Heritage Tours
504-451-1082

4:00 PM

Arrh! Jean Lafitte's Blacksmith Shop

Built between 1722 and 1732, Lafitte's is reputed to be the oldest structure used as a bar in the United States, and it looks it, but the thoroughly modern rum punch makes it worth a visit.
941 Bourbon Street, 504-593-9761
www.lafittesblacksmithshop.com

6:00 PM

Dinner at Palace Café

Part of the ever-growing number of restaurants operated by members of the venerable Brennan family, the Palace Café is a beautiful spot for New Orleans Creole cuisine with an up-to-date flair.

605 Canal Street, 504-532-1661
www.palacecafe.com

8:00 PM

Southern Repertory Theater

Southern Rep presents classic and contemporary plays
and also develops and produces new plays that reflect the
diversity of New Orleans.
See website for venues, 504-522-6545
www.southernrep.com

Day Two

9:00 AM

A morning by the river

Start with beignets for breakfast at Café du Monde. Don't
wear black if you're going to eat these powdered-sugar-piled
little gems of deep-fried dough. Do drink lots of chicory
coffee and plan to pay with cash.
800 Decatur Street, 800-772-2927
www.cafedumonde.com

Then wander the rest of the historic French Market
(www.frenchmarket.org) and take a leisurely walk along
the Mississippi River on the promenade called the Moon
Walk, named after former mayor Maurice "Moon" Landrieu,
during whose tenure the promenade was built. Cross back
over Decatur to Jackson Square, site of the famous statue
of Andrew Jackson on horseback and check out St. Louis
Cathedral. Blanche Dubois said that the sound of the
cathedral's bells was the only clean thing in the French
Quarter.

Just off Jackson Square, opposite St. Louis Cathedral's
rear garden, you'll find the tiny Pirate's Alley, the home of
Faulkner House Books, so charming you'll want to ask for a

job there. They offer a great selection of New Orleans authors, as well as rare editions, especially books by Faulkner, who lived in the same space that houses the bookstore today. It is where he wrote his first novel, *Soldier's Pay*.
624 Pirate's Alley, 504-524-2940
www.faulknerhouse.net

12:00 PM

Lunch at Napoleon House
The building's first occupant was the mayor of New Orleans from 1812 to 1815. He offered his residence to Napoleon in 1821 as a refuge during his exile, hence the name, though Napoleon never made it. The place oozes New Orleans ambiance, looks every bit its age, and offers a spectacular patio and some of the best muffuletta sandwiches in town.
500 Chartres Street, 504-524-9752
www.napoleonhouse.com

1:30 PM

The Streetcar, the Garden District, and Magazine Street
There's no longer a streetcar named Desire, but you can take the St. Charles Street trolley from Canal Street, through the Garden District, along one of the world's most charming boulevards. Hop off at Jackson Avenue. Go by Garden District Book Shop at 2727 Prytania (www.gardendistrictbookshop.com) and Anne Rice's former home at 1239 First Street (the inspiration for Mayfair Manor). Peek in at Lafayette Cemetery No. 1 (Washington Avenue at Coliseum), seen in the movie *Interview with the Vampire*. It doesn't get any more gothic than this. (The nonprofit organization Save Our Cemeteries offers tours of this City of the Dead Monday through Saturday at 10:30 AM. Their motto is "Bringing the dead back to life." www.saveourcemeteries.org) Since your blood is running cold at this point anyway, indulge in an ice cream cone at Sucre

(3025 Magazine) before you continue on Magazine Street, an eclectic mix of art, antiques, and fashion.
www.magazinestreet.com

If you're not shopped out, wander Royal Street in the French Quarter.

7:00 PM

Dinner at Stanley

Stanley is the more casual counterpart to another restaurant—you guessed it, Stella!—and serves sandwiches, gumbo, and all-day breakfast. This was the first restaurant to open after Katrina (no reservations).
547 St. Ann Street, 504-587-0093
www.stanleyrestaurant.com

9:00 PM

Music on Frenchman Street

You'll find some of New Orleans's best music just outside the French Quarter in the Faubourg Marigny neighborhood.
Three Muses
536 Frenchmen, 504-252-4801
www.thethreemuses.com
d.b.a.
618 Frenchman, 504-942-3731
www.dbabars.com/dbano
Snug Harbor (shows at 8:00 and 10:00, book ahead)
626 Frenchmen Street, 504-949-0696
www.snugjazz.com

Day Three

9:00 AM

Breakfast at Antoine's Annex

This offshoot of the famous Antoine's offers a yummy selection

of pastries and other breakfast baked goods and coffee.
513 Royal Street, 504-525-8045
www.antoines.com/antoines-annex.html

10:00 AM

New Orleans School of Cooking

Learn to cook a few New Orleans standards, such as
jambalaya, crawfish étouffée, gumbo, and bananas Foster . . .
with a dollop of humor and New Orleans folklore. Leave with
recipes and a full tummy. Special participation classes are
available for groups of eight or more.
524 St. Louis Street, 800-237-4841
www.neworleansschoolofcooking.com

1:00 PM

Shopping on Royal Street

Wrap up your trip with a stroll down Royal Street, which
features an assortment of antiques, touristy stuff, galleries,
and street entertainment.

Where to Stay

Hotel Montelone

For generations this hotel has been a hub for writers,
including Williams, Faulkner, Hemingway, and many more.
Truman Capote's mother lived here, but he wasn't born in the
hotel as he claimed.
214 Royal Street, 866-338-4684
www.hotelmonteleone.com

Le Richelieu

A smaller hotel in a quiet edge of the French Quarter.
1234 Chartres Street, 504-529-2492
www.lerichelieuhotel.com

ADD-ON (OR, IN NEW ORLEANS, A "LAGNIAPPE")

If your book group is in town in late March, you'll want to attend at least a portion of the Tennessee Williams/New Orelans Literary Festival. Like New Orleans, the festival offers a lively study in contrasts. You'll find highbrow literary presentations by impressive authors about their works, previews of plays, readings, and discussions of Tennessee Williams's works by famous actors, along with activities tied to the city's food and music scene. At the other end of the spectrum, as an example of "only in New Orleans" behavior, I offer the Stanley and Stella Shouting Contest, the hilarious event in which competitors, often under the influence, do their best to mimic Brando's famous scene from *A Streetcar Named Desire*. Judges in the balcony above offer rowdy encouragement.

www.tennesseewilliams.net

13

Boulder

BREATHLESS IN BOULDER

For Wendy, it was discovering truth in a cliché: her breath was taken away. For a moment she was unable to breathe at all; the view had knocked the wind from her.
—Stephen King, *The Shining*

Looking down at Boulder from its iconic landmark, the jagged rock formations called the Flatirons, it's easy to see why the city is continually labeled with superlatives—it's the happiest place, fittest, foodiest, smartest, and many more. The city sits at the intersection of Colorado's High Plains and the Front Range of the magnificent Rocky Mountains, and from this vantage point the Boulder area is certainly one of the prettiest places, with scenery to satisfy the soul.

But as I sit here on my perch at fifty-four hundred feet, panting from the hike and the altitude, I learn that the scenery isn't all that's breathtaking in Boulder. I catch my breath and begin to feel superlative myself, with a sense of accomplishment from just getting here. The pines rustle around me and the breeze feels cool and crisp in contrast to the hot sun on my skin. Maybe it's the thin air, but one starts to feel a sense of well-being here, and a connection with the mountains and with nature. One of the most famous travelers to Colorado, Isabella Bird, describes the area as "a glorious region where the air and the life are intoxicating."

The amazing Isabella Bird was an Englishwoman who lived a life of continual travel and was, as a result, the first woman to be elected to the Royal Geographical Society. She came to Colorado in 1873, three years before it became a state. She traveled solo through the wilderness and covered more than eight hundred miles during her journey around Colorado, which she described in letters that she wrote to her younger sister in Scotland. The letters were published in 1879 as *A Lady's Life in the Rocky Mountains*, part travelogue, part memoir, part character study of the people who settled here on the frontier, especially "Mountain Jim," a handsome trapper and "desperado" with whom she was fascinated. Bird was also one of the first of a genre that we now call "environmental writers."

She loved the mountains, especially the area of Estes Park, about forty miles from Boulder. But Boulder, not so much. She described it as "a hideous collection of frame houses on the burning plain, but it aspires to be a 'city' in virtue of being a 'distributing point' for the settlements up the Boulder Canyon, and of the discovery of a coal-seam." No superlatives there. How things have changed. Boulder retains a few of those Victorian frame buildings and some of its quaint historic character. But it's now the home of the University of Colorado and a substantial number of high-tech businesses that have made Boulder quite affluent. Bird would be dumbfounded by the bounty of Boulder's famous farmers' market and its trendy restaurants, which prompted *Bon Appétit* magazine to dub it the "foodiest town in America." The city's liberal streak and a contingent of laid-back free spirits and enduring hippies all contribute to its funky atmosphere and a significant arts and music scene. It's all on display at the Pearl Street pedestrian mall, where you'll see more men with ponytails per capita than just about anywhere else. You'll also find shops with unusual and handcrafted goodies that aren't available in the typical shopping mall.

Pearl Street also provides a great opportunity to sit down, rest your weary hiking shoes, and people watch. But, perhaps fueled by an espresso from one of the many local coffee shops, you'll soon feel the urge to get back in motion. The more time I spend in Boulder, the more I'm aware that my little Flatiron hikes are small-time stuff in this, the "outdoorsiest" of places. People run by, they cycle past, they climb the rocks. Boulder, as the *New York Times* writer Susan Enfield Esrey wrote, "sees itself as a community apart, a sort of Front Range Shangri-La that blends hardcore athleticism, latter-day hippie sensibilities and university-town liberalism—often melded into the same Teva-wearing individual. On any given day, you're never far from a preternaturally fit resident burning up calories like crazy: knots of Lance Armstrong look-alikes clotting the bike lanes; wiry climbers toting crash pads; indefatigable young moms towing helmeted toddlers in bike trailers."

If all the activity doesn't make a visitor breathless, a good fright, courtesy of Stephen King, should do the trick. Looking for a place to write without distraction, King came to Boulder back in the early 1970s, after the success of *Carrie* and *Salem's Lot*. King and his wife drove up to the Stanley Hotel in Estes Park, a fabulous setting at the gateway to Rocky Mountain National Park. The story goes that they arrived just before the hotel was about to close for the season (it's open year-round now) and it was nearly empty. Such emptiness would be a tad creepy even in the happiest of hotels, and it was more than enough to set King's powerful imagination in motion. He returned to Boulder, where he wrote what is probably his most famous novel, *The Shining*. He says in his introduction to the 2001 edition of the book that *The Shining* was for him a "'crossroads novel,' where the writer is presented with a choice: either do what you have done before, or try to reach a little higher." So in his study in Boulder, overlooking the Flatirons, he did just that and cranked out a breathtaking three thousand words a day.

Fans of *The Shining* or of the intrepid Isabella Bird will want to make the trip to Estes Park for a look at the rocky scenery and the Stanley Hotel. Fortunately, it only takes an hour now to travel a distance that it took Isabella Bird nine hours to cover. It's a bit odd to compare Stephen King with Isabella Bird, but in both cases it's easy to understand how the isolation of this setting could inspire a writer. Read Bird's description of Estes Park as winter set in: "The Park never had looked so utterly walled in; it was fearful in its loneliness, the ghastliest of white peaks lay sharply outlined against the black snow-clouds, the bright river was ice-bound, the pines were all black, the lawns of the Park were deserted of living things, the world was absolutely shut out." Now, imagine *The Shinings's* Wendy Torrance, completely snowed in at the Overlook Hotel, with the phone lines cut, the road closed, and her husband going berserk.

Stanley Kubrick didn't shoot his famous film adaptation of *The Shining* at the Stanley Hotel, but King returned later to make a television version of the novel. Judging from the number of people who stay in this lovely hotel, the Stanley's spirits must not be as malevolent as those in King's novel. You can find out for yourself, because the hotel offers several types of ghost tours that give visitors the chance to visit the lounges and travel the halls that inspired King's vision, the Overlook Hotel where little Danny Torrance wandered, "the dark and booming place where some hideously familiar figure sought him down the long corridors carpeted with jungle." This, thinks Danny, "is the place Tony has warned him against. It was here. It was here. Whatever Redrum was, it was here." Yikes!

Stressed? After so many breathtaking experiences, you deserve a little pampering. Head back to Boulder and one of several lovely spas there. Take a deep breath; then heave a sigh of relief and contentment.

Kent Haruf and the Nobility of Rural America

Kent Haruf uses the power of simple yet elegant language to portray the drama of everyday life, particularly life on the farms and the plains of eastern Colorado. Born in Pueblo, Haruf is the son of a Methodist minister who moved frequently from congregation to congregation in this section of the state. Consequently, Haruf gained an intimate knowledge of Colorado small-town and farm life and sets his fictional stories in that landscape.

Critics compare his style in novels such as *Plainsong, Eventide, The Tie That Binds,* and *Where You Once Belonged* with that of Hemingway and Faulkner. He uses spare sentences that portray the specific details of small-town life and the universal nature of the stories underneath. Haruf was an English teacher in the Peace Corps in Turkey and later taught writing at the university level, but the success of his books (*Plainsong* was a National Book Award finalist) has allowed him to write full time and to return to Colorado, where he now lives in a small town called Salida. In 2012, Haruf received the Stegner Award from The Center of the American West at the University of Colorado in Boulder. The award goes to an individual who, in the spirit of writer Wallace Stegner, has made a sustained contribution to the cultural identity of the West through literature, art, history, lore, or an understanding of the West.

COLORADO READING

Below you'll find an eclectic reading list of authors who live in Colorado or who set their books there.

James Galvin, *Fencing the Sky.* Set in northern Colorado, about the disappearance of the American West in the face of development.

Kent Haruf, *Plainsong,* a lyrical novel of small-town life on the high plains of Colorado, *Eventide*, the sequel to *Plainsong*, *The Tie That Binds*, and *Where You Once Belonged*.

Pam Houston, *Cowboys Are My Weakness* and *Waltzing the Cat*, two collections of linked short stories, and *A Little More About Me*, essays on the author's globe-trotting adventures.

Stephen King, *The Shining*, King's famous horror story set in Boulder and Estes Park, and *The Stand*, an apocalyptic story set in Boulder.

Esri Rose, *Bound to Love Her* and *Stolen Magic*. Fantasy, romance, and suspense books that mention places in Boulder.

COLORADO MYSTERIES AND MYSTERY WRITERS

Nevada Barr, *Hard Truth*. A thriller set in Rocky Mountain National Park.

Margaret Coel, *The Perfect Suspect* and *Blood Memory*. Train buffs will also appreciate her nonfiction work with Sam Speas, *Goin' Railroading*.

Clive Cussler, *Raise the Titanic*, *Pacific Vortex*, and many other fiction and nonfiction works, mostly related to maritime adventures.

Robert Greer, *First of State*, *The Devil's Hatband*, and other novels that feature Denver bail bondsman C. J. Floyd.

Stephanie Kane, *Seeds of Doubt* and *Extreme Indifference*. Lawyer mysteries set around Denver.

Diane Davidson Mott, *Fatally Flaky*, *Dark Tort*, and *The Main Corpse*. Mott has been called queen of the "culinary mystery."

Stephen White, *Line of Fire*, *The Last Lie*, and others. White, himself a psychologist, writes mysteries that feature Boulder psychologist Alan Gregory.

HISTORY AND HISTORICAL FICTION

Isabella Bird, *A Lady's Life in the Rocky Mountains*. Bird's travels are amazing for a woman in her era, and the people she encounters are equally interesting. See also *This Grand*

Beyond: Travels of Isabella Bird Bishop, an anthology of her travel writing, and Robert Root, *Following Isabella: Travels in Colorado Then and Now*.

Sandra Dallas, *The Diary of Mattie Spenser*. A historical novel based on the fictional life of a woman who comes west with her new husband; a story of harsh reality and triumphant survival.

Kristen Iversen, *Molly Brown: Unraveling the Myth*. This is the real story behind the most famous Titanic survivor, the unsinkable Denver folk legend, and her rags-to-riches life story.

Helen Hunt Jackson, *Ramona* and *A Century of Dishonor*. Hunt lived in Colorado Springs and was a fiery and prolific writer, especially about the plight of Native Americans.

James Michener, *Centennial*. A historical fiction epic of Colorado history.

Sylvia Pettem, *Only in Boulder* and *Boulder: A Sense of Time and Place*. The quirky characters and history behind the Boulder of today.

Frank Waters, *Pike's Peak*. A saga of the fictional Rogier family that features real characters from Colorado's early history.

Dorothy Wickenden, *Nothing Daunted: The Unexpected Education of Two Society Girls in the West*. The author tells of two friends, one of whom is her grandmother, and their adventure as teachers in Colorado in the early 1900s.

BOULDER ITINERARY

Boulder rocks, as they say, especially if you're an outdoorsy person, a foodie, or a Stephen King fan. Within easy reach of downtown Boulder, there's a great variety of outdoor activity, though at 5,430 feet a brisk walk taxes the lungs of flatlanders. So this itinerary includes leisurely dining and a spa day.

Day One

2:00 PM

Boulder Dushanbe Teahouse

Built completely by hand, the Teahouse was constructed
in Dushanbe, Tajikistan, as a gift to its sister city, Boulder.
From 1987 to 1990, more than forty artisans carved and
painted the intricate Persian motifs and decorative elements
of the Teahouse, including its hand-carved and hand-painted
ceiling, tables, stools, columns, and exterior ceramic panels.
1770 Thirteenth Street, 303-442-4993
www.boulderteahouse.com

3:30 PM

Stroll Boulder Creek Trail

Walk along Boulder Creek as it winds through the heart
of the city.

5:45 PM (or later, depending on time of year, June through October)

Sunset mountain tour

Take an easy, two-hour hike with Colorado Wilderness Rides
and Guides to watch the sun set over the Continental Divide,
see the city of Boulder light up, and learn about natural and
local history.
Tour departs from 900 Walnut Street, 720-242-9828
www.coloradowildernessridesandguides.com/sightseeing
/index.html

9:00 PM

Dinner at the Kitchen

1039 Pearl Street, 303-544-5973
www.thekitchencafe.com

Day Two

8:30 AM

Breakfast at your hotel or grab coffee and a pastry at Boulder Farmers' Market

The season runs every Saturday, beginning the first Saturday in April and continuing through the third Saturday in November, 8:00 AM to 2:00 PM. The Wednesday evening season runs every Wednesday beginning in May and continuing through the first Wednesday in October, 4:00 PM to 8:00 PM.

Boulder Farmers' Market

Thirteenth Street between Arapahoe and Canyon, next to Central Park in downtown Boulder

www.boulderfarmers.org

10:00 AM

Head for Estes Park

Take in the scenery that dazzled and challenged Isabella Bird as you follow the route that she traveled on the way to Estes Park.

11:30 AM

Stanley Hotel Ghost and History Tour

Visit the hotel that inspired Stephen King to write *The Shining* for a one-and-a-half-hour tour.

333 Wonderview Avenue, Estes Park, 800-976-1377

To book tours, call 970-577-4111 to speak to a tour guide or book online at stanleyhotel.com/tours/.

1:00 PM

Follow the tour with lunch at the hotel, and then head back to Boulder

4:00 PM

Shopping Pearl Street

Offbeat shopping, great coffee shops, and the Boulder Book Store. Pearl Street is also home to a number of other independent bookstores, with both new and used books.

6:00 PM

Dinner at Centro Latin Kitchen and Refreshment Palace

950 Pearl Street, Boulder, 303-442-7771
www.centrolatinkitchen.com

Boulder nightlife (without the ghosts)

Along with bars and restaurants, the city has many live entertainment opportunities to choose from, such as the following:

Boulder Theater

This venue offers everything from movies to a wildly diverse calendar of musical acts, both national and local. See the website for show times.
2032 Fourteenth Street, 303-786-7030
www.bouldertheater.com

Colorado Chautauqua House

This historic landmark began with the turn-of-the-century movement to educate and enlighten working-class citizens by creating gathering places dedicated to learning. Known as Chautauquas, the public spaces offered a place for traveling lecturers, politicians, writers, and entertainers to deliver their message to large crowds. Now the Colorado Chautauqua is one of only three remaining Chautauquas in the country and home to concerts, cultural events, theatrical productions, and educational programs.
900 Baseline Road, 303-442-3282
www.chautauqua.com

Day Three

9:00 AM

Breakfast and spa at the St. Julien Hotel
The hotel offers Sunday morning yoga, too.
900 Walnut Street, 720-406-8218
www.stjulien.com/spa-at-st-julien

OR

Bike a bit of Boulder
For those not ready for too much relaxation, rent bikes
at University Bicycles to cruise Boulder's residential
neighborhoods and the Boulder Creek Trail, and ride up the
hill to the University of Colorado campus, where you can look
around the Boulder History Museum. That should keep you
breathless enough.
University Bicycles
839 Pearl Street (Ninth and Pearl), 303-444-4196
www.ubikes.com
Boulder History Museum
1206 Euclid Avenue (on University Hill), 303-449-3464
Tuesday through Friday from 10:00 AM to 5:00 PM and
weekends noon to 4:00 PM
www.boulderhistorymuseum.org

Where to Stay

Hotel Boulderado
Isabella Bird might have thought more of Boulder if she could
have stayed at the Boulderado. It's been a landmark since it
opened in 1909.
2115 Thirteenth Street, 303-442-4344
www.boulderado.com

St. Julien Hotel and Spa

One of Boulder's newest and most luxurious hotels, with a great location and a great spa.

900 Walnut Street, 1-877-303-0900

www.stjulien.com

Chautauqua Cottages

For groups, these cottages may be the perfect choice. They're a bit far from downtown activities but sit directly adjacent to the Flatirons, hiking trails, and Chautauqua entertainment. No TV or phone, but they have fully equipped kitchens—a great value.

900 Baseline Road, 303-442-3282, extension 611

www.chautauqua.com

14

Austin

BUCKAROOS AND BOHEMIANS

You can't capture Austin in one book, or one song, or one lifetime. The best you can do is to experience it.
—**Kinky Friedman,** *The Great Psychedelic Armadillo Picnic*

The Texas State Capitol in Austin is a very persuasive place. It's immense—the largest state capitol building in the country—and it quickly delivers a wallop of larger-than-life Texas. At the center of the rotunda's terrazzo floor, builders embedded a giant Lone Star surrounded by the words "Republic of Texas," just in case you weren't aware that Texas was an independent nation before it became a state. Symbols of past and present "occupiers" of Texas—France, Spain, Mexico, the Confederacy, and the United States—are relegated to a smaller orbit around the Lone Star. A star also stares down from the Capitol dome two hundred feet above. Standing beneath it, you quickly get the feeling that, here, at least one eye of Texas is upon you.

The Capitol is just the start. Say "Texas" and a whole herd of larger-than-life and distinctively Texan images come to mind: giant ranches like the famous King Ranch, big ol' longhorn cattle, Texas-style ten-gallon hats, fancy boots, big hair, and big politicians such as US presidents Lyndon Baines Johnson and George Bush Senior and Junior, to name a few. In the 1950s, the story of "big oil" in the state inspired Edna Ferber to write her novel *Giant*, which later became a movie with Liz Taylor, Rock Hudson, and James Dean. The 1980s TV show *Dallas* added juicy plotlines of family scandal, double dealing, and even murder to the ostentatious image of Texas oilmen. Author Bryan Burrough says in *The Big Rich: The Rise and Fall of the Greatest Texas Oil Fortunes*, "There is a legend in America, about Texas, about the fabulously wealthy oilmen there who turned gushers of sweet black crude into raw political power, who cruised their personal jets over ranches measured in Rhode Islands, who sipped bourbon-and-branch on their private island as they plotted and schemed to corner an entire international market." He adds, "There is truth behind the legend, a surprising amount in fact."

The most enduring image of Texas, though, is that of the cowboy riding the open range. You know the one: ruggedly handsome, tough as nails, but with a heart of gold. He squints as he scans the horizon for any form of danger while singing "Don't Fence Me In." The famous cattle drives that traveled from the Texas-Mexico border to stockyards in Nebraska and Kansas lasted only about twenty-five years, until the invention of barbed wire allowed ranchers to fence in the open range. But the legend of those brave and independent cowboys endures—and we love it.

No one has captured the cowboy legend better than Larry McMurtry in his epic novel *Lonesome Dove*, winner of the Pulitzer Prize for fiction. (McMurtry's body of work, with a list of novels, screenplays, essays, and memoirs a mile long, stacks up to Texas-sized proportions, too.) In 2010, at the twenty-fifth anniversary of *Lonesome Dove*'s release, *Texas Monthly* said of the book, "It is the great hero myth of Texas, the state's favorite depiction of itself and the world's favorite depiction of Texas. . . . It's our *Gone with the Wind*." So if your idea of a cattle drive is an air-conditioned car ride to the nearest steakhouse, *Lonesome Dove* is required reading before your trip to Austin.

With rich detail and panoramic scenery but a less romanticized portrayal of the cowboys than that first popularized in the old dime novels, critics credit *Lonesome Dove* with reforming the Western genre and making the myth of the cowboy even more appealing to modern readers. Loosely based on the real-world cattle drive of Charles Goodnight and Oliver Loving, *Lonesome Dove* tells the story of Woodrow Call and Augustus McCrae, retired captains in the Texas Rangers who now run the Hat Creek Cattle Company in the dusty settlement of Lonesome Dove. But finding life a little too tame they set out on an epic Texas-to-Montana trail drive, a final grand adventure. Ultimately, the book is about the settlement of the frontier and the disillusionment of aging characters resistant to change in a changing world, but McMurtry subsumes these themes in a page-turning story complete with stampedes, hangings, romance, gunfights, snakes, and hilarious banter.

Cattle drives like theirs used to pass right by Austin, along the famous Chisholm Trail, but it's hard to imagine dusty herds of cattle and cowpokes anywhere close to Austin today. You'll get a glimmer of those days at the Bob Bullock Texas State History Museum, which offers a great introduction to Texas's proud history. Formerly known as Waterloo, Austin began as nothing more than a low crossing point on the Colorado River. After some Austin-versus-Houston dissention, Austin became the capital.

Since then, the city has developed a larger-than-life reputation of its own, not only as the capital of the Lone Star State (hence its political hub) but also as Texas's cultural center. As such, Austin defies many of the aforementioned stereotypes of Texas. Politically, it's a progressive blue dot in the center of an overwhelmingly conservative red state. You're as likely to meet hipsters or people

with elaborate piercings and tattoos as you are to encounter people sporting armadillo cowboy boots or hair big enough to hide
a six-shooter. Austin treasures them all and just about anything
goes in this laid-back town. Shannon Sedwick, a founder and
actor at the Austin comedy club Esther's Follies, says, "Everybody
gets along with each other here. Hippies next to conservatives;
it's very laissez-faire," a fact that she attributes largely to the fact
that Austin is home to the University of Texas. The city takes its
reputation as a bohemian and liberal outpost very seriously. Its
unofficial motto is "Keep Austin Weird." A visit to South Congress
Avenue confirms the success of that effort.

That environment has made Austin a hip haven for artists,
writers, and especially musicians. Rock, blues, and jazz light up
the nightlife right along with the classic country and honky-tonk
that are Texas's musical roots. Kinky Friedman, author, musician,
and sometimes candidate for governor of Texas, says in his Austin tour book *The Great Psychedelic Armadillo Picnic*, "When Willie
Nelson came on the national scene, ten minutes later everyone
wanted to come to Austin to have their hip cards punched." Austin
has become the live music capital of the United States; the famed
music and film festival South by SouthWest, the Austin City Limits
Music Festival, and other events draw thousands of visitors annu-
ally. Yet it's not necessary to visit Austin during a major music fest
because—be they cowboy, hiking, or stiletto-heeled—your boots
will be knocked off any night of the year by the city's music scene.

By comparison, Texas's literary culture seems to play second
fiddle. Don Graham, author and J. Frank Dobie Regents Professor
of American and English Literature at the University of Texas, says
that's partly because of Texans' own reticence to recognize their
literary culture and partly because the stereotypes that dominate
the state's image make it hard to take its literary efforts seriously.
Graham says in *State of Minds: Texas Culture and Its Discontents*,
"The fact is, Texas has done a much better job of exporting its
mystique than it has its truths—aided and abetted, of course, by

Yankee expectations." And, he told the *Austin Chronicle*, "To tell you the truth, I got kind of worked up by people at UT, faculty members saying, 'There isn't such a thing as Texas culture. It's an oxymoron.'" According to Graham, "There's a big advantage in being identified as a Southern writer. But a Texas and a Western writer, they just never had the kind of standing nationally. . . . My theory is that the East Coast is only interested in Southern writing so much because it's about race and it's Gothic. It fits their idea of the South—that the South is full of crazies, religious nuts, and racists. Whereas, they don't really have any idea about the West at all."

But Texans don't take belittlement lying down. The organizers of the annual October Texas Book Festival, hardworking booksellers such as the folks at Book People, and Texas writers themselves, are working to elevate the state in the eyes of the literary world. In addition, members of the Austin literati such as Sarah Bird, Oscar Casares, Karen Valby, Stephen Harrigan, and Dagoberto Gilb are adding to the region's literary "anthology." You won't find much of the larger-than-life aspect of Texas in their books. What you will find is down-home good reading, with portraits of life specific to Texas but also with universal themes and experiences that we all share. Like Texas barbeque, you can't put these books down. And like a visit to Austin, you'll want to share them with friends.

Oscar Casares: Life Along the Border

Born and raised in the border town of Brownsville, Texas, Oscar Casares comes from a family that he says had a tradition of storytelling rather than reading. After a short career in advertising, Casares realized that people loved to hear his stories about his family and growing up along the Texas-Mexico border, so he left advertising for the writing life. Since 2003, his essays have appeared in the *New York Times*, on *All Things*

Considered for National Public Radio, and in *Texas Monthly*, where he is known as the Bard of the Border. He has written two noted books—a novel, *Amigoland*, and a collection of stories, *Brownsville*—and garnered fellowships from the National Endowment for the Arts, the Copernicus Society of America, and the Texas Institute of Letters. The Mayor's Book Club in Austin chose *Amigoland* for its 2010 citywide reading campaign.

His books weave the realities of life along the border with pathos and humor, and he credits his uncles Hector and Nico, whom he calls master storytellers (perhaps models for the main characters in *Amigoland*) for their influence on his literary abilities. Casares now teaches creative writing at the University of Texas at Austin and directs its new Master of Fine Arts Program in English. He lives in Austin with his wife and two young children.

LONE STAR READING

FICTION

Rick Bass, *The Diezmo*. A novel about the ill-fated Mier expedition in the Texas border country.

Sarah Bird, *Virgin of the Rodeo, How Perfect Is That*. Comedic Texas fiction.

Oscar Casares, *Amigoland, Brownsville*. A tremendously engaging novel and short story collection about people living in two cultures.

Edna Ferber, *Giant*. A sensational story of power, love, cattle barons, and oil tycoons.

Dagoberto Gilb, *Hecho En Tejas: An Anthology of Texas-Mexican Literature*. A comprehensive collection that showcases Texas-Mexican writers. Also *The Magic of Blood, The Flowers*, and *Woodcuts of Women*, tales of working-class Mexican Americans in the Southwest.

Fred Gipson, *Old Yeller.* This is technically a children's book, but who can resist this classic three-Kleenex read?

Don Graham, Larry McMurtry (foreword), *Lone Star Literature: From the Red River to the Rio Grande: A Texas Anthology.* Fiction and nonfiction Texas stories from the state's best writers.

Stephen Harrigan, *Remember Ben Clayton* (the story of a sculptor and the rancher who commissions a statue) and *The Gates of the Alamo* (a fictionalized account of the fall of the Alamo).

O. Henry (aka William Henry Porter), *The Best Short Stories of O. Henry.* Some of the best works from a favorite American storyteller.

Paulett Jiles, *The Color of Lightning* and *Stormy Weather.* Historical fiction.

Cormac McCarthy, *Blood Meridian, No Country for Old Men, All the Pretty Horses.* Many of McCarthy's gripping novels are set in the border country.

Larry McMurtry, *Lonesome Dove, The Last Picture Show, Terms of Endearment, Texasville,* and nonfiction such as *In a Narrow Grave: Essays on Texas,* memoirs such as *Books* and *Literary Life,* and scads of other books.

James Michener, *Texas.* A fictionalized history of the state.

George Sessions Perry, *Hold Autumn in Your Hand.* Perry won the National Book Award in 1941 for this novel about a year in the life of a Depression-era Texas sharecropper. See also Perry's *Texas: A World in Itself,* about the history, tradition, and folklore of Texas.

Katherine Anne Porter, *Ship of Fools* (in which a wide cast of characters sails from Mexico to Europe) and *The Collected Stories of Katherine Anne Porter.*

Rick Riordan, *The Devil Went Down to Austin.* A wisecracking private investigator and English professor moves to Austin, where he expects simply to teach at the University of Texas.

NONFICTION

H. G. Bissinger, *Friday Night Lights: A Town, a Team, and a Dream.* A Pulitzer Prize–winning journalist covers the Permian Panthers of Odessa, a famously winning high-school football team.

Bryan Burrough, *The Big Rich: The Rise and Fall of the Greatest Texas Oil Fortunes.* The real stories of the legendary Texas oilmen.

Randolph Campbell, *Gone to Texas.* Tells the stories of the colorful individuals and events that shaped the history of Texas, giving equal treatment to the lives of men like Sam Houston and to women and minorities in Texas's history.

Mike Cox, *The Texas Rangers Wearing the Cinco Peso, 1821–1900.* The reality and the myth behind the early Rangers.

J. Frank Dobie, *The Longhorns, Tales of Old-Time Texas, Cow People,* and many others. Before there was McMurtry, there was Dobie. Considered Texas's master storyteller, he wove together fact and folklore.

T. R. Fehrenbach, *Lone Star: A History of Texas and the Texans.* The Texas story from prehistory to the oil boom.

Kinky Friedman, *The Great Psychedelic Armadillo Picnic: A "Walk" in Austin, Kinky Friedman's Guide to Texas Etiquette: Or How to Get to Heaven or Hell Without Going Through Dallas–Fort Worth,* and *Heroes of a Texas Childhood.* Humorous observations from this country-and-western singer, novelist, and politician.

Don Graham, *Kings of Texas: The 150-Year Saga of an American Ranching Empire Life on the King Ranch, Giant Country: Essays on Texas,* and *States of Minds: Texas Culture and Its Discontents.* Observations of Texas culture.

John Graves, *Texas Hill Country.* A prose and photographic portrait of this lovely section of the state.

S. C. Gwynne, *Empire of the Summer Moon: Quanah Parker and the Rise and Fall of the Comanches, the Most Powerful Indian Tribe in American History.* Finally, a view from the Indians' side.

Mary Karr, *The Liar's Club.* A memoir of the author's childhood growing up in an über dysfunctional family in an East Texas refinery town.

Frederick Law Olmsted, *A Journey Through Texas: Or a Saddle-Trip on the Southwestern Frontier.* Before he became America's foremost landscape architect, Frederick Law Olmsted had a variety of jobs, including traveling newspaper correspondent.

Américo Paredes, *With His Pistol in His Hand: A Border Ballad and Its Hero.* An analysis of Mexican American folklore through the story of ballad singer Gregorio Cortez.

Jessie Gunn Stephens, *A Book Lover's Tour of Texas,* a literary visit to various regions of the state.

Calvin Trillin, *Trillin on Texas.* A collection of Trillin's magazine articles about the Lone Star State.

Karen Valby, *Welcome to Utopia: Notes from a Small Town.* A fascinating portrait of a West Texas community.

Red Wassenich, *Keep Austin Weird: A Guide to the Odd Side of Town.* Wassenich coined the phrase "Keep Austin Weird." This lavishly photographed book makes a good souvenir.

AUSTIN ITINERARY

Be sure to tailor this itinerary to whether you are staying south of the river or north of the river. Also, don't forget to make restaurant reservations and book show tickets in advance for venues with specific show times—they sell out. Consult the *Austin Chronicle* or *Austin360* for entertainment calendars.

Day One

2:00 PM

The SoCo scene

Launch your trip to Austin with the funkiest and most retro section of the city, the South Congress neighborhood, south of the river. It's filled with vintage shops, amazing cowboy boot stores, clothing stores, and galleries. Other establishments defy categorization. Check out Allens Boots, Lucy in Disguise, Mi Casa Gallery, Parts and Labour, and some great eateries including an assortment of food trailers near Congress and Elizabeth. Go ahead and indulge in a cone at Amy's Ice Creams.

6:00 PM

Sixth Street serenade
Head to one of the hubs of Austin nightlife: the historic downtown entertainment district based around Sixth Street, roughly from Red River Street to Brazos. Every night of the week, the smell of great food and the sound of music of all genres pour forth from just about every building in this neighborhood. Start with dinner at . . .

El Sol y La Luna
Traditional and contemporary Mexican food, including a variety of vegetarian and seafood selections.
600 East Sixth Street, 512-444-7770
www.elsolylalunaaustin.com

7:30 PM

Austin humor at Esther's Follies
A hilarious comedy, music, and magic revue heavy on timely political humor, Esther's pokes good-natured fun at women, men, liberals, conservatives—you name it. You'll also enjoy the antics from passersby on the sidewalk outside during the show. (The show starts at 8:00 PM, Thursday through Saturday. There's also a 10:00 PM show on Friday and Saturday.)
525 East Sixth Street, 512-320-0553
www.esthersfollies.com

10:00 PM

The music scene

See why Austin is considered the live-music capital of the world with a stroll along Sixth. Pop in at establishments where you hear your favorite kind of music; most don't charge a cover. Especially recommended, Blue Moon Blues and Rock (422 East Sixth). Thursday through Saturday nights the police close off Sixth Street and it becomes a pedestrian thoroughfare. If you're looking for a quieter place for a nightcap, head up the street to Austin's grand dame, the Driskill Hotel (604 Brazos at Sixth). The Victorian landmark was built in 1886 by cattle baron Jesse Driskill. The bar here also features live music and decor that mixes velvet with cowhide and horns—elegance with Texas style.

Day Two

9:00 AM

Breakfast at the Old Pecan Street Café

Breakfast goodies baked on site, served in a former hardware store.
310 East Sixth Street, 512-478-2491
www.oldpecanstcafe.com

10:30 AM

The Bob Bullock Texas State History Museum

Pass by the thirty-five-foot-tall bronze Lone Star sculpture outside to learn what makes Texas Texas from the indigenous people, the struggle for independence from Mexico, and on to oil and astronauts. You'll find the history of the cowboys and cattle drives at the center of Larry McMurtry's novel *Lonesome Dove*.
1800 North Congress Avenue at the intersection of Martin Luther King Jr. Boulevard, 512-936-8746 or, for ticket

reservations, 512-936-4649
www.thestoryoftexas.com

12:30 PM

A short call at O. Henry's house

The tiny house William Henry Porter, aka O. Henry, rented
for several years is tucked in right next to the Hilton. Before
he wrote his famous short story "The Gift of the Magi," Porter
lived in Austin drawing maps for the General Land Office and
publishing a paper called the *Rolling Stone*.
409 East Fifth Street, 512-472-1903
http://austintexas.gov/department/o-henry-museum

1:30 PM

Lunch at Chuy's

You can't beat great Tex-Mex food and an Elvis shrine.
1728 Barton Springs Road, 512-474-4452
www.chuys.com

2:30 PM

Biking through Zilker Park

Right across the street from Chuy's, you'll find Barton Springs
Bike Rental, a convenient spot to pick up bicycles to explore
one of Austin's signature features, Zilker Park and Barton
Springs Pools. It's an easy ride along the Colorado River
(known here as Lady Bird Lake) to enjoy this lovely green
area and visit the iconic statue of Stevie Ray Vaughn. This
shop offers guided tours of the park by bike. Depending on
the time of sunset, you may want to make sure you're at the
Congress Avenue Bridge around dusk (spring through fall)
when the famous bats pour out from under the bridge.
1707 Barton Springs Road, 512-480-0200
bartonspringsbikerental.com

7:00 PM

Dinner at Stubb's Bar-B-Q
Roll up your sleeves and dig in at Stubbs, an Austin classic, known for both its barbecue and its live music.
801 Red River, 512-480-8341
www.stubbsaustin.com

The Broken Spoke
Put on your two-steppin' shoes and mosey over to the Broken Spoke, a true Texas honky-tonk dance hall, where the likes of Willie Nelson, George Strait, and many others have played. Dance lessons 8:00 to 9:00 PM (Wednesday through Saturday).
3201 South Lamar, 512-442-6189
www.brokenspokeaustintx.com
   In a jazzier mood? Head to the . . .

The Elephant Room
315 Congress Avenue, 512-473-2279
www.elephantroom.com

Day Three

Breakfast at Annie's Café and Bar
Hearty fresh-baked breakfast in a French brasserie atmosphere.
319 Congress Avenue, 512-472-1884
www.anniescafebar.com

10:30 AM

Book People
Austin's biggest indie bookstore, with a section on local Austin writers, Texas history, a staff that's eager to talk books, and a continuing parade of author appearances. They're right across the street from one of the last physical

places to buy music, Waterloo Records (600 North Lamar Boulevard), and right next door to REI, Anthropologie, and the Whole Foods flagship store.
603 North Lamar Boulevard, 800-853-9757
www.bookpeople.com

11:30 PM

Lone Star State Capitol
You can simply park next to the beautiful capital grounds and stroll inside for a look at the impressive capital rotunda, the portraits of Texas governors, and the chambers of the legislature.
112 East Eleventh Street, 512-305-8400
www.tspb.state.tx.us/SPB/capitol/texcap.htm

12:30 PM

Lyndon Baines Johnson Library and Museum
The most visited of all presidential libraries, this one does a great job of tracing the personal history of our thirty-sixth president and weaving it with some of the most important events of the twentieth century, including the Kennedy assassination, the Civil Rights era, and the Vietnam War.
2313 Red River Street, one block west of I-35 between MLK (Twenty-First Street) and Dean Keeton (Twenty-Sixth Street; parking is free), 512-721-0200
www.lbjlibrary.org

2:30 PM

Late lunch at Z'Tejas Southwestern Grill
Sit outside and enjoy anything from catfish tacos to wild mushroom enchiladas.
1110 West Sixth Street, 512-478-5355
www.ztejas.com/locations/#!/texas/austin-6th-street

ADD-ON: TEXAS HILL COUNTRY

If you have an extra day, the Hill Country west of Austin offers a chance to see the Texas countryside, with stunning wildflowers in spring and even a few longhorn cattle. Head to Fredericksburg (www.fredericksburgtexas-online.com), a charming town that German settlers founded. A trip down Main Street here is like a walk back into the Old West, only with shops that cater to tourists. On your way back to Austin, visit the LBJ Ranch (be sure to read Doris Kearns Goodwin's LBJ bio, *Lyndon Johnson and the American Dream*, first), which is now operated by the National Park Service. You can tour both a historic Texas farm and the Texas White House, circa 1968 (www.nps.gov/lyjo/planyourvisit /visitlbjranch.htm). End your day with a stop in Driftwood at the legendary rib joint and meat lover's heaven, the Salt Lick (www .saltlickbbq.com).

Where to Stay

Hilton Austin
This is a beautiful hotel, centrally located downtown, and if they're not fully booked for a convention or other events, it offers great rates, and a spa, too.
500 East Fourth Street, 512-482-8000
www1.hilton.com/en_US/hi/hotel/AUSCVHH-Hilton-Austin -Texas/index.do

Hotel San Jose
With a Zen-like atmosphere, this small but supercool hotel is an oasis amid the South Congress shops and eateries and offers a peaceful courtyard for gathering. (If you have a large group, they may not have enough rooms.)
1316 South Congress Avenue, 512-444-7322 or 800-574-8897
www.sanjosehotel.com

Austin Motel

Another SoCo location, the Austin Motel offers funky decor and great rates. Their motto is "So close and yet so far out." 1220 South Congress Avenue, 512-441-1157 www.austinmotel.com

15

Santa Fe

THE ARCHBISHOP COMES TO LIFE

The moment I saw the brilliant, proud morning shine high up over the deserts of Santa Fé, something stood still in my soul, and I started to attend. . . . In the magnificent fierce morning of New Mexico one sprang awake, a new part of the soul woke up suddenly, and the old world gave way to a new.

— **D. H. Lawrence**, "New Mexico"

Fair warning: it's hard to keep a group on course in Santa Fe. Here in the country's second-largest art market, shopping opportunities cry out like Sirens on the rocks. If you can stroll without stopping past art galleries of every description, gorgeous Native American weavings and pottery, or beautiful jewelry sold by local artisans beneath the portal of the Palace of the Governors, you're a better woman (or man) than I. But it's not only the temptation to buy beautiful things that diverts you. Bands play music in the city's historic downtown plaza. Bells peal from St. Louis Cathedral. Adobe architecture draped in purple wisteria, courtyards full of giant sculptures that spin like whirligigs or softly sing as they resonate with the wind, and even the crisp, dry air—everything about Santa Fe beckons the visitor to ooh, aah, and stop.

My advice: Don't fight it. Odysseus ordered his sailors to put beeswax in their ears and tie him to the mast of their ship to avoid the Siren's calls. Silly man. In Santa Fe, make sure each person has the cell-phone number of every other person so you can find each other later, because a few of you are bound to stray.

Once you adjust to the sensory fiesta that is Santa Fe, you'll be free to focus on a more ethereal odyssey that Willa Cather lays out in her classic *Death Comes for the Archbishop*. Set in the latter half of the nineteenth century, the book is a barely fictional retelling of the lives of two French priests, Father Jean-Baptiste Lamy and Father Joseph Machebeuf (appearing in the book as Father Latour and Father Vaillant, respectively), who were sent to the New Mexico Territory with the goal of creating order in the Catholic Church and enlarging the flock there. Before my book club read *Archbishop* we had read Cather's *My Antonia*, which isn't exactly a cliffhanger. Still, I thought *Archbishop* offered all the ingredients for an action western: a perilous unsettled landscape, a rogue priest, and the famous frontiersman and Indian fighter Kit Carson. Even the name implies drama: *Death Comes for the Archbishop* conjures a fighting man of action, like John Wayne in a black cassock.

Cather's aim, however, was entirely different. *Archbishop*, which she called a *narrative* rather than a novel, is more experimental in its form than her previous books. In response to readers' many questions about her sources for the book and its historical accuracy, Cather explained in a letter that appeared in *The Commonweal*, "I had all my life wanted to do something in the style of legend which is absolutely the reverse of dramatic treatment. Since I first saw the Puvis de Chavannes frescoes of the life of Saint Genevieve in my student days, I have wished that I could try something a little like that in prose; something without accent, with none of the artificial elements of composition." So, in *Archbishop*, she foregoes the dramatic highs, lows, and plot twists of more conventional novels. Instead, her "fresco" gives equal importance to most incidents in Archbishop Lamy's life, whether he is excommunicating a priest or weathering a blizzard. Even if you prefer more plot-driven books (and you'll see plenty on the reading list for this chapter), you'll find *Archbishop* a perfect read for your Santa Fe trip. I read it again before my most recent visit there and saw both the book and the city in a new light.

Willa Cather made several trips to Arizona and New Mexico and, like so many people, fell in love with the Southwest. Archbishop Lamy, in particular, piqued her interest. "I never passed the life-size bronze of Archbishop Lamy which stands under a locust tree before the Cathedral in Santa Fe without wishing that I could learn more about a pioneer churchman." She found his story laid out in great detail in *Life of the Right Reverend Joseph P. Machebeuf*, by the priest William Joseph Howlett. Cather, blending Lamy's and Machbeuf's history with her own experience and observations in the region, created a vivid picture of life in the territory in which the sense of place itself takes a starring role. You can't envision *Death Comes for the Archbishop* without appreciating the landscape Cather so beautifully paints with words. Rebecca West, in her 1927 review of *Archbishop*, calls Cather "the most sensuous of writers," and one of the delights of visiting Santa Fe is that the fresco Cather paints in her fiction is still there for you to see, down to the last detail.

The first thing you'll notice when you arrive in New Mexico's high desert is the light, which at this altitude is clear and stunningly bright. (Note to self: bring sunglasses.) Cather wrote in *Archbishop*, "The desert, the mountains and mesas, were continually re-formed and re-coloured by the cloud shadows. The whole country seemed fluid to the eye under this constant change of accent, this ever-varying distribution of light." It's no wonder that the distinctive character of the New Mexico light attracted a cadre of famous artists, including Georgia O'Keefe and Alfred Stieglitz, as well as writers such as Cather and the British author D. H. Lawrence. Cather had a special affinity for the New Mexico sky, which she describes in *Archbishop* as "full of motion and change as the desert beneath it was monotonous and still—and there was so much sky, more than at sea, more than anywhere else in the world. The plain was there, under one's feet, but what one saw when one looked about was the brilliant blue world of stinging air and moving cloud. Even the mountains were mere anthills under it. Elsewhere the sky is the roof of the world; but here the earth was the floor of the sky. The landscape one longed for when one was far away, the thing all about one, the world one actually lived in, was the sky, the sky!"

Still, the New Mexico sky rolls over some pretty remarkable terrain. On the drive to Santa Fe from Albuquerque, it was easy to imagine the endurance and determination required for Lamy to travel around his arid, expansive diocese on the back of a mule. As Cather describes it, "As far as he could see, on every side, the landscape was heaped up into monotonous red sand-hills, not much larger than haycocks. . . . Every conical hill was potted with smaller cones of juniper, a uniform yellowish green, as the hills were a uniform red. The hills thrust out of the ground so thickly that they seemed to be pushing each other, elbowing each other aside, tipping each other over." During your time in Santa Fe, you'll also get a feel for how desperate the characters must have been for water, not to mention ChapStick.

Near the center of old Santa Fe are the archbishop's architectural projects, the Cathedral Basilica of St. Francis of Assisi and the Loretto Chapel, which are built in the style of the Romanesque churches of France and stand in contrast to the adobe buildings around them. On a less grand scale, just north of town, the house and tiny chapel Lamy built for his retirement sit just as he left them. Joseph Pulitzer, the newspaper publisher, purchased the archbishop's retreat, preserved it, and added two new houses to turn the property into a summer home for his family. In 1918, new owners turned the hacienda into the resort now called Bishop's Lodge, where you can see the property Cather describes in the book. "Once when he was riding out to visit the Tesuque mission, he had followed a stream and come upon this spot, where he found a little Mexican house and a garden shaded by an apricot tree of such great size as he had never seen before. It had two trunks, each of them thicker than a man's body, and though evidently very old, it was full of fruit." As of this writing the huge, gnarly old tree is still there, though quite dead, with no hope of resurrection.

Archbishop Lamy planted new plants and coaxed them to bloom here in the high desert where no one had seen them before. But with the region's mix of people and cultures—indigenous, Mexican, and white European—he often found it more challenging to cultivate the souls of his flock and to keep them growing in the straight rows of church doctrine. In *Archbishop*, Father Latour, a man who obviously seeks to show his devotion to God by building churches, can't understand why the Indians lack a similar desire to build something permanent, like a cathedral. He comes to recognize that their cathedrals stand in nature. "They actually lived upon their Rock; were born upon it and died upon it. There was an element of exaggeration in anything so simple!" In the "Stone Lips" chapter, Bishop Latour's Indian guide Jacinto finds shelter for them during a blizzard in a cave that serves as a religious site. Its entry looks like a pair of stone lips and it's a mystical place where the line between earth and heaven is a fine one. Latour begins to see the cavern as a "lofty gothic chamber" and, though he finds in Indian life "a strange literalness, often shocking and disconcerting," he seems to recognize and respect the Native Americans' brand of spirituality and its connection to the earth. Jacinto kneels down over a fissure in the cave and tells the bishop to lay with his ear to the crack, where "he told himself he was listening to one of the oldest voices of the earth. What he heard was the sound of a great underground river flowing through a resounding cave."

In Santa Fe and throughout the Southwest, Native Americans have been less absorbed into mainstream culture and have held on to their traditions and spirituality more successfully than most other tribes in the country. The spirit of nature that the bishop heard persists today among the many elements that have lured artists and writers to Santa Fe. The sky, the land, and the mystical spirituality are all there, both in fiction and in fact. You'll want to add your own layer of experience to the fresco that Cather creates in *Death Comes for the Archbishop* and take it home with you, along with some great silver earrings.

Cormac McCarthy

Cormac McCarthy is almost as famous for avoiding interviews as he is for his critically acclaimed writing. The *New York Times* writer Richard B. Woodward once called him a "hermitic author, who may be the best unknown novelist in America." That was before *All the Pretty Horses* hit the market in 1992. Unlike McCarthy's earlier books, this one became a publishing sensation. The other two volumes in his Border Trilogy, *The Crossing* and *Cities of the Plain*, followed and also garnered both critical acclaim and a devoted following of readers.

The trilogy and several other McCarthy works are set in the Southwest, a place where history and the natural world seem a perfect backdrop for his brand of fiction. Yet the fiction that emerges couldn't be more different from what resulted from Willa Cather's experience here. McCarthy's stories are as brutal as their prose is poetic. Saul Bellow commented on his "absolutely overpowering use of language, his life-giving and death-dealing sentences." His 2005 crime thriller *No Country for Old Men* was adapted into an award-winning film by Joel and Ethan Coen. In 2006, his apocalyptic novel, *The Road*, hit the bookstores, won the Pulitzer Prize for Literature, and was turned into a movie with Viggo Mortensen.

McCarthy lives in Tesuque, on the outskirts of Santa Fe, and is a trustee at the Santa Fe Institute, a theoretical-science think tank, where he has a chance to talk about science rather than writing. He occasionally copyedits the work of scientists, doggedly rooting out exclamation points and semicolons the way he does in his own writing.

SANTA FE READING

FICTION

Rudolfo A. Anaya, *Bless Me, Ultima*, the coming-of-age story of a young boy in 1940s New Mexico, and *Alburquerque: A Novel*, in which a young man searches for his real father.

Elspeth Grant Bobbs, *Done from Life*. A mystery set in the fictional version of Canyon Road.

Richard Bradford, *Red Sky at Morning*. A boy comes of age in a New Mexico town. The story is often compared to *The Catcher in the Rye*.

Willa Cather, *Death Comes for the Archbishop*. Cather's classic tale of two priests on the New Mexico frontier. See also Phyllis C. Robinson's biography *Willa: The Life of Willa Cather*.

Rick Collignon, *Perdido*. Tense relations among racial groups intensify when an Anglo man living in a small New Mexico town becomes intrigued with the story of a young woman who was found hanging from a bridge more than two decades before.

Laura Hendrie, *Remember Me*. The story of a woman who is an outcast in her New Mexico town, where embroidery is a key activity.

Tony Hillerman, his many mystery novels, including *Skinwalkers*, *Listening Woman*, *Dance Hall of the Dead*, and *People of Darkness*, are set in New Mexico and Arizona. He also edited *The Spell of New Mexico*, an anthology.

Oliver LaFarge, *Laughing Boy: A Navajo Story*. The Pulitzer Prize–winning story of a Navajo romance and the changing life of the American West.

N. Scott Momaday, *In the Bear's House* and *The Way to Rainy Mountain*. He also wrote the Pulitzer Prize–winning *House Made of Dawn* about a young man struggling to adjust to life after World War II, when he is torn between life in his pueblo and the white man's realm. Momaday is one of the country's most acclaimed Native American writers.

John Nichols, *The Milagro Beanfield War*. A humorous book about a mini–class war that pits small-town farmers against Anglo businessmen and land developers.

Conrad Richter, *The Sea of Grass*. An epic tale of the settling of the Southwest.

Leslie Marmon Silko, *Ceremony*. A classic about the clash between the creation of the atom bomb and Native Americans' worldview.

Frank Waters, *The Woman at Otowi Crossing*. A fictional portrayal of the story of Edith Warner, who owned a café that catered to Los Alamos scientists. His book *The Man Who Killed the Deer*, about a crime at Taos Pueblo, explores the conflict between Native American and white culture and the mystical qualities of the land.

NONFICTION

Jennet Conant, *109 East Palace: Robert Oppenheimer and the Secret City of Los Alamos*. The story of life in the desert outpost where scientists and their families lived as they worked to create the atomic bomb.

Peggy Pond Church, *The House at Otowi Bridge: The Story of Edith Warner and Los Alamos.* The story of a woman who lived near Los Alamos and her relationships with people in the area, who ranged from Native Americans to atomic scientists Niels Bohr, Robert Oppenheimer, and the others who worked at Los Alamos during World War II.

Lynn Cline, *Literary Pilgrims: The Santa Fe and Taos Writers' Colonies, 1917–1950.* About the writers of the area's literary heyday.

Barbara Harrelson, *Walks in Literary Santa Fe: A Guide to Landmarks, Legends, and Lore.* Harrelson, who leads literary walking tours in Santa Fe, offers a literary look at each segment of the city.

Paul Horgan, *Lamy of Santa Fe.* A Pulitzer Prize–winning biography of the first bishop of Santa Fe.

John Pen LaFarge, *Turn Left at the Sleeping Dog: Scripting the Santa Fe Legend, 1920–1955.* A collection of interviews with a cross section of the city's residents, written by a Santa Fean who knew them.

Mabel Dodge Luhan, *Edge of Taos Desert: An Escape to Reality.* The wealthy Taos arts patron's tale of personal transformation and her fascination with Native American culture. *Lorenzo in Taos* is her personal account of her relationship with the novelist D. H. Lawrence.

Charles C. Mann, *1491.* A fast-paced history of the Americas before Columbus.

Hampton Sides, *Blood and Thunder: The Epic Story of Kit Carson and the Conquest of the American West.* The story of the campaign against the Indians and other aspects of settling the American West.

Frank Waters, *To Possess the Land: A Biography of Arthur Rochford Manby.* The story of a land swindler and his mysterious murder.

SANTA FE ITINERARY

In *Death Comes for the Archbishop*, Willa Cather tells the tale of Archbishop Lamy while painting a sensory portrait of the Santa Fe area. Keep your eyes open, because you will see much of what was in the novel on this itinerary.

Day One

2:00 PM

An afternoon in Old Santa Fe

A literary walking tour of Old Santa Fe
Barbara Harrelson, the author of *Walks in Literary Santa Fe*, offers walking tours, by appointment only.
505-989-4561

If she's not available, grab a copy of her book at Collected Works Bookstore and Coffeehouse (202 Galisteo Street) and take your own tour of old Santa Fe. Be sure to do some browsing at Collected Works, because they have a wonderful selection of books, including works by regional authors. During your walking tour, you'll visit the Cathedral of St. Francis. In front is the statue of Archbishop Lamy that piqued Cather's interest in his story; the archbishop is buried in a crypt behind the altar.
131 Cathedral Place
www.cbsfa.org

After your tour, give in to temptation and take a look in the shops that adjoin the plaza.

6:00 PM

Cocktails in the Bell Tower at La Fonda (in warm weather)

Located literally at the end of the Santa Fe Trail, there has been an inn on this site for hundreds of years. Willa Cather stayed at La Fonda, as have countless writers, artists, actors, and other dignitaries. The Bell Tower offers a great view of the city and its surroundings.

100 East San Francisco Street, 800-523-5002
www.lafondasantafe.com

8:00 PM

Dinner at Pasqual's
Between the creative southwestern cuisine and the decor,
Pasqual's will put you in a fiesta mood. Hand-painted Mexican
tiles and murals by the renowned Mexican painter Leovigildo
Martinez line the dining room. This is a tiny restaurant, so
reserve well in advance.
121 Don Gaspar, 800-722-7672
www.pasquals.com

Day Two

10:00 AM

An amazing art race
This art-based treasure hunt is an action-packed way for your
group to get a taste of a huge variety of the art, artists, and
museums of Santa Fe, and even try your own hand at a sketch
or two. They'll tailor the activities to the needs/interests of
your group.
505-795-8137, artisthire@yahoo.com
www.nmartistsforhire.com

12:00 PM

Shidoni Foundry and Galleries
Self-guided tours weekdays from noon to 1:00 PM. Visitors
have the opportunity to visit the indoor art galleries, stroll
the outdoor sculpture gardens, and take a self-guided tour of
the foundry to see how bronze statues and monuments are
made. Note: if you're there on a Saturday, you'll want to alter
your schedule to watch a "pour," in which workers pour two-
thousand-degree molten bronze into ceramic shell molds to
make sculptures. Call for times.

1508 Bishops Lodge Road, Tesuque (five miles north of Santa
Fe), 505-988-8001
www.shidoni.com

1:00 PM

Lunch at Tesuque Market

Just down the road from the foundry is a "general store with
a hipster aesthetic." The market serves soup, salad, awesome
deli sandwiches, and mouth-watering baked goods.
138 Tesuque Village Road, 505-988-8848
www.tesuquevillagemarket.com

2:30 PM

New Mexico History Museum

Comprised of several buildings, including the Palace of the
Governors, where Lew Wallace, the author of *Ben Hur*, served
as territorial governor. Exhibits cover the early history
of indigenous people, Spanish colonization, travel and
commerce on the legendary Santa Fe Trail, and New Mexico's
path to statehood. Be sure to visit the museum's bookstore
and the portal in front where New Mexico Native American
artists display and sell their handmade arts and crafts. This
is a regulated market in which artisans must be members of
New Mexico tribes and pueblos and must follow stringent
rules designed to ensure the authenticity of their goods.
113 Lincoln Avenue, 505-476-5200
www.nmhistorymuseum.org

4:00 PM

Stroll Canyon Road

Along this road, you'll find more than one hundred galleries,
specialty shops, and restaurants.
www.canyonroadarts.com

7:00 PM

Dinner at the Shed

You'd never know there's such a lively restaurant tucked behind the walls of this hacienda, which dates back to 1692. Southwestern cuisine, with an emphasis on homegrown chilies. 113½ East Palace Avenue, 505-982-9030 www.sfshed.com

Music and a nightcap at El Farol

This Canyon Road establishment offers live entertainment and tapas every night. 808 Canyon Road, 505-983-9912 www.elfarolsf.com

Day Three

9:00 AM

Morning with the Archbishop

A horseback ride at Bishop's Lodge Ranch Resort and Spa offers a great way to get out into the New Mexico countryside, with views of the Sangre de Cristo Mountains as well as the hillside retreats of well-known actors. For those less intrepid, the lodge offers a lovely array of spa services.

Follow up with a tour of Archbishop Lamy's house and chapel. Ask the concierge for details.

12:00 PM

Lunch at the Lodge's Las Fuentes Bar and Grill

Great view of the property outside and the art inside. 1297 Bishop's Lodge Road, 800-768-3586 www.bishopslodge.com

Where to Stay

Inn on the Alameda
Close to downtown and the Canyon Road art district.
303 East Alameda, 505-984-2121
www.innonthealameda.com

Inn of the Governors
Close to downtown sites and restaurants.
101 West Alameda, 800-234-4534
www.innofthegovernors.com

ADD-ON: TAOS

If you have an extra day, a trip to Taos is in order. Getting there is half the pleasure. Take the beautiful High Road on the way and return by the equally beautiful Low Road, which runs along the Rio Grande River. Be sure to see Taos Pueblo, a living community that is also a UNESCO World Heritage site.
120 Veterans Highway, 575-758-1028
www.taospueblo.com

Also in Taos: **Hacienda de los Martinez,** which was the home of Padre Antonio Martinez (Bishop Lamy's adversary), offers a glimpse of the rugged frontier life and times of the early 1800s.
708 Hacienda Way (off Lower Ranchitos Road), 575-758-1000
www.taoshistoricmuseums.com

16

Seattle

WEARING LAYERS

I dreamed I was flying over a map of America until I stopped above the vast green oasis that was Washington State. Taking the dream as a sign, I made plans to move to Seattle at once. I didn't know a soul there, which was partially why I came. Seattle was the kind of place where you could tell people this story and they wouldn't call you a flake.
—**Natalia Rachel Singer,** "Blurred Vision: How the Eighties Began in One American Household"

My friends and I are sipping lattes, but other than that, it's a rare day in Seattle. We've peeled off our rain jackets. The sun is shining, and sitting here in the Olympic Sculpture Park on the city's northern waterfront, we can see the Olympic Mountains stretching out across from us on Puget Sound. Even shy Mount Rainier is treating us to his presence. If Seattle's weather were always like this, everyone in the world would want to move here.

We're perched on a bench near Alexander Calder's giant red metal sculpture, *The Eagle*, with its curving wings and pointy abstract beak. From this vantage point, it feels like sitting in the middle of Seattle history. In front of us, as old as time, stretch the blue ocean, gray mountains, and lush, green, tree-covered islands. But next to me the eagle's sharp beak seems to point toward the famous Space Needle that rises up behind us like George Jetson's office building. It's a 1960s vision of the future from the Seattle world's fair, formally known as the Century 21 Exposition. Next to that is downtown Seattle, a forest of shiny metal and glass office buildings, full of people from high-tech companies that no one at the world's fair could have imagined, such as Amazon, Microsoft, RealNetworks, and ZymoGenetics.

Unlike many cities, Seattle's historical strata are on display for all to see. The city adds new layers each time it reinvents itself. As Timothy Egan puts it, "Seattle is a city that can't decide what to wear." In his book *The Good Rain: Across Time and Terrain in the Pacific Northwest*, Egan says, "It has changed its look three times in the last thirty years and half a dozen times in the last century." He refers to changes in the look of the city that come with new building and development. "Every wave of fresh tenants wants to remodel." Seattleites have cut the timber from the hills, lopped off the tops of the hills themselves, and slid the soil downhill to fill in the waterfront. Take the Seattle Underground Tour and walk the former streets that are now at basement level, and you'll see what I mean.

Seattle began as a gold rush city, like San Francisco but about fifty years later, when gold was discovered in the Yukon. Once the "gateway to Alaska," Seattle's proximity to Asia also made it a portal for international trade with the continent. Boeing later made Seattle a hub of the aircraft industry; then Microsoft, Amazon, and their progeny altered the tech landscape as well as the city's skyline; and Starbucks turned a single coffee shop into an international phenomenon. Maybe that's why Seattle has more nicknames than any other city: the Queen City, the Gateway to Alaska, the Jet City, and the Coffee Capital, to name a few. And through its reinventions, Seattle has morphed into one of the country's hippest, most progressive urban centers, the home of grunge rock, high-tech business without the business suit, and a passion for recreation and the outdoors.

Yet no matter how many times a new industry or trend changes in Seattle, it will still be the Emerald City, with a year-round lush and green look due to the fact that it's also Rain City. The rainy landscape is one of the things that makes Seattle and the Pacific Northwest so unique and such interesting places to visit. So despite Seattle's acclaim as a youthful urban paradise, it's not surprising that the landscape of the Pacific Northwest—with its craggy wilderness, lush green beauty, and blue-gray seas—tends to dominate its literature. In the anthology *Reading Seattle: The City in Prose*, Seattle author Peter Donahue rues the fact that Seattle lacks a large body of *urban* literature. "Because of the region's stunning natural beauty and frontier past, the outdoors focus of its literature is understandable. Unfortunately, this focus has too often excluded writings about the Northwest urban experience. Within the canon of Northwest literature, cities seem anathema to the idealization of the region as a land of mountains, forests, lakes, wildlife, loggers, and fishermen, where nary a high-rise, housing project, freeway, back alley, or apartment dweller is seen." True enough, but you can find freeways and back alleys just about everywhere. Not so with mountains, lakes, and forests where trees grow so big you can drive a car through them. For the creative mind, the lush landscape can inspire flights of imagination or simply serve as a great backdrop for drama. For a writer to shun Seattle's environment would be like ordering a glass of water at Ben and Jerry's.

So Seattle writers have donned their rain gear and taken up their pens. In her funny (and distinctly un-PC) memoir, *The Egg and I*, Betty MacDonald recounts her life on a chicken farm in the wilderness of the Olympic Peninsula from 1927 to 1931. What her family lacks in running water, electricity, and indoor plumbing they make up for in stunning scenery, a lot of nasty chickens, and some truly unusual neighbors, Ma and Pa Kettle. MacDonald describes the constant effort it takes to keep the wilderness from retaking their property. "Clearing land there in the mountains," she says, "was like holding back a mob at a fire. As long as the fences held and we were ever watchful, we were safe enough but one break and the trees surged in. We were constantly pushing them back from the garden, the road, the driveway, the chicken yard; and the mountains were carelessly letting them slide down on us. I expected to look up some day and see a mountain bare shouldered and grabbing frantically for her trees."

In *Still Life with Woodpecker*, Tom Robbins offers one of my favorite descriptions of how the rain makes plants flourish around Seattle. "In the wet months, blackberries spread so wildly, so rapidly that dogs and small children were sometimes engulfed and never heard from again. In the peak of the season, even adults dared not go berry picking without a military escort. Blackberry vines pushed up through solid concrete, forced their way into polite society, entwined the legs of virgins, and tried to loop themselves over passing clouds." Now, I'm betting that the blackberries have never really looped over passing clouds. But I know that rainy forests *do* offer just the right habitat for vampires and werewolves. No wonder Stephanie Meyer chose to set her *Twilight* stories of Edward and Bella's vampire romance in Forks, Washington, about three hours from Seattle. "For my setting," says Meyer, "I knew I needed someplace ridiculously rainy. This turned out to be the Olympic Peninsula in Washington State. I pulled up maps of the area and studied them, looking for something small, out of the way, surrounded by forest. . . . And there, right where I wanted it to be, was a tiny town called Forks."

The Seattle area isn't as downright drippy as those rainforests in Forks, but it certainly has a misty and evocative atmosphere, which David Guterson employs in his novel *Snow Falling on*

Cedars. The story takes place on fictional San Piedro, an island of "five thousand damp souls." A map in the book shows it as part of the San Juan Islands to the northwest of Seattle, but Bainbridge Island, where the author lives, provides both the atmosphere and the historical backdrop. Structured somewhat like *To Kill a Mockingbird*, Guterson's story revolves around a double plot line involving a murder trial set against the story of Japanese residents during World War II. "San Piedro had . . . a brand of verdant beauty that inclined its residents toward the poetical," writes Guterson. "Enormous hills, soft green with cedars, rose and fell in every direction. The island homes were damp and moss-covered and lay in solitary fields and vales of alfalfa, feed corn, and strawberries." Here the cedar trees grow big enough to shelter Ishmael and Hatsue for a little forbidden romance. They take refuge in a hollow cedar when it starts to rain, safe from the prejudices of the outside world.

From Seattle's busy waterfront along Alaskan Way, we hop onto a ferry to Bainbridge Island, a forty-minute ride to another world and a slower time. Today it's a bedroom community for Seattle, but the picturesque harbor, the trees, the greenery, and the misty hills give it just the right rich ambiance for romance and drama. We get off the ferry in the little village of Winslow, which runs alongside Eagle Harbor. It certainly isn't "downtrodden and mildewed," like Amity Harbor in *Snow Falling on Cedars*. The Bainbridge Island Historical Museum, housed in a red 1908 schoolhouse, tells the story of the Japanese internment as it really played out on the island. After the bombing of Pearl Harbor, Japanese citizens became the focus of suspicion, even though many were second-generation Americans, known as Nisei. Considered a security threat, 110,000 Japanese men, women, and children from all over the West Coast were rounded up and sent into exile in military-style camps. One of the museum's most moving exhibits shows class pictures from Bainbridge Island's high school classes of 1941 and 1942. The Japanese students missing from the latter picture say it all.

After lunch and a tour of Winslow's charming shops and art studios, it's time to board the return ferry for Seattle. The modern skyline seems to grow as the boat gets closer. The clouds start to roll in, smoothing the rough edge of the modern buildings. Wisps of fog add a misty layer over the Space Needle and soften *The Eagle*'s hard edges. I think again that it's good that the weather isn't perfect here. There would be too many people. And too few stories.

Sherman Alexie: Scaring the Right People

Poet, novelist, and filmmaker Sherman Alexie grew up on the Spokane Indian reservation in Wellpinit, Washington. His stories about life on the reservation are often far from the mainstream portrayal of Native Americans. As such, Alexie's writings are often targets of protest and even censorship, which, to Alexie, simply means he's doing something right. He considers it an honor that his book *The Absolutely True Diary of a Part-Time Indian* is regularly on the American Library Association's Top Ten List of Challenged Books. As he says on his website, "It means I'm scaring the right people. Hooray! I keep hoping somebody will organize a national boycott against me."

Alexie weaves together memory, fantasy, humor, and the harsh reality of reservation life in his books, which seems to be a winning formula for all but the most conservative critics. His twenty-two books have won numerous awards. Along with the American Library Association "honor," *The Absolutely True Diary of a Part-Time Indian* won the 2007 National Book Award for Young People's Literature; *War Dances* won the 2010 PEN Faulkner Award; *The Lone Ranger and Tonto Fistfight in Heaven* garnered a PEN Hemingway Special Citation; and *Smoke Signals*, the film he wrote and coproduced, won the Audience Award and Filmmakers' Trophy at the 1998 Sundance Film Festival. He regularly returns to the reservation, but as he told the

Los Angeles Times, important as his heritage is to him, it's not his sole focus. "People's ethnicity is the first floor of their house," he says. "But the real interesting stuff is in the cellar and the attic."

Alexie is known not only for his lyrical writing style but also for his love of basketball, his sense of humor, quick wit, and outspoken attitudes. That combination makes him a popular public speaker everywhere from high school graduations to bookstores to *The Colbert Report*, where he gives even Stephen Colbert a run for his money. When his book *War Dances* came out, Alexie and Colbert discussed the reasons why he doesn't allow his books to be published in a digital format. Alexie spoke out in favor of the printed book, independent bookstores, and the celebration of books on a local level. He said that he has made a career going from bookstore to bookstore, university to university, and person to person, reading from his books like a storyteller around a fire. "I think white folks should be ashamed that it's taking an Indian to save part of their culture."

SEATTLE READING

FICTION

Sherman Alexie, *The Lone Ranger and Tonto Fistfight in Heaven, Reservation Blues, Indian Killer,* and many others, all focus on Native American life. *The Absolutely True Diary of a Part-Time Indian* is a semiautobiographical novel for young adults.

Erica Bauermeister, *The School of Essential Ingredients.* The story of eight students who gather every week for cooking classes.

Ryan Boudinot, *Blueprints for the Afterlife.* Science fiction set in Seattle.

Michael Byers, *Long for This World: A Novel.* A cure for a childhood disease versus the ethical dilemma it poses, set against the backdrop of 1990s Seattle.

Megan Chance, *City of Ash*. The intertwining tale of a young actress and an exiled society lady set against the Great Seattle Fire.

Annie Dillard, *The Living*. A novel of pioneer life on the frontier of the Northwest.

Peter Donahue, ed., *Reading Seattle: The City in Prose*. An anthology of prose set in the city. And two works of historical fiction: *Clara and Merritt*, set against the violent strife between longshoremen and Teamsters in Seattle in the 1930s and 1940s, and *Madison House*, the story of Maddie Ingram, who runs a Seattle boardinghouse in the late 1800s.

Earl Emerson, *Cape Disappointment* and *Catfish Café*. Feature Seattle private eye Thomas Black.

G. M. Ford, *Thicker than Water*, *The Deader the Better*, and others. Mysteries featuring Seattle PI Leo Waterman.

Jamie Ford, *Hotel on the Corner of Bitter and Sweet*. The story of a Chinese boy and a Japanese girl who face the prejudices of their relatives and the greater society during World War II.

David Guterson, *Snow Falling on Cedars*. A murder trial and love story set against the true story of Japanese internment during World War II. His books *The Other* and *Ed King* are set in Seattle.

Richard Hugo, *A Run of Jacks*, *Death of the Kapowsin Tavern*, *Good Luck in Cracked Italian*, and other collections of poetry of the Northwest.

J. A. Jance, *Betrayal of Trust*, *Failure to Appear*, *Lying in Wait*. Mysteries with J. P. Beaumont, set in the Northwest.

Laura Kalpakian, *Educating Waverley*. The story of a romance writer, set on Isadora Island in Puget Sound.

Jim Lynch, *The Highest Tide*, a coming-of-age novel about a boy who finds a giant squid in Puget Sound, and *Truth Like the Sun*, based on the Century 21 Exposition.

Stephanie Meyer, *Twilight*, *New Moon*, *Breaking Dawn*, *Eclipse*. The books in Meyer's outrageously popular series are set primarily in Forks, Washington, but in *Eclipse* a set of really nasty vampires come down from Seattle.

Cherie Priest, *Boneshaker*. A steampunk novel (think science-fiction technology, zombies, and the Klondike era) set in Seattle.

Jonathan Raban, *Waxwings*. A story that blends in the issues of American life at the turn of the millennium.

Tom Robbins, cult novels such as *Another Roadside Attraction*, which features a cast of characters in Captain Kendrick's Memorial Hot Dog Wildlife Preserve of Skagit County, and *Still Life with Woodpecker*, a romance between a princess and an outlaw in suburban Seattle.

Maria Semple, *Where'd You Go, Bernadette*. A comic novel that takes place in modern-day Seattle.

Garth Stein, *The Art of Racing in the Rain*. A race car driver and a family tragedy as seen through the eyes of his dog.

Urban Waite, *The Terror of Living*. Drug smuggling in the Pacific Northwest.

NONFICTION

June Burn, *Living High: An Unconventional Autobiography*. An inspiring story of homesteading on Sentinel Island in the Puget Sound, teaching school in isolated Alaska, and other adventures.

Bruce Brown, *Mountain in the Clouds*. About the demise of the salmon runs in Puget Sound.

Ivan Doig, *Winter Brothers: A Season at the Edge of America*. A travel narrative in which Doig retraces the life and journeys of an adventurer who left detailed daily diaries of life on Washington's Olympic Peninsula during the 1850s.

Timothy Egan, *The Good Rain: Across Time and Terrain in the Pacific Northwest*. Personal observation, history, and ecology from Puget Sound, Indian reservations, formal gardens, and other Northwest landscapes.

Alexandra Harmon, *Indians in the Making: Ethnic Relations and Indian Identities Around Puget Sound.* Explores native people's regional history from their interaction with settlers in the 1820s to the activism of the 1970s.

Erik Larson, *The Devil in the White City, In the Garden of Beasts, Thunderstruck,* and others. His books aren't set in Seattle, but he is one of the area's most prominent authors.

Mary McCarthy, *How I Grew.* A memoir from the author of *The Group,* who grew up in Seattle.

Murray Morgan, *Skid Road.* An anecdotal history of Seattle.

Ann Rule, true crime stories including *The Stranger Beside Me,* her own story of working at a crisis hotline where she slowly discovers that one of her coworkers is the notorious serial killer Ted Bundy.

Roger Sale, *Seattle Past to Present.* A history that highlights the city's major periods from founding to Boeing.

Monica Sone, *Nisei Daughter.* The memoir of a Japanese American coming of age in the 1930s and 1940s.

William C. Speidel, *Sons of the Profits: Or, There's No Business Like Grow Business! The Seattle Story, 1851–1901.* An irreverent take on Seattle history.

Tobias Wolff, *This Boy's Life.* A memoir of growing up with a sadistic stepfather.

Mary Woodward, *In Defense of Our Neighbors: The Walt and Milly Woodward Story.* How the publishers of Bainbridge Island's community newspaper fought the forced internment of their Japanese neighbors during World War II.

SEATTLE ITINERARY

Rain or shine, Seattle offers plenty to do inside or out.

Day One

2:00 PM

Chihuly Garden and Glass
Take the monorail to Seattle Center, where you'll find the newest addition to Seattle's arts and entertainment complex, Chihuly Garden and Glass, which presents a comprehensive collection of the work of glass artist Dale Chihuly. It's adjacent to the Space Needle, which was erected for the 1962 world's fair (as seen in Jim Lynch's *Truth Like the Sun*).
305 Harrison Street, 206-753-4940
www.chihulygardenandglass.com

4:00 PM

Washington wine tasting
Return to Westlake Center on the Monorail (which puts you in the middle of a Seattle shopping mecca including Nordstrom's flagship store at Pacific Place, which may require a quick detour). Then head toward the Tasting Room, nestled in Post Alley right near Pike Place market, for a chance to taste wines from Washington State in a charming cellar-like atmosphere.
The Tasting Room
1924 Post Alley, 206-770-9463
www.tastingroomseattle.com

8:00 PM

Dinner at Steelhead Diner
Located in Pike Place Market, with a view out to Elliott Bay and the Olympic mountains.
95 Pine Street, Pike Place Market, 206-625-0129
www.steelheaddiner.com

10:00 PM

Triple Door

A live music venue with a variety of music styles. There's a
main stage with a hefty minimum, but there's no cover in the
Musicquarium Lounge.
216 Union Street, 206-838-4333
www.thetripledoor.net

Day Two

8:30 AM

Pike Place Market

Grab coffee at the original Starbucks and pastries at Le Panier
and watch as this working market goes into action with
flower stands, fruit and veggie vendors, and the famous fish-
throwing fishmongers. The market is a sensory delight.

10:30 AM

Snow Falling on Cedars Bainbridge Island Tour

Take the ferry for a thirty-five-minute trip to Bainbridge
Island. (Ferry schedules vary with the time of year.) The
island is home to David Guterson, author of *Snow Falling on
Cedars*, and served as an inspiration for the story's San Piedro
Island. A cozy, small seaside town, founded on its timber
industry, Winslow, located on Eagle Harbor, is a great place to
explore on foot, with charming shops. For those who want to
go further, and depending on the weather, bikes are available
to rent at Classic Cycle (www.classiccycleus.com) by the ferry
or call Bainbridge Island Taxi, 206-842-1021

Then there's the Bainbridge Island Historical Museum.
Housed in a little red schoolhouse, the museum traces the
island's history including the Japanese exclusion during
World War II, which features prominently in Guterson's book.
Pick up their brochure, *Walking Tour of Historic Winslow*.

215 Ericksen Avenue Northeast, 206-842-2773
www.bainbridgehistory.org

12:00 PM

Lunch at Café Nola
An eclectic bistro.
101 Winslow Way East, Bainbridge Island, 206-842-3822
www.cafenola.com
    Then wander the shops, including Eagle Harbor Books
(157 Winslow Way East), where they're happy to tell you about
regional authors. Walk down to the docks and marina. It's a
half-hour bike ride or a ten-minute cab ride to the Bainbridge
Island Japanese American Exclusion Memorial, around the bay
from the ferry landing. This is the site from which Japanese
Americans were removed from their homes and sent to Seattle
and then internment camps on March 30, 1942.
Located at Pritchard Park, 4192 Eagle Harbor Drive
www.bijac.org

2:30 PM

Return to Seattle

3:30 PM

Art on the waterfront
The Seattle Art Museum's Olympic Sculpture Park is a great
place to sit next to Alexander Calder's *The Eagle* and admire the
view of the Olympic Mountains and Puget Sound in front of
you and the Space Needle and downtown Seattle behind you.
Olympic Sculpture Park, 2901 Western Avenue,
206-654-3100
www.seattleartmuseum.org/visit/osp

5:30 PM

Happy hour/dinner at Chandler's on Lake Union

Take the trolley to this lovely spot on Lake Union, home of the houseboat in *Sleepless in Seattle*. In good weather you can sit outside and watch seaplanes land and take off and check out the yachts moored here while enjoying a substantial happy hour, for which Seattle bars and dining establishments are famous.
Chandler's Crabhouse
901 Fairview Avenue North, 206-223-2722
www.schwartzbros.com/chandlers-crabhouse

7:15 PM

Books onstage

Book-It Repertory Theater creates world-premiere adaptations of classic and contemporary literature for the stage, preserving the narrative text as it is spoken, not by a single "narrator" but as dialogue by the characters in the production. It has covered literary works ranging from *Great Expectations* to *A Confederacy of Dunces* to *The Art of Racing in the Rain*.
Seattle Center House, 305 Harrison Street, 206-216-0833
www.book-it.org

Day Three

9:00 AM

Breakfast at Bacco Cafe

86 Pine Street, Pike Place Market, 206-443-5443
www.baccocafe.net

11:00 AM

Beneath Old Seattle

In Seattle's oldest neighborhood, Pioneer Square, this very funny Underground Tour takes you through the subterranean

world of Seattle's first settlement, as it was before the city elevated this section of town in order to prevent flooding, with a blend of gold rush history.
608 First Avenue, 206-682-4646
www.undergroundtour.com

1:00 PM

The International District

This is the location of Jamie Ford's *The Hotel at the Corner of Bitter and Sweet*. Start with lunch at the Jade Garden (424 Seventh Avenue South, 206-622-8181); then stroll through the famous Uwajimaya Market (600 Fifth Avenue South, 206-624-6248, www.uwajimaya.com).

The Wing Luke Museum

The museum is in the heart of Seattle's vibrant Chinatown-International District and includes the hotel where countless immigrants first found a home, a meal, and refuge. They offer a Bitter and Sweet Tour based on the book.
719 South King Street, 206-623-5124
www.wingluke.org

Where to Stay

Inn at the Market

Great central location with a rooftop terrace that overlooks Puget Sound.
86 Pine Street, 206-443-3600
www.innatthemarket.com

Hotel Monaco

Centrally located, decorated in the Kimpton Hotel chain's eclectic style.
1101 Fourth Avenue, 206-621-1770
www.monaco-seattle.com

ADD-ONS

Elliot Bay Books

If you have extra time in Seattle, you'll want to stop by one of the city's venerable indie bookstores, Elliot Bay Book Company, in the city's trendy Capitol Hill neighborhood. Check out their events calendar, which is chock-full of author appearances.

1521 Tenth Avenue, 206-624-6600

www.elliottbaybook.com

Twilight in Forks

Put on a Team Edward or Team Jacob T-shirt and carry a little garlic for a visit to Forks, Washington, about three hours from Seattle. This area provides a perfect setting for the drama and romance of the undead, so it's no wonder that fans of Meyer's *Twilight* series of teen vampire novels are flocking to Forks, pumping "new blood" into tourism in and around Seattle. For those whose interest lies more with nature than the supernatural, there's plenty to do near Forks, including a hike into the Olympic National Forest.

17

San Francisco

IMMIGRANTS AND ICONOCLASTS, POETS AND SEEKERS

I see a vision of a great rucksack revolution thousands or even millions of young Americans wandering around with rucksacks, going up mountains to pray, making children laugh and old men glad, making young girls happy and old girls happier, all of 'em Zen Lunatics who go about writing poems that happen to appear in their heads for no reason and also by being kind and also by strange unexpected acts keep giving visions of eternal freedom to everybody and to all living creatures . . .
—**Jack Kerouac**, *Dharma Bums*

The elderly Chinese woman picks a huge bullfrog from a white plastic bucket and, dangling it by its back legs, examines it closely. Too small. She plops it back into the bucket, digs out another, approvingly slips it into a plastic bag, and starts the process over again. Around her, throngs of people vie for the best crabs, live turtles, fish, and produce, all identified with signs written in Chinese characters. The aroma of fish and exotic spices is everywhere. A cacophony of voices bounces around the market asking in various Chinese dialects for the best and the freshest items. If you're used to shopping in pristine supermarkets with everything tightly wrapped in Styrofoam and cellophane, perhaps with a little Muzak playing in the background, this grocery melee is enough to leave you dazed and amazed. And if you've read Amy Tan's novel *The Joy Luck Club*, about the lives of four Chinese immigrant women and their four American-born daughters, it will feel familiar, too. Tan describes a similar fictional locale, the Ping Yuen Fish Market, where "the front window displayed a tank crowded with doomed fish and turtles struggling to gain footing on the slimy green-tiled sides. A hand-written sign informed tourists, 'within this store, is all for food, not for pet.'"

It's a scene that has played out in San Francisco since the Chinese, along with thousands of others, began racing to the California gold fields in 1849. They proved to be more successful catering to the needs of miners by doing their laundry than they were at prospecting. Thousands more Chinese came later, imported to work on the Central Pacific Railroad. Since those days, Chinese people have settled in Chinatown, lived in cramped quarters, worked like crazy, and saved money to move to more affluent sections of the city and the suburbs. Chinatown remains a vibrant mecca for newcomers and the place where generations of Bay Area Chinese return for both cultural renewal and shopping opportunities, for everything from clothing to, well, bullfrogs.

As our group strolls though Chinatown's bustling streets, Linda Lee, who leads "All About Chinatown" tours, tells us stories about growing up here. "We used to sleep four to a bed," she says. "My aunt and my sisters slept across the top and I slept across the bottom with their feet on my back." We snake our way down streets that, but for the bilingual street signs, could easily be in Beijing or Shanghai. We arrive at the shop of an herbalist who carefully prepares medicinal concoctions of herbs, roots, plants, and various animal parts from a "prescription," a page full of Chinese characters written by a practitioner of Chinese medicine. Further down the street, we enter a store where the shelves are loaded with intricate miniature replicas of mansions, clothing, food, and many other items—all made of paper, to be burned on ancestors' graves. Like the characters in Amy Tan's novels, Chinese Americans balance modern life with ancient tradition, building their own version of the American dream while retaining at least a little of their Chinese heritage. Sometimes they merge the two cultures. We turn down an alley to visit a fortune cookie manufacturer, stamping out dough and rolling it up with a fortune inside. Though they're served in every Chinese restaurant in the United States, "they've never heard of fortune cookies in China," says Lee. "They're strictly American." But San Francisco is fertile soil for all sorts of cultural twists and transformations to take root. Anything goes, which is perhaps one reason Amy Tan told the *Washington Post*, "This city is like an opera—very dramatic, historical, tragic, funny, lyrical, beautiful, over-the-top."

The city has never lacked for drama. In the opera that is San Francisco, the city's unique landscape offers a stunning backdrop, with hills and ocean, fog and sun, and a shaky geology that keeps residents on the edge of their seats. The opening scene of San Francisco's libretto takes place on the Barbary Coast, the city's former port area, which was a lurid wasteland of gambling, prostitution, and opium dens—Las Vegas times fifty. An influx of rowdy sailors and traders regularly returned not just with exotic goods but also with stories of their adventures around the world. The chorus in San Francisco's opera has always been composed of "seekers," men and women who came from around the world seeking their fortune in the gold rush and immigrants searching for the American dream. Later the city's liberality and general "go to hell" attitude attracted seekers of a cultural and spiritual variety. Those grandmothers in the Chinese market would be shocked to be compared in any way to the beatniks, hippies, protesters, and flamboyant gay rights activists who made San Francisco famous. But they're part of a line of people who have come to San Francisco, added their own imprint on its culture, and ultimately influenced the rest of the country. They all made San Francisco a place in which to expand beyond boundaries, push limits, and change perceptions.

That iconoclastic spirit made the city fertile ground for writers. Mark Twain, Robert Louis Stevenson, and Bret Harte made San Francisco their home for a while. Jack London, who grew up across the bay in Oakland, was the prototype of the footloose adventurer/author who depicted life from the point of view of the workingman. London drew upon his own adventures and experiences for his novels *White Fang*, *The Call of the Wild*, *The Sea Wolf*, and *Martin Eden*. Like his character Martin Eden, London grew up poor, was largely self-educated, and worked his way up in the literary world after working as a seaman. London was the literary forefather of the Beat generation (particularly Jack Kerouac) that followed him in the 1950s.

The Beats, or "beatniks" as they came to be known, came together in North Beach, the Italian community that became San Francisco's center of bohemian culture and where the city's counterculture reputation took root. The Beats were a fundamental catalyst for the beginning of the post–World War II avant-garde movement in literature and the arts. There are many explanations for the term "beat," but it basically meant that they felt beaten down and wearied by the forms and conventions in the world, and they consequently turned to a different literary style that reduced writing to the essentials. In both their creative and their personal lives, they challenged the materialism and conformity of postwar America, the buttoned-down "squares" of the Eisenhower era. These bad boys and girls wore jeans, sandals, sweat shirts, and, yes, berets. They took drugs, drank to excess, read poetry, listened to jazz, and embarked on spiritual quests investigating Eastern religions. They challenged obscenity laws and rules about morality. In a word, they *rebelled*. In the Beat Museum, a North Beach shrine to these iconoclasts, a sign sums it up: WHAT ELVIS WAS TO MUSIC, WHAT JAMES DEAN AND MARLON BRANDO WERE TO FILM, THE BEAT GENERATION WAS TO LITERATURE.

Jack Kerouac shone like a fire in that rebellious crowd. Born in Massachusetts, Kerouac traveled the county "on the road" before coming to San Francisco, where his New York friends had migrated. In 1957, the story of Kerouac's travels with his friend Neal Cassidy (known as Dean Moriarty in the book) were published in *On the Road*, which instantly topped the bestseller list. Kerouac wrote with a whole new style, using jazz-like rhythms and spontaneous, unstructured composition to convey the immediacy of experience. Many critics didn't know what to make of it. Kerouac was either a genius or a literary Neanderthal whose prose Truman Capote called "not writing, but typewriting." In her 1957 review of *On the Road* in the *Atlantic*, critic Phoebe-Lou Adams wrote that the book contained so much "dope, liquor, girls, jazz, and fast cars, in that order" that it was hard to keep track of the larger narrative of the story "behind all the scuttling about." Nevertheless, she went on, "the novel contains a great deal of excellent writing. Mr. Kerouac has a distinctive style, part severe simplicity, part hep-cat jargon, part baroque fireworks. He uses each of these elements with a sure touch, works innumerable combinations and contrasts with them, and never slackens the speed of his narrative, which proceeds, like Dean at the wheel, at a steady hundred and ten miles an hour."

Following closely in the Beats' footprints were San Francisco's hippies, who made Haight-Ashbury their own in the 1960s. Acid, free love, and psychedelic rock aren't among the traditional ingredients of great literature, but Tom Wolfe's *The Electric Kool-Aid Acid Test* neatly depicts an era that shook American culture to its bedrock foundation. By the late 1960s, another group that had found acceptance in San Francisco, the gay community, began to shake things up. They helped launch the gay rights movement that galvanized and swept the county. The reporting of Randy Shilts in *And the Band Played On: Politics, People, and the AIDS Epidemic* and *The Mayor of Castro Street: The Life and Times of Harvey Milk* and Armistead Maupin's *Tales of the City* series brought the stories of gay people to readers far beyond San Francisco.

Visit San Francisco today and you'll discover that the landmarks left by these cultural iconoclasts and free thinkers aren't hard to find. Go to North Beach and spend some time in the Vesuvio Cafe or the City Lights Bookstore, made famous by the Beats and Allen Ginsberg's 1955 poem, *Howl*, and the famous obscenity trial that followed its publication. Hit the Beat Museum and watch a segment of *The Steve Allen Show* from 1959 in which Kerouac reads from *On the Road* while Allen punctuates his words with jazz piano. It's pure poetry.

Walk the streets of North Beach and Chinatown or ride a bike in the Marina District and over the Golden Gate Bridge. No matter where you go, the beat of the city is inescapable. Kerouac describes it in *Desolation Angels*:

> It's seeing the rooftops of Frisco that makes you excited and believe, the big downtown hulk of buildings, Standard Oil's flying red horse, Montgomery Street highbuildings, Hotel St. Francis, the hills, magic Telegraph with her Coit-top, magic Russian, magic Nob, and magic Mission beyond with the cross of all sorrows I'd seen long ago in a purple sunset with Cody on a little railroad bridge—San Francisco, North Beach, Chinatown, Market Street, the bars, the Bay-Oom, the Bell Hotel, the wine, the alleys, the poorboys, Third Street, poets, painters, Buddhists, bums, junkies, girls, millionaires, MGs, the whole fabulous movie of San Francisco seen from the bus or train on the Bridge coming in, the tug at your heart like New York.

Even if you're not a poet or a seeker, it's easy to get swept up in the drama and the beauty of the City by the Bay.

Armistead Maupin's Tales Continue

≈ Since the 1970s, Armistead Maupin has become *the* author associated with San Francisco, much the way Charles Dickens is associated with London. As with Dickens's work, readers first became acquainted with Maupin's tales in serial installments in newspapers. First a Marin County paper and later the *San Francisco Chronicle* introduced readers to "Tales of the City" (subsequently the title of the first book and the series by the same name) and its quirky and sometimes bizarre collection of transsexual, straight, and gay characters who reside at 28 Barbary Lane. The groundbreaking stories incorporated the politics of the era but also focused on universal themes of love and longing that have made the "Tales" endure over the course of the six *Tales of the City* books and several additional books with the same characters. The stories have been made into a three-part miniseries and a musical.

You'd never guess that Maupin, who in his writing and his personal life has been an outspoken advocate for gay rights, was once a campus conservative. He grew up in North Carolina and later served as a naval officer in the Mediterranean and with the River Patrol Force in Vietnam. He launched his career in journalism in North Carolina and later moved to join the San Francisco bureau of the Associated Press. Though Maupin recently announced that he and his husband, Christopher Turner, were planning to move to Santa Fe, there are still new tales on the horizon. Look for *The Days of Anna Madrigal*, which continues the saga of one of the main characters.

You can find a map of the San Francisco sites in his books on his website, www.armisteadmaupin.com/TalesMap.html.

SAN FRANCISCO READING

FICTION

San Francisco's diversity, eccentric characters, and geographic scenery have provided a backdrop for many works of fiction and fascinating nonfiction.

THE CLASSICS

Dashiell Hammett, *The Maltese Falcon*. One of the first and finest of noir crime fiction.

Jack Kerouac, *Dharma Bums, San Francisco Blues, Desolation Angels*, and his masterpiece *On the Road*. All show the bohemian life of the "king of the beats." See also Ann Charters, ed., *Kerouac: A Biography, The Portable Beat Reader*, and many other works by this noted scholar of the Beats; Bill Morgan and Lawrence Ferlinghetti, *The Beat Generation in San Francisco: A Literary Tour*; Lawrence Ferlinghetti, *Starting from San Francisco*; and Steven Watson, *The Birth of the Beat Generation: Visionaries, Rebels and Hipsters, 1944–1960*.

Jack London, *Martin Eden*, a story of a sailor who educates himself in order to win the heart of a wealthy, educated woman; *John Barleycorn*, London's mostly humorous autobiographical account of his struggles with alcohol; and *Tales of the Fish Patrol*, London's adventure stories about his time as both an oyster pirate and someone who chased the oyster pirates.

Armistead Maupin, *Tales of the City* series, *Mary Ann in Autumn, Significant Others*, and more novels that weave together the lives of the diverse crowd of characters in a San Francisco neighborhood.

John Miller, ed., *San Francisco Stories: Great Writers on the City*. An anthology of the classics.

Frank Norris, *McTeague: A Story of San Francisco*. About poverty, avarice, and murder in 1890s San Francisco.

William Saroyan, *The Time of Your Life*. A classic play set in a run-down San Francisco bar.

Amy Tan, *The Joy Luck Club*, *The Bonesetter's Daughter*, *The Kitchen God's Wife*, and others. Books that deal with the experiences of Chinese American women.

OTHER SAN FRANCISCO FICTION

Isabel Allende, *Daughter of Fortune*. A young Chilean woman pursues her love to the gold fields of California.

Gwen Bristow, *Calico Palace*. A novel of the gold rush and how it transformed San Francisco.

Philip K. Dick, *Do Androids Dream of Electric Sheep?* Science fiction set in a post–world war Bay Area; the basis for the movie *Blade Runner*.

James Fadiman, *The Other Side of Haight*. A novel about the hippie scene during the "summer of love."

Howard Fast, *The Immigrants* and *Second Generation*. Both are family sagas about the people who settled California.

Kathryn Forbes, *Mama's Bank Account*. About a Norwegian family living in San Francisco; the basis for the movie *I Remember Mama*.

Glen David Gold, *Carter Beats the Devil*. Fiction based on real-life stage magician Charles Carter, set in the 1920s.

Maria Hong, *Growing Up Asian American*. An anthology of stories, essays, and excerpts from prominent writers.

Gus Lee, *China Boy*. An autobiographical novel about assimilating in San Francisco in the 1950s.

JoAnn Levy, *Daughter of Joy: A Novel of Gold Rush California*. The gold rush through the eyes of a Chinese woman.

Christopher Moore, *Bite Me: A Love Story*, *Bloodsucking Fiends: A Love Story*, and others. Novels about the San Francisco vampire scene.

Fae Ng, *Bone*. Two generations of a family in contemporary Chinatown.

Julie Otsuka, *The Buddha in the Attic.* About a group of young Japanese women brought to San Francisco as "picture brides" in the 1920s. A finalist for the National Book Award.

Michelle Richmond, *The Year of Fog.* A family's struggle after a child disappears into the San Francisco fog.

Vikram Seth, *The Golden Gate.* A novel in verse about a group of San Francisco yuppies.

Karen Tei Yamashita, *I Hotel.* Stories of civil rights struggles in Chinatown.

NONFICTION

Herbert Asbury, *The Barbary Coast: An Informal History of the San Francisco Underworld.* A look at San Francisco's post–gold rush underworld, similar to Asbury's *Gangs of New York.*

H. W. Brands, *The Age of Gold: The California Gold Rush and the New American Dream.* The gold rush seen through the stories of men like Leland Stanford, Levi Strauss, and less famous forty-niners.

Herb Caen, *Herb Caen's San Francisco: 1976–1991.* A view of the city from the beloved San Francisco newspaper columnist.

Dave Eggers, *A Heartbreaking Work of Staggering Genius.* Eggers's memoir of raising his younger brother in San Francisco.

Shirley Fong-Torres, *San Francisco Chinatown: A Walking Tour.* A peek inside the nooks and crannies often overlooked by tourists; includes recipes.

Maxine Hong Kingston, *The Woman Warrior.* A mystical memoir of childhood in San Francisco.

Randy Shilts, *And the Band Played On: Politics, People, and the AIDs Epidemic* and *The Mayor of Castro Street: The Life and Times of Harvey Milk.* Two classics that portray critical events in San Francisco gay culture.

Rebecca Solnit, *Infinite City: A San Francisco Atlas.* Maps of the city as seen through the eyes of artists, writers, and cartographers.

W. A. Swanberg, *Citizen Hearst.* A biography of the newspaper magnate.

David Talbot, *Season of the Witch.* A look at the city's decline and rebirth from 1967 to 1982.

Simon Winchester, *A Crack in the Edge of the World: America and the Great California Earthquake of 1906.* About the quake, the geological forces that caused it, and the fire afterward.

Tom Wolfe, *The Electric Kool-Aid Acid Test.* A classic look at the hippie era with Ken Kesey's band of Merry Pranksters.

Jade Snow Wong, *Fifth Chinese Daughter.* A memoir of growing up in Chinatown.

SAN FRANCISCO ITINERARY

This itinerary takes you to some of San Francisco's most picturesque areas and neighborhoods, which have been hubs for the city's immigrants, bohemians, and iconoclasts.

Day One

2:00 PM

A walk on the Barbary Coast

Bronze medallions mark the course through San Francisco's most illustrious, famous, and sometimes infamous, neighborhoods. You can download the tour at www.barbarycoasttrail.org/. Though now it's full of fancy office buildings, the Embarcadero, the Ferry Building, restaurants and retailers, this was once a favorite area for shanghaiing sailors. Be sure to go inside the Ferry Building for a snack. Eat it outside, where you have a view of the bay. The Ferry Building is also a great place to pick up breakfast.

Embarcadero at Market Street
www.ferrybuildingmarketplace.com

7:30 PM

Dinner at Palio D'Asti
Italian food in a beautiful setting.
640 Sacramento Street, 415-395-9800
www.paliodasti.com

9:30 PM

Dessert and jazz at John's Grill
One of the first restaurants to open after the Great Fire and
one of the locations featured in Dashiell Hammett's *The
Maltese Falcon*.
63 Ellis Street, 415-986-3274
www.johnsgrill.com

Day Two

8:30 AM

Breakfast near Union Square
There are plenty of coffee shops and small cafés in the Union
Square area, but if you're in the mood for something more
substantial, Sears Fine Foods is a San Francisco institution.
This restaurant has an old-time mom-and-pop feel and is
known for its "world famous" Swedish pancakes. Bear in mind
that you'll be eating a fantastic Chinese lunch at noon.
Sears Fine Foods
439 Powell Street, 415-986-0700
www.searsfinefood.com

10:00 AM

Dim sum and then some
A visit to Chinatown with former resident Linda Lee. You'll
see things you'd never see on your own.
All About Chinatown Tours
415-982-8839

www.allaboutchinatown.com
www.chinatownla.com/calendar.php?eventId=366

12:00 PM

Stick with your tour for a dim sum lunch in Chinatown

1:30 PM

North Beach and the Beats: The Beat Museum
Learn about the ways in which Jack Kerouac, Allen Ginsberg, and other "Beats" influenced literature and life, leading to the emergence of the counterculture of the 1960s.
540 Broadway, 1-800-KEROUAC (537-6822)
www.kerouac.com

2:30 PM

City Lights Bookstore
Founded in 1953 by poet Lawrence Ferlinghetti and Peter D. Martin, the bookstore was ground zero for the Beats and still offers a fabulous selection of all sorts of books.
261 Columbus Avenue at Broadway, 415-362-8193
www.citylights.com

3:00 PM

Taste of the neighborhood
Look down Jack Kerouac Alley, next to City Lights, to see if there's an "Art in the Alley" event with merchandise from local artists. Pop in at Vesuvio Cafe just across the alley from City Lights for a look at the beat hot spot (that still attracts a colorful crowd of patrons) and have a drink.
255 Columbus Avenue
www.vesuvio.com

OR

Coffee at Caffe Puccini

411 Columbus Avenue, 415-989-7033

Artfully presented coffee drinks, cannoli, and biscotti.

Then walk up to Washington Square, a park that is not a square in the heart of North Beach.

6:00 PM

Dinner at Lemongrass Thai Cuisine

2348 Polk Street, 415-929-1183

www.lemongrasssf.com

8:00 PM

An evening of arts

Depending on the time of year, choose from the following:

San Francisco Ballet

War Memorial Opera House

301 Van Ness Avenue, 415-861-5600

www.sfballet.org

American Conservatory Theater

415 Geary Street, 415.749.2228

www.act-sf.org

Or, if the night is clear, simply opt for a drink with a view of the city from Nob Hill at the . . .

Top of the Mark

Intercontinental Mark Hopkins

One Nob Hill, Nineteenth Floor, 415-616-6940

www.intercontinentalmarkhopkins.com/top_of_the_mark

Day Three

9:00 AM

Breakfast at the café at Boudin Bakery at Fisherman's Wharf

You can pick up goodies here if you want to have a picnic in the park in Sausalito.

160 Jefferson Street, 415-928-1849, ext. 3

www.boudinbakery.com/at-the-wharf

10:00 AM

The Golden Gate to Sausalito

Rent bikes from Blazing Saddles

721 Beach Street, 415-202-8888

www.blazingsaddles.com/san-francisco.aspx

Ride along the waterfront, then across the Golden Gate Bridge. Once you're across, it's an easy downhill ride into the charming town of Sausalito. Then ride back on the ferry. (You can get tickets at Blazing Saddles.) On your trips, you'll see great views of San Francisco, the Marin Headlands where Jack Kerouac roamed with his friends in *Dharma Bums*, and the route from which Jack London's character Humphrey van Weyden was taken captive in *Sea Wolf*. Not inclined to bike? You can take the ferry both ways.

Where to Stay

Kensington Park Hotel

450 Post Street, 415-788-6400

www.kensingtonparkhotel.com

Hotel Monaco

501 Geary Street, 415-292-0100

www.monaco-sf.com

18

Santa Monica

SUN AND SHADOW

There was a desert wind blowing that night. It was one of those hot dry Santa Anas that come down through the mountain passes and curl your hair and make your nerves jump and your skin itch. On nights like that every booze party ends in a fight. Meek little wives feel the edge of the carving knife and study their husbands' necks.
> **—Raymond Chandler,** *Red Wind*

Passages like that make *my* nerves jump and my skin itch. I don't have the carving knife out yet, but my husband looks as worried as a musician on the *Titanic*. I've never been a huge fan of crime fiction, but I've found I can't resist Raymond Chandler, the king of the detective novel, who could turn a phrase the way a stubble-jowled mechanic cranks his monkey wrench around a #12 hex nut.

In these days of political correctness, Chandler's prose is jarring, especially if you're a person of color or a woman. He depicts African Americans condescendingly and with strange slang terms. Chandler's women are either leggy blond femmes fatales or boozy chain-smokers with faces like ten miles of bad road. Either way, these dames are neither trustworthy nor intelligent. And, yes, he populates the pages with words like dame, copper, rat, and joint that seem archaic now. Yet somehow his misogynistic prose fits the dark outlook of his stories. Sit down with one of his classics, *Farewell, My Lovely* or *The Long Goodbye*, for example, and you'll soon find yourself on the hunt for "Chandlerisms" like "as conspicuous as a tarantula on a slice of angel food." His dialogue and similes are so crazy and over the top that I want to write them down and bring them up in my own conversation. Beyond the similes, you start to recognize in Chandler's work all of the hallmarks of "hard-boiled" detective fiction—the shadowy scenery, the sleazy criminals, and Phillip Marlowe, the epitome of the tough and surprisingly idealistic private eye. The dialogue, the setting, and the characters are all as familiar as the nose on a washed-up boxer's ugly mug, but it was Chandler who created them and, in the process, pioneered a uniquely American genre and style.

Some of his impact came as a screenwriter. Chandler adapted James M. Cain's *Double Indemnity* for the movie and wrote the original screenplay for *The Blue Dahlia*. And it was through films based on his books such as *The Big Sleep* that his books gained huge popularity. Bogie and Bacall brought his hard-boiled characters to life on the big screen, and his stories have been the subject of parody by everyone from Woody Allen to Steve Martin to Garrison Keillor. As Paul Auster, a modern crime writer, says, "Raymond Chandler invented a new way of talking about America, and America has never looked the same to us since."

But Chandler was much more than a five-and-dime gumshoe novelist. He believed that great writing was the key to the crime fiction genre's success, and he lambasted anyone who sought, in his view, to water it down. In a famous essay, "The Simple Art of Murder," Chandler lamented the huge number of detective novels that were published no matter how poor the quality. "Even Einstein," he said, "couldn't get very far if three hundred treatises of the higher physics were published every year." He reserved special scorn for English crime novelists in the Agatha Christie mold, whose detectives "all did the same old futzing around with timetables and bits of charred paper and who trampled the jolly old flowering arbutus under the library window." He said, "The English may not always be the best writers in the world, but they are incomparably the best dull writers." Chandler credited Dashiell Hammett, author of *The Maltese Falcon*, with changing all that. He says, "Hammett took murder out of the Venetian vase and dropped it into the alley; it doesn't have to stay there forever, but it was a good idea to begin by getting as far as possible from Emily Post's idea of how a well-bred debutante gnaws a chicken wing." Hammett, wrote Chandler, "gave murder back to the kind of people that commit it for reasons, not just to provide a corpse; and with the means at hand, not with hand-wrought dueling pistols, curare and tropical fish."

You won't find any perky old ladies or flowering arbutus in Chandler's stories. Realism was his touchstone, and despite the sunny Los Angeles setting where he worked, his worldview is one of overwhelming cynicism.

The realist in murder writes of a world in which gangsters can rule nations and almost rule cities, in which hotels and apartment houses and celebrated restaurants are owned by men who made their money out of brothels, in which a screen star can be the fingerman for a mob, and the nice man down the hall is a boss of the numbers racket; a world where a judge with a cellar full of bootleg liquor can send a man to jail for having a pint in his pocket, where the mayor of your town may have condoned murder as an instrument of money making, where no man can walk down a dark street in safety because law and order are things we talk about but refrain from practicing. . . . It is not a very fragrant world, but it is the world you live in.

Living in Los Angeles of the 1930s and 1940s no doubt shaped his attitudes and prose. In those years, L.A. was the fastest-growing city in the world, a sunny Eden, the City of Angels. But, with such an influx of people and money, it was also an unruly frontier, with organized crime, greed, and celebrity scandals, a city of sunlight with a very dark soul. And in Santa Monica, the beachfront town on the western edge of Los Angeles where he lived for a time, and which appears as Bay City in his books, the daily papers had plenty of material from which Chandler could draw his stories.

In Chandler's day, Santa Monica was the embarkation point for an infamous fleet of gambling ships anchored just far enough offshore to be beyond the jurisdiction of California state law. Thus in *Farewell, My Lovely*, for example, Chandler depicted Bay City as a dingy and corrupt little beach town with gambling ships offshore and police corruption on shore, where there were "lots of churches and almost as many bars." In one of his personal letters, he comments about the policemen from Santa Monica who went along on a raid with a couple of DAs, "The cops went along with the natural reluctance of good cops to enforce the law against a paying customer." He was particularly fascinated with the story of a Santa Monica doctor who was tried in 1940 for the murder of his wife five years after she had supposedly committed suicide, and he eventually used that story in *The Lady in the Lake*.

Chandler offers a light of redemption in the form of his persistent hero, Marlowe, who repeatedly picks himself up after being bludgeoned, blackjacked, and constantly clobbered for practically no pay at all. Chandler says of his ideal fictional detective, "He is the avenging justice, the bringer of order out of chaos. . . . His moral and intellectual force is that he gets nothing but his fee, for which he will if he can protect the innocent, guard the help-less, and destroy the wicked, and the fact that he must do this while earning a meager living in a corrupt world is what makes him stand out." You just have to love a big lug like that. Chandler concluded, "If there were enough like him, I think the world would be a very safe place to live in, and yet not too dull to be worth living in."

Chandler's unmistakable style lives on through new genera-tions of Los Angeles crime novel writers, including Ross MacDon-ald, Michael Connelly, and Walter Mosley, who have followed in his path and made Los Angeles the capitol of crime fiction.

Like so many cities that are symbolized, satirized, and scru-tinized in American literature, the real L.A. area moved on. The gambling ships of *Farewell, My Lovely* are gone now, ultimately banished as a public nuisance, and so are many of the old Santa Monica buildings of Chandler's era. The "mean streets" have been replaced by shopping thoroughfares such as Montana Avenue and the Third Street Promenade. Yet enough of the old Bay City remains today to get your imagination moving, including the famous Santa Monica Pier and Main Street's deco-era city hall, the scene of many of Marlowe's comings and goings. There's still the harbor and "beyond it the huge emptiness of the Pacific, purple-gray" that trudges "into shore like a scrubwoman going home."

Visit Santa Monica and let your imagination soar into the noir. You never know what you might find, because when the Santa Ana winds blow, anything can happen.

"G" Is for Grafton

Move over, you hard-boiled tough guys. Sue Grafton carries on the detective novel tradition with a female private eye, Kinsey Millhone, a tough loner and a wisecracking cynic, like the male PIs who have preceded her. Kinsey is the heroine of Grafton's famous alphabet series, *A Is for Alibi* on down to *V Is for Vengeance*, set in the fictional Santa Theresa, which, like Santa Barbara, where the author lives, is located south of Los Angeles. Grafton says that Kinsey is much like herself, "only younger, smarter, and thinner."

Like so many other Southern California writers, Sue Grafton spent time writing screenplays. She started the alphabet series in 1982, and critics say her books get better with each new installment in the series. While two things—the heroine and an unsolved murder—remain constant in each book, Grafton says she works hard to make each one very different. Each installment weaves in other issues, such as false memory syndrome, elder abuse, identity theft, and other complexities. So crime fans await the crimes that will come unleashed in *W, X, Y,* and *Z*.

SANTA MONICA/LOS ANGELES READING

CRIME

James Cain, *Mildred Pierce,* about a woman's rise to success during the Depression and her unreasonable devotion to her horrible daughter; *Double Indemnity,* in which a femme fatale persuades a small-time insurance salesman to get rid of her husband; and *The Postman Always Rings Twice,* about a drifter and a waitress who have an affair and plot to kill her husband.

Raymond Chandler, *The Big Sleep, The Lady in the Lake, Farewell, My Lovely,* and *The Long Goodbye.* Chandler's crime classics depict the classic noir image of L.A. and Santa Monica. See also Tom Hiney's *Raymond Chandler,* a biography of the famous crime writer, and the all-things-Chandler website, www.shamustown.com.

Michael Connelly, the series including *The Lincoln Lawyer* and *The Brass Verdict* feature defense attorney Mickey Haller.

Connelly's other series includes *The Overlook*, *The Black Echo*, and *The Narrows* and features the detective Harry Bosch.

James Ellroy, *L.A. Confidential*, includes L.A. cops, crooks, and a gangland heroine; and *My Dark Places: An L.A. Crime Memoir*, about Elroy returning to the scene of his mother's murder.

Denise Hamilton, ed., *Los Angeles Noir 2: The Classics*. An anthology of great stories of love, lust, and murder in the City of Angels.

Susan Kandel, *I Dreamed I Married Perry Mason*. A cross between chick lit and crime fiction.

Ross MacDonald, *The Doomsters* and *The Moving Target*. Stories with private eye Lew Archer.

Walter Mosley, *Devil in a Blue Dress*, *A Red Death*, *White Butterfly*, and many other Mosley works feature the private eye Easy Rawlins.

Joseph Wambaugh, *The Choirboys*, a novel about L.A. police in the 1970s, and *The Onion Field*, the true story of two L.A. cops who were murdered in 1963.

OTHER FICTION

Michael J. Atwood, *HiStory of Santa Monica*. Short stories set in Santa Monica.

T. C. Boyle, *The Tortilla Curtain*. The lives of an L.A. couple and illegal immigrants collide.

Charles Bukowski, *Post Office*, *The Women: A Novel*, and many others. A writer, poet, and essayist, Bukowski's work emphasizes ordinary lives of poor Americans.

Bebe Moore Campbell, *Brothers and Sisters*. A black woman's struggle for success in the banking world, set against the backdrop of L.A. after the Rodney King verdict.

Sandra Tsing Loh, *If You Lived Here, You'd Be Home by Now* and *Depth Takes a Holiday: Essays from Lesser Los Angeles*. A novel and a book of essays, respectively, that focus on modern L.A. culture.

Allison Lurie, *The Nowhere City.* About 1960s Los Angeles and the differences between East and West Coast culture.

Horace McCoy, *They Shoot Horses, Don't They?* A dance marathon during the Depression is a metaphor for the loss of the American dream. Takes place on the Santa Monica Pier.

Upton Sinclair, *Oil!,* The fictional story of big oil in California and the Teapot Dome scandal.

Helen Maria Viramontes, *Their Dogs Came with Them.* East L.A. Latino life in the 1960s.

Nathaniel West, *The Day of the Locust.* A classic novel of desperate people on the fringes of the movie industry.

NONFICTION

Colleen Dunn Bates, ed., *Hometown Santa Monica: The Bay Cities Book.* A guide to the city.

John Buntin, *L.A. Noir: The Struggle for the Soul of America's Most Seductive City.* A true story of gangsters and cops, vice, and movie stars.

Mark C. Carnes, *Past Imperfect: History According to the Movies.* A look at the historical accuracy of classic films.

Marion Davies, *The Times We Had: Life with William Randolph Hearst.* By the actress who was Hearst's longtime girlfriend.

Margaret Leslie Davis, *Rivers in the Desert: William Mulholland and the Inventing of Los Angeles.* How water engineer Mulholland masterminded the water supply that allowed the development of Los Angeles.

Joan Didion, *Slouching Towards Bethlehem* and *The White Album.* Essays on American (and California) life from a pioneer of "new journalism."

James D. Houston, *Californians; Searching for the Golden State.* Essays about the search for the California dream.

Richard Rayner, *A Bright and Guilty Place: Murder; Corruption, and L.A.'s Scandalous Coming of Age.* Los Angeles in the 1920s and 1930s.

Marc Reisner, *Cadillac Desert: The American West and Its Disappearing Water.* The economics, politics, and ecology of water in California.

Peter Theroux, *Translating LA: A Tour of the Rainbow City.* A look at the city's quirky characters.

GETTY MUSEUM PREPARATION

Jason Felch and Ralph Frammolino, *Chasing Aphrodite: The Hunt for Looted Antiquities at the World's Richest Museum.* An investigation of the museum's dealing in illegal antiquities from two *Los Angeles Times* reporters.

J. Paul Getty, *As I See It: The Autobiography of J. Paul Getty.* Several instances in Getty's life would be perfect for a Chandler novel.

SANTA MONICA ITINERARY

This trip focuses mainly on Santa Monica, on the west side of Los Angeles, which is very walkable, with shops, restaurants, and the beach at your fingertips. You'll see some of the places in Chandler's novels, but all isn't noir in greater L.A. You'll enjoy the sunny side at the beach and the Pier, and cap it off with a visit to the fabulous Getty Museum.

Day One

2:00 PM

Hit the beach

7:30 PM

Dinner at Stella Rossa Pizza Bar
2000 Main Street, 310-396-9250
stellarossapizzabar.com

9:30 PM

Santa Monica old and new

Stroll Third Street Promenade for window shopping (many stores are open until 10:00 or 11:00 PM on Friday and Saturday nights), street entertainers, and people watching, then go over to the waterfront and Santa Monica Pier. (Check the schedule for free concerts on the pier in summer.)
www.santamonicapier.org
www.downtownsm.com

Day Two

10:00 AM

A look back at the Santa Monica of Chandler's day with a walking tour

Docent-guided walking tours occur at 10:00 AM every Saturday morning. Reservations are suggested. Self-guided tour booklets providing a map and detailed information on the city's history and the historic buildings featured on the tour are available for three dollars at the Visitors Center, 1920 Main Street, and the Hostelling International Travel Store, 1434 Second Street.
www.smconservancy.org/walking_tour.shtml

Combine the walking tour with a stop at the . . .

Santa Monica History Museum

1350 Seventh Street, 310-395-2290
www.santamonicahistory.org

A tour company called Esotouric also occasionally offers tours relating to true crime and literary L.A. Check their website for their schedule.
www.esotouric.com/chandlerpage

12:30 PM

Beach 'n' biking

Pick up goodies for a picnic at Whole Foods.
2201 Wilshire Boulevard, 310-315-0662
wholefoodsmarket.com/stores/santamonica

With locations up and down the beach, Perry's Café and Rentals is a good place to rent bikes. They offer bike tours, too. You'll want to head up toward Malibu and picnic at Will Rogers State Beach. Along the way, check out the Annenberg Community Beach House and the guest house that was part of the actress Marion Davies's beach estate. Turn around and continue down to Venice Beach.
2600 Ocean Front Walk, 310-584-9306
www.perryscafe.com

4:00 PM

Shopping on Montana Avenue, home to high-end boutiques and restaurants

5:00 PM

Watch the sunset at the Penthouse at the Huntley Hotel

Eighteen stories up, this lounge offers a stunning view of the Los Angeles coastline and a fantastic happy hour. Make dinner out of it.
1111 Second Street, 310-394-5454
www.thehuntleyhotel.com

8:00 PM

Santa Monica Playhouse

Take in a show at Santa Monica's famous repertory theater.
1211 Fourth Street, 310-394-9779
www.santamonicaplayhouse.com

Day Three

10:00 AM

The Getty Center

Spend the morning at the Getty Museum, a must-see on your visit to L.A. You'll pass through some great neighborhoods on the way, including Westwood, the UCLA campus, and Bel Air. The museum is a work of art in itself and took thirteen years to build. It's perched on a mountaintop and commands a fabulous view of Los Angeles, downtown, and the ocean. The architecture is amazing, and so are the grounds. Grab lunch at the café and eat outside on the terrace.

1200 Getty Center Drive, Los Angeles, 310-440-7300
www.getty.edu

Where to Stay

The Ambrose

A little far from the beach, but that makes this luxurious spot more affordable.

1255 Twentieth Street, 310-315-1555
www.ambrosehotel.com

The Georgian Hotel

A 1930s deco gem on the beachfront, straight out of Raymond Chandler's era.

1415 Ocean Avenue, 800-538-8147
www.georgianhotel.com

APPENDIX

BOOK FESTIVALS ACROSS THE COUNTRY

Book festivals offer readers and authors from around the world a chance to come together over their favorite topic: books. Here is a list of some of the most exciting book festivals across the United States.

MARCH

Tennessee Williams/New Orleans Literary Festival
www.tennesseewilliams.net
New Orleans, Louisiana

Tucson Festival of Books
http://tucsonfestivalofbooks.org
Tucson, Arizona

APRIL

Los Angeles Times Festival of Books
http://events.latimes.com/festivalofbooks
Los Angeles, California

JUNE

Chicago Tribune Printers Row Lit Fest
www.chicagotribune.com/entertainment/books
/printersrowlitfest
Chicago, Illinois

SEPTEMBER

Decatur Book Festival
www.decaturbookfestival.com
Decatur, Georgia

Brooklyn Book Festival
www.brooklynbookfestival.org
Brooklyn, New York

Library of Congress National Book Festival
www.loc.gov/bookfest
Washington, DC

OCTOBER

Boston Book Festival
www.bostonbookfest.org
Boston, Massachusetts

Southern Festival of Books
www.humanitiestennessee.org/programs/southern-festival
-books-celebration-written-word
Nashville, Tennessee

Twin Cities Book Festival
www.raintaxi.com/bookfest
Minneapolis, Minnesota

Texas Book Festival
www.texasbookfestival.org
Austin, Texas

NOVEMBER

Wisconsin Book Festival
www.wisconsinbookfestival.org
Madison, Wisconsin

Miami Book Fair International
www.miamibookfair.com
Miami, Florida

JUST ONE LOVE: AUTHOR SOCIETIES

If you have a passion for a particular author or your group would like to focus on reading the works of one author and base a trip around his or her work, there are plenty of festivals and societies devoted to famous writers. These organizations are like high-brow fan clubs. They have conferences and other events, newsletters, and offer information on places to visit that are related to the author. They're also helpful if your book group would simply like biographical information or articles of literary criticism on the author in conjunction with reading one of his or her books, all in one website. Here are a few examples:

Jane Austen Society of North America
www.jasna.org
This site has links to local Jane Austen groups. Many celebrate her birthday on December 16.

The Brontë Parsonage Museum & Brontë Society
www.bronte.org.uk
This site will make you want to visit the museum.

The Dickens Fellowship
www.dickensfellowship.org
A worldwide society with local branches, such as the Dickens Fellowship of New York and those of many other US cities.

The William Faulkner Society

www.faulknersociety.com

This group "fosters the study of Faulkner" and holds a Faulkner and Yoknapatawpha Conference in Oxford, Mississippi.

F. Scott Fitzgerald Society

www.fscottfitzgeraldsociety.org

In addition to academic activities, the society holds conferences and lectures across the country.

Ernest Hemingway Society

www.hemingwaysociety.org

This organization's website has helpful links to places associated with Hemingway.

The Michigan Hemingway Society

www.michiganhemingwaysociety.org

The Michigan Hemingway Society is particularly active. (This is the land of his Nick Adams stories.)

Dorothy Parker Society

www.dorothyparker.com

The society's annual Parkerfest celebrates all things Dorothy, with walking tours and recently a birthday party at a New York distillery that named a gin in her honor.

National Steinbeck Center

www.steinbeck.org/pages/steinbeck-festival--2

They hold the Steinbeck Festival every year in Salinas, California, to study and celebrate the works of John Steinbeck.

CONNECTING TO FELLOW READERS

If you'd like to connect with other people over reading, there's no better way to do it than through a book club. Organize your own, or join or create a chapter of an established reading group. If you or your book club would like to meet other kindered spirits or engage in projects to foster reading in your community, there are many groups out there waiting to hear from you.

BookCrossing

www.bookcrossing.com

Got too many books? Pass them on. This site allows you to register the books you want to pass on. You put a label in each book with a BookCrossing code and then release it in a variety of ways. You can pass it on to someone you know or send it to a fellow BookCrosser who is looking for that book. You can also take the book(s) to a designated "Crossing Site."

Little Free Library

www.littlefreelibrary.org

This organization prompts book lovers to build tiny libraries, put them in their front yard, and create a place where neighbors can exchange books.

National Book Club Conference

www.nationalbookclubconference.com

With a focus on African American authors, "the mission of the National Book Club Conference is to create the world's largest book club meeting once a year, to promote the value of reading and formulating book clubs among adults and in the nation's public school systems for the purposes of advancing literacy, broadening youths' minds and knowledge through reading and dialogue."

National Reading Group Month

www.nationalreadinggroupmonth.org

October is National Reading Group Month. Check out their website to find events and ways to get involved that promote books and reading. The site features a great reading list, too.

The Pulpwood Queens
www.beautyandthebook.com/pulpwood.html
This book group started in Texas and has spread across the country and gone international. They also have an annual lit-related Girlfriend Getaway.

World Book Night
www.us.worldbooknight.org
"An annual celebration dedicated to spreading the love of reading. Each year on April 23, tens of thousands of people go out into their communities and give half a million free . . . paperback books to light readers and nonreaders." The goal is to "[encourage] reading in those who don't ordinarily do so." You can make a donation to the effort or apply to be a "giver."

INDEX